Easiest & Best!

Coffee Cakes
and
Quick Breads

with Love, ♥ Renny Darling

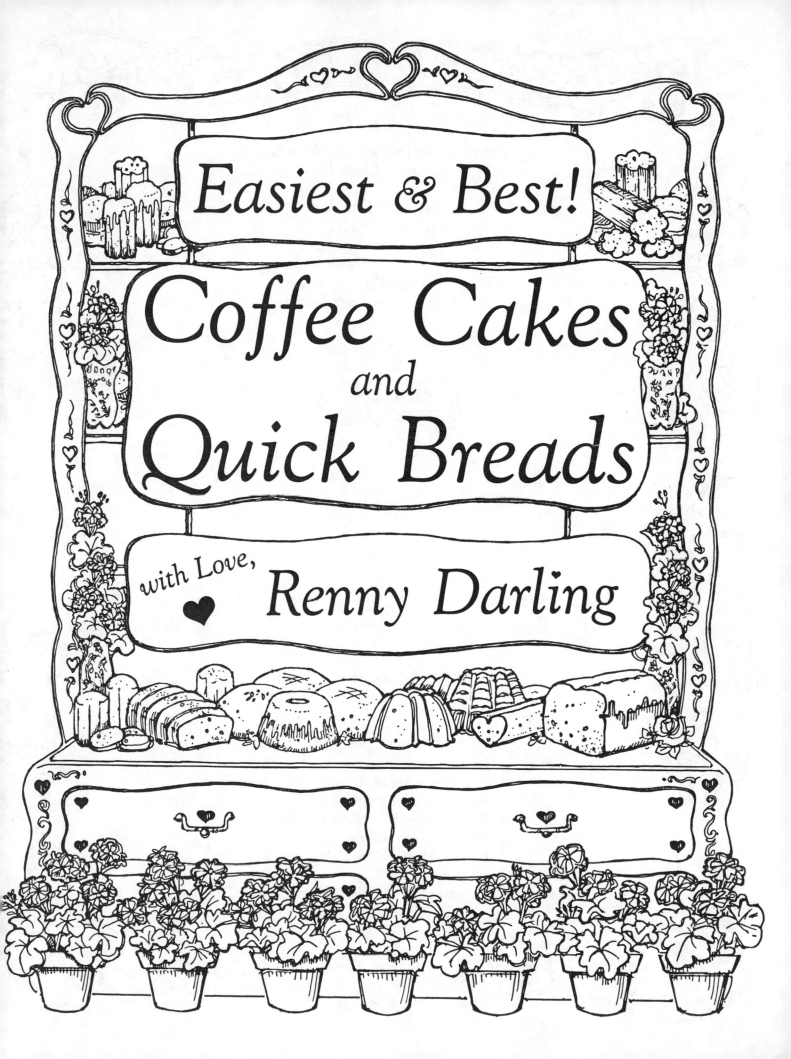

Other Simply Delicious Cookbooks
by Renny Darling

The Joy of Eating
The Love of Eating
The Joy of Entertaining
The Joy of Eating French Food
Great Beginnings & Happy Endings
With Love from Darling's Kitchen

Third Edition

Published by Royal House Publishing Co., Inc.
9465 Wilshire Boulevard
Beverly Hills, CA 90210
Printed in the United States of America
Library of Congress Catalog Card Number: 85-60770
ISBN: 0-930440-19-6

The Introduction

Baking coffeecakes and quick breads is one of the true joys and pleasures of the culinary experience. It has a magic all its own. Starting with the simplest of everyday ingredients and seeing how they transform into cakes or breads or muffins is little short of a miracle.

There is something unbelievably comforting about the aroma of cake or bread baking in the oven. It fills a home with a sense of love and caring that is impossible to describe. The wonderful fragrance of bread, baking in the oven, assures you that love is very close by.

Baking is the stuff memories are made of. When we are growing up, many were the times when we awakened to the aroma of bread, baking in the oven. It could be zero outside, and we could barely get our toes out from under the covers, but we would still race to the kitchen for the happiness that awaited us. The memories of those cold mornings ... of warm bread with sweet, creamy butter melting into each one of its little pores ... still fills me with nostalgia.

Sharing a slice of cake or bread with coffee or tea or a cup of hot cider, is one of the great feasts of the world. And offering a freshly baked cake or bread is very much like an embrace ... a big hug or a tight squeeze. Offering a freshly-baked bread is like giving someone a juicy kiss. **You only bake for those you love.**

Coffeecakes and quick breads are incredibly popular these days. There is talk that gooey desserts are out and coffeecakes are in. Coffeecakes seem to be in tune with the American preoccupation for lighter, less caloric desserts. And, more and more, American tastes are heading toward informal entertaining. "Come for dessert." or "Join us for coffee." is replacing the formal, time-consuming dinner party.

And, interestingly, it is now a time, when so many of us, are going back to the basics ... we are finding comfort in tradition. Consider how, the old-fashioned American breads, the cherished cakes and muffins are becoming more and more popular. It is hard to believe that America's darling, the plump muffin, is now becoming trendy.

Also, Americans are very, very busy. They choose not to spend inordinate amounts of time preparing in the kitchen. This book could easily have been called "Minute Magic" as most of these grand confections and glorious breads can be prepared in literally minutes. Imagine, making those incredible tortes in minutes, in a processor. Imagine coffeecakes, quick breads, the marvellous savory breads, that need only to be stirred and baked. Even bagels, made with yeast, are simply beaten and baked. You will feel like a magician, I promise you.

Included are hundreds of glazes and frostings. Except for the tortes, these are optional, for all the cakes and breads stand alone, quite well. They can be decorated with a faint sprinkle of sifted powdered sugar, and that will do very nicely. But there may come a time, when a more festive presentation is called for, and the frostings and glazes, designed to balance the flavors, will prove very useful.

Baking is a labor of love ... but in this book, I have taken away the labor ... so all that's left is an act of love. It has taken 3½ years to bring this to you, and could you believe, one of the happiest thoughts to cross my mind, is that in a little while, many of my cherished fans, will be sharing this with me.

As always, enjoy with love.

Renny Darling

Renny Darling
Beverly Hills, California
April, 1985

INGREDIENTS

Baking Powder
All recipes were tested with double-acting baking powder.

Bran
Recipes calling for 100% Bran refer to the packaged ready-to-eat cereal. Unprocessed Bran Flakes cannot be substituted.

Brown Sugar
Brown sugar should be packed when measured. Be certain to sift it, if it has become lumpy.

Butter
Sweet (unsalted) butter was used in testing the recipes. Lightly salted butter can be substituted. In most cases, margarine can be substituted, but check the label for preservatives, artificial colors and other additives.

Buttermilk
If a recipe calls for Buttermilk, Sour Milk can be substituted. To make Sour Milk, place 1 tablespoon lemon juice in a measuring cup and then add milk to measure 1 cup. Stir and allow to set for 1 minute; then add to the recipe as indicated. If you need less than 1 cup, then use proportionate amounts of lemon juice and milk. Milk that has gone sour is never to be used.

Chocolate
Always use pure chocolate, not flavored chocolate. If you happen to be out of chocolate, 3 tablespoons of cocoa and 1 tablespoon of butter can be substituted for 1 ounce of unsweetened chocolate.

To melt chocolate, place it in the top of a double boiler, over hot, not simmering, water. Make certain that the water does not touch the upper pan. If you own a microwave oven, place chocolate in a bowl and microwave for 1 minute on High. Turn the bowl ½ turn and microwave for ½ minute longer. Do not overdo it, or chocolate will become a stubborn mess.

Cinnamon Sugar
To make Cinnamon Sugar, place 1 cup sugar and 3 teaspoons cinnamon in a glass jar, with a tight-fitting lid, and shake until blended. If you like it spicier, add more cinnamon to taste.

Cocoa
When cocoa is called for, it refers to unsweetened powdered cocoa. Cocoa should be sifted, for it has a tendency to lump.

Cream
Where cream is indicated, use heavy cream or whipping cream.

Eggs

All recipes were tested with Large Grade AA eggs.

Extracts

Always use pure domestic vanilla. Pure almond and maple extracts are far superior to any imitations.

Flour

When Flour is called for, it refers to all-purpose white flour. Bleached or unbleached can be used. In practically all the cake and bread recipes, ½ of the flour called for in the recipe can be substituted with whole wheat pastry flour. If you use stone-ground or milled whole wheat flour, the finished bread or cake will be a little denser. There is no need to sift flour.

Fruit—Dried

Chop prunes, raisins, apricots in food processor, with a little sugar taken from the amount in the recipe. This keeps the dried fruit from getting gummed together.

If dried fruits are extra hard, they should be plumped. Raisins, currants, apricots can be plumped overnight in orange juice, sherry or liqueur. Or, they can be soaked for 5 minutes in boiling water and drained.

Fruit—Fresh

As a general rule, fresh is better than frozen, and frozen is better than canned... with the exception of canned crushed pineapple, which adds a lovely moistness and flavor to cakes and breads.

When a recipe calls for GRATED ORANGE or GRATED LEMON, it means to use the grated fruit, which includes the peel, juice and fruit. The orange or lemon can be grated on the 3rd largest side of a 4-sided hand grater, by using short, quick strokes. If the orange or lemon is very thick-skinned, peel off the zest (the yellow or orange part) and remove the pith (the white part). Finely chop (not puree) the zest with the fruit in the food processor. As a general rule, 1 medium orange will yield about 6 tablespoons of grated fruit, juice and peel. Cakes and breads using the whole fruit are far more flavorful than those using only the peel.

Nuts and Seeds

To toast walnuts, almonds, pecans, sesame seeds, place them in a thin layer of a shallow pan and toast in a 350° oven for 8 minutes, stirring now and again.

If you have any doubts as to the freshness of the nuts, it is important to taste one or two to make certain nuts are not rancid. Nuts that have turned rancid will spoil your cake or bread, for the bad taste can never be camouflaged, even with the most delicious ingredients.

Oats

Quick-cooking oats were used wherever oats or oatmeal is called for. Do not substitute instant-cooking oatmeal.

Oil

Use a bland, unflavored vegetable oil.

Powdered Sugar

Also called Confectioner's Sugar, is best sifted. Little unsightly lumps can ruin a glaze or frosting.

Salt

Notice that very few recipes contain salt. The breads and cakes are sweet and delicious without it. However, if you must, you can add a few shakes of salt, and it will not spoil the taste.

Sour Cream

If a recipe calls for sour cream, unflavored yogurt can be substituted, with a slight variation in taste.

Spices

Always use ground cinnamon, nutmeg or cloves. Do not use cinnamon sticks or whole cloves.

Vanilla Sugar

To make Vanilla Sugar, place 1 pound of sifted powdered sugar in a cannister or jar with a tight-fitting lid. Snap 2 vanilla beans sharply in thirds and bury them in the sugar. Use on pastries, cakes and wherever powdered sugar is called for. Sugar will take on a gentle hint of vanilla.

Wheat Germ

In recipes calling for Wheat Germ, either the sweetened or unsweetened can be used.

Yogurt

If a recipe calls for yogurt, sour cream can be substituted.

PREPARATION HINTS

You will find that there are 5 basic methods used in preparing cakes and breads. I will recap them here briefly, as they are fully described in each recipe.

1. **The Bread Method:** Basically, start with 2 bowls. In one, blend the wet ingredients. In the 2nd, mix the dry ingredients. Combine the contents of the 2 bowls and stir, just to blend.

2. **The Cake Method:** In this instance, cream the butter with the sugar; beat in the eggs and then the liquids. Beat in the dry ingredients until nicely blended.

3. **Biscuit and Scone Method:** Beat dry ingredients with butter until mixture resembles coarse meal. Add the liquids, all at once, and stir until just blended. Do not overmix. As most catastrophes occur from improper handling or kneading, the recipes in this book eliminate this step. Biscuits are dropped and scones are cut after baking.

4. Brownie Method: There are several ways to prepare brownies. Some are mentioned above. But in this method, the eggs are beaten with the sugar until light and foamy, and then the chocolate and butter are folded in. Dry ingredients are folded in at the end.

5. Processor Method: Except for the incredible tortes, where all the ingredients are processed together, cakes and breads can be prepared in the food processor, using a light touch. Liquid ingredients can be processed until blended. Dry ingredients are then added and blended with an on and off pulsing action. Do not overprocess.

KINDS OF BAKING PANS

As you read on, you will notice my personal preference for baking breads in smaller pans. There are many reasons for this. Smaller loaves can be individually frozen, and you can defrost only those that you plan to use. It is far more attractive to serve a small whole loaf than ½ of a started one. Little loaves never look like leftovers. Also, most of the basic recipes (4 mini-loaves) will yield 16 servings. So, unless you are expecting lots of friends, you will surely have leftovers. Baking the smaller loaves, you can immediately freeze those you do not plan to use. Little loaves are also great for sharing. A small loaf from your kitchen looks so much nicer than a few slices of bread.

The breads and cakes can be baked in so many interesting shapes. Today, one can find the most beautiful and unusually shaped baking pans. Aside from the traditional round, square and rectangle pans, you will find heart-shapes, cloverleafs, flowers, animals... the list is endless. Except for the tortes, the cakes can be baked in many shapes, right down to cupcakes. Similarly, the breads (except the savory dinner breads), can be baked in any number of shapes, right down to muffins. Simply grease and flour the pan and fill ⅔ full with batter. Any leftover batter can be made into muffins.

PREPARING PANS

To easily remove cakes or breads from baking pans, pans should be greased with shortening and dusted lightly with flour. Bread pans can also be dusted with wheat germ, bread crumbs, cracker crumbs, nuts, oats (depending on a complimentary blend with the recipe). Cake pans can be greased and dusted with cookie crumbs or nuts.

BAKING HINTS

To avoid too-peaked-a-crown, which will create a deep crack, pour batter into the pan and, with a spatula, build up the sides a little, leaving the center slightly indented. This will result in a more level cake or bread.

If top is browning too quickly, tent the cake loosely with foil. (This means to simply lay a piece of foil loosely over the cake.)

Bake small loaves on a cookie sheet for easier handling in and out of the oven.

TESTING FOR DONENESS

It is important to know when a cake is "done" to avoid the problem of overbaking, which will make the cake dry... or underbaking, which will leave the cake soggy or gummy. Use the suggested baking time only as a guide, as oven temperatures vary. Use a cake tester. In absence of one, a long, wooden toothpick can be used. Look at the color. After a few trials, you can almost tell by the appearance when a cake is done.

When a cake or bread is crusty, the crust may scrape the tester clean. To avoid this, probe a little circle in the center of the cake (about 1/16th-inch will do), so that when you test, the tester does not touch the crust. Except for brownies, tester should come out clean.

STORING

Always refrigerate breads or cakes made with fresh fruit, to retard the formation of bacteria or mold.

To store breads, cover with plastic wrap and refrigerate. They can be stored in this manner for several days. For longer storage, cakes and breads should be frozen. To freeze breads or cakes, wrap in double thicknesses of plastic wrap, and then with foil. I find it far more satisfactory to remove wrapper while defrosting to avoid the accumulation of moisture on the cake.

Do not glaze breads or cakes until after defrosting, for purely cosmetic reasons. Glazed breads or cakes can successfully be frozen but they look prettier and fresher when glazed on the day of serving.

LEFTOVERS

There is never any need to throw away a single crumb. Any leftover cake or bread can be toasted to produce the finest tasting crisp cookie, very much like Mandelbread. These crisp cookies are a treat to serve. They are great for munching and dunking. Slice any leftover bread or cake into ⅓-inch thick slices. Place in one layer in a baking pan, and bake at 350° for about 15 minutes, or until the bottom is toasted. Turn each slice and continue baking until lightly browned on both sides. These can be frozen for months in double freezer bags, or stored for weeks in a cannister. They are lovely served with coffee, tea or hot cider... and are a joy for dunking in milk.

CONVERSIONS

Many of the coffeecakes and quick breads can be baked in alternative shapes or sizes. At best, the following can only be a general guide for conversions. Please keep in mind that you may end up with a slightly taller or flatter cake or bread. Baking times will vary, also, so use a cake tester and watch for color.

With all this in mind, a recipe, calling for 2 to 2 1/2 cups of flour can be baked in the following pan sizes.

---

4 (6x3x2-inch) mini-loaf pans

---

12 muffins (2 1/2 x 1 1/4-inches)

---

2 (8x4-inch) loaf pans

---

1 (9x5-inch) loaf pan

---

1 (10-inch) springform pan

---

1 (10-inch) tube, kugelhopf, or decorative mold

---

2 (10-inch) deerback loaf pans

1 (9x13-inch) baking pan

2 (8x8-inch) baking pans

2 (10-inch) layer pans

1 (10-inch) fluted deep quiche pan

2 (1 1/2-quart) souffle dishes

1 (8x12-inch) fluted baking pan

2 (3-cup) heart molds

SUBSTITUTIONS

Rather than suffer the embarrassment of excess, I had to use colossal restraint not to include about 200 more wonderful cakes and breads that I tested. Many, many of the coffeecakes, quick breads and muffins (not tortes), can be transformed into new versions by the substitution of flavors.

Again, at best, please keep in mind that the following can only serve as a guide. I would recommend that you first prepare a recipe as indicated, and then, when you are familiar with its performance, experiment with it to include other fruits or vegetables. This will be expanded upon in the different chapters.

If a Recipe Calls For:	You Can Use:
Fruit — Chopped, Diced, Sliced	Apples, pears, peaches, apricots, plums, cherries, papaya
Fruit — Mashed, Pureed, Pulp	Pumpkin, applesauce, mango, avocado, persimmons, bananas, cooked rhubarb, papaya, crushed pineapple (with a little juice)
Berries	Raspberries, strawberries, blueberries, blackberries, cranberries, boysenberries
Dried Fruit	Dates, apricots, raisins, prunes, currants, figs, glaceed fruits
Nuts	Walnuts, pecans
Vegetables — Grated	Carrots, zucchini, apples
Orange — Grated	Tangerine, grapefruit
Lemon — Grated	Lime

Mix and Match

You can achieve exciting and new combinations by mixing and matching fruits or vegetables with dried fruits or nuts. For example, a carrot cake can be enhanced with the addition of dates or apricots or a zucchini cake can be enriched with currants or figs.

Streusel Topping

Many of the coffeecakes, quick breads and muffins can be dressed up with a Streusel Topping. Find a recipe that pleases you (see Toppings in index) and sprinkle tops lightly before baking. Bake for a minute or two longer.

The Contents

INTRODUCTION 3

COFFEECAKES WITH FRUITS & VEGETABLES 21-58

Royal Sour Cream Apple Coffeecake 24
Sour Cream Apple Kuchen 25
Fresh Apple & Walnut Honey Cake 26
Majestic Apple Cake with Orange 27
Fresh Apple Spiced Cake with Walnuts 28
Easiest & Best Apple Cake with Pecans 29
Cinnamon Apple Cake with Raisins 30
Fresh Apple Sour Cream Cake 31
Spiced Applesauce Cake with Raisins 32
Spiced Banana Cake 33
Country Home Carrot & Raisin Cake 34
California Carrot Cake with Pineapple 35
Cooked Carrot Spice Cake 36
Easiest & Best Carrot Cake with Orange 37
Farmhouse Carrot Cake with Pineapple 38
French Clafouti with Bing Cherries 39
Black Cherry & Almond Cake with Streusel 40
Red Cherry Almond Cake with Almond Cream Glaze 41
Glazed Cranberry Cake with Orange 42
Cranberry Orange & Lemon Tea Cake 43
Daffodil Lemon Cake 44
Extra Tart Springtime Lemon Cake 45
Lemon Pound Cake with Lemon Creme Fraiche 46
Lemon Cream Cheese Coffeecake 47
Spicy Nectarine Ginger Cake 48
Fantastic Spiced Orange Cake 49
Buttery Orange Walnut Coffeecake 50
World's Best Orange & Lemon Sponge Cake 51
Peach & Walnut Cinnamon Coffeecake 52
Fresh Peach & Orange Cake with Streusel 53
Pear Cobbler with Orange & Pecans 54
Ginger Snap Pumpkin Cake with Raisins 55
Honey & Spice Pumpkin Cake 56
Royal Raspberry & Almond Cake 57
Old-Fashioned Zucchini Cake 58

OTHER COFFEECAKES WITH DRIED FRUITS, NUTS, JAMS 59-80

Sour Cream Almond Cake with Almond Glaze 62
Royal Apricot Cake with Vanilla Glaze 63
Apricot Pecan Yogurt Cake 64
Apricot Jam & Macaroon Cake 65
California Date Nut Cake 66
Old-Fashioned Marble Poundcake 67
Poppyseed Orange Cake 68
Old-Fashioned Spiced Prune & Walnut Cake 69
Bara Brith-Welsh Raisin Date Nut Cake 70
Buttery Scotch Shortcake with Raspberries 71
Strawberry Jam & Almond Cake 72
Golden Bourbon Fruit & Nut Cake 73
Bourbon & Eggnog Spiced Cake 74
Cappucino Poundcake 75
English Sherry Spice Cake 76
Sunny California Sour Cream Pineapple Cake 77
Old-Fashioned Spiced Honey Cake 78
Orange & Walnut Cake 79
Orange & Yogurt Cake with Cinnamon Streusel Swirl 80

CAKES WITH CHOCOLATE & CHOCOLATE CHIPS 81-104

Sour Cream & Chocolate Banana Cake 84
Chocolate Banana Cake 85
Chocolate Carrot Almond Cake 86
Swiss Chocolate Cake with Cherries 87
Chocolate Fudge Decadence with Rum & Raisins 88
Chocolate Chestnut Cake 89
Chocolate Chip Buttermilk Cake 90
Sour Cream Chocolate Chip Chocolate Cake 91
Chocolate Chip Chocolate Cake 92
Sour Cream Chocolate Fudge Cake 93
Sour Cream Poundcake with Chocolate Chips 94
Bittersweet Chocolate Fudge Cake 95
Mocha Chocolate Cake 96
Chocolate Pumpkin Pecan Cake 97
Chocolate Pumpkin Spiced Cake 98
Raspberry & Chocolate Chip Cake 99
Anniversary Chocolate & Raspberry Cake 100
Vanilla Poundcake with Chocolate Chips 101
Basic Chocolate Sponge Cake 102
Chocolate Velvet Cake 103
Chocolate Zucchini Cake 104

DESSERT TORTES 105-124

    Almond Torte with Chocolate Chip Crust 108
    Almond Torte with Glazed Strawberries 109
    Chocolate Almond Torte 110
    Fresh Apple & Orange Pecan Torte 111
    Easiest & Best Carrot & Pecan Torte 112
    Chocolate Torte with Apricot 113
    Chocolate Chip Graham Torte 114
    Gateau au Chocolate 115
    Easiest & Best Torte au Chocolate 116
    Grand Duke's Pecan Torte with Apricot Jam 117
    Hungarian Pecan Torte 118
    Hungarian Chocolate Torte 119
    Easiest & Best Macaroon Torte 120
    Easiest & Best Walnut Torte 121
    Coffee & Chocolate Walnut Torte 122
    Yogurt Chocolate Fudge Torte 123
    Viennese Nut Torte 124

QUICK BREADS WITH FRUITS & VEGETABLES 125-162

    Apple Orange Raisin Bread 128
    Upside Down Honey Bran Bread 129
    Spiced Applesauce Bread with Currants 130
    Fresh Apricot & Cottage Cheese Bread 131
    Old-Fashioned Banana Chocolate Chip Bread 132
    Sour Cream Banana Bread 133
    Whole Wheat Banana & Chocolate Chip Bread 134
    Banana & Orange Raisin Bran Bread 135
    Whole Wheat & Oatmeal Blueberry Bread 136
    Spiced Carrot & Orange Bread 137
    Pineapple Cranberry Bread 138
    Holiday Cranberry Almond Bread 139
    Sour Cream Lemon Tea Bread 140
    Extra Tart Lemon Nut Bread 141
    Sour Cream Orange & Pecan Bread 142
    Orange Tea Bread 143
    Honey Bran Bread with Peaches 144
    Fresh Peach & Almond Bread 145
    Orange Peach Bread 146
    Peach & Orange Yogurt Bread 147
    Honey Whole Wheat Pineapple Bread 148
    Pineapple & Orange Bran Bread 149

QUICK BREADS WITH FRUITS & VEGETABLES   (Continued)

Pineapple Raisin Bran Bread   150
Pineapple Orange & Coconut Bread   151
The Best Pumpkin Bread   152
Orange & Raisin Pumpkin Bread   153
Whole Wheat Pumpkin Pecan Bread   154
Spicy Pumpkin Bread   155
Raspberry & Pecan Lemon Bread   156
Rhubarb Oatmeal Bread   157
Strawberry Pecan Bread   158
Strawberry Yogurt Banana Bread   159
Strawberry Banana Bread   160
Cinnamon Zucchini Bread   161
Spiced Zucchini Walnut Bread   162

QUICK BREADS WITH DRIED FRUITS, NUTS, SPIRITS   163-200

Honey Almond Bread   166
Mississippi Mud Pie Bread   167
Apricot & Orange Almond Bread   168
Apricot Jam & Almond Bread   169
Christmas Eggnog Cherry Bread   170
Buttermilk Chocolate Bread   171
Cafe Creme Chocolate Nut Bread   172
Two-Minute Cinnamon Swirl Bread   173
Cinnamon Cottage Cheese Bread   174
Old-Fashioned Date Nut Bread   175
Orange Date Nut Bread   176
Date Nut Orange Bread   177
Fig & Honey Pecan Bread   178
California Fruit & Nut Bread   179
Sticky Honey Gingerbread   180
Farmhouse Spiced Raisin Gingerbread   181
Oatmeal Bread with Orange & Prunes   182
Orange Marmalade Bread   183
Peanut Butter & Jam Bread   184
Danish Prune Bread   185
Old-Fashioned Honey Prune Walnut Bread   186
Sour Cream Walnut Tea Bread   187
Country Walnut & Raisin Bread   188
Honey-Spiced Walnut Bread   189
Wheat Germ Bread with Apricots   190
Bourbon Fruit & Nut Bread   191

QUICK BREADS WITH DRIED FRUITS, NUTS, SPIRITS (Continued)

Spiced Raisin & Walnut Sherry Bread 192
Holiday Brandy Fruit & Pecan Bread 193
St. Patrick's Day Bread 194
Christmas Sherry Fruit & Nut Bread 195
Health Bread with Yogurt, Oatmeal & Whole Wheat 196
Whole Wheat & Buttermilk Prune Bread 197
Molasses & Buttermilk Bran Bread 198
Whole Wheat & Oat Bran Bread with Dates 199
Irish Breakfast Soda Bread 200

BAR CAKES & COOKIES 201-226

Rocky Road Bars 204
Rocky Road Chewies 205
Butterscotch Brownies 205
Chewy Fudgy California Brownies 206
World's Best Velvet Chocolate Brownies 207
Best Sour Cream Bittersweet Brownies 208
Chocolate Fudge Brownies 209
Chocolate Cream Cheese Bars 210
German Chocolate Bar Cookies 211
Chewy Bar Cookies 212
Goldies 213
Walnut & Butterscotch Cookie Bars 214
Friendship Caramel Pecan Bars 215
Apricot Bars with Pecan Meringue 216
Red Raspberry Butter Bars 217
Lemon Butter Bars 218
Creamy Chocolate Squares 219
Coffeecake Bars 220
Chocolate Granola Bars 221
Chocolate Chip Walnut Chewies 222
World's Best Chocolate Chip Raisin Cookies 223
Victorian Pretty Maids of Honor Bars 224
Holiday Fruit & Nut Chewies 225
Biscotti di Amaretto-Almond Biscuits 226

STRUDELS & DANISH 227-238

Flaky Strudel Pastry with Apricot Jam 230
Flaky Strudel Pastry with Cinnamon Raisin 231
Flaky Strudel with Rugalach Filling 231
Flaky Strudel with Pecan Raisin Filling 231

STRUDELS & DANISH (Continued)

Flaky Strudel with Chocolate Chip Filling 231
Danish Apple Strudel 232
Danish Pastry Rolls 233
Strudelettes with Walnuts & Strawberry Jam 234
Scandinavian Cinnamon Date Nut Roll 235
Danish Crescents with Strawberry Jam 236
Viennese Crescents with Cinnamon & Walnuts 237
Cinnamon Breakfast Croissants 238

SAVORY DINNER BREADS 239-266

Easiest & Best Onion Sesame Bagels 242
Onion Kuchen with Sour Cream & Poppyseeds 243
Poppyseed Onion Rolls for Passover 244
Red Hot Pastelle with Onions & Swiss Cheese 245
Pesto Bread with Cheese & Pine Nuts 246
Pizza Bread with Tomatoes, Onions & Cheese 247
Green Onion Buttermilk Bread with Lemon & Sesame 248
Parmesan Herb & Onion Cheese Bread 249
Poppyseed Bread with Green Onions & Cheese 250
Greek Lemon Bread with Green Onions, Tomato & Feta 251
Sweet & Sour Red Cabbage Bread with Apples & Raisins 252
Sauerkraut Rye Bread with Yogurt, Onions & Bacon 253
Russian Black Bread with Sour Cream & Raisins 254
Burgundian Cheese & Chive Bread 255
Two-Minute Cheese Bread with Onions & Herbs 256
Country Kitchen Cornbread 257
Mexican-Style Cornbread with Chiles & Cheese 258
Giant Popovers with Chives & Cheese 259
Giant Popovers - Alternate Method 260
Chewy Cheese Sticks with Onions 261
Whole Wheat Raisin Soda Bread 262
Apple Cheddar Cheese Oatmeal Bread 263
Cheese & Onion Crescents 264
Cheddar Cheese Muffins 265
Bacon & Swiss Cheese Muffins 266

MUFFINS, SCONES, BISCUITS, WAFERS 267-296

All-American Macaroon Muffins with Dates 270
Cinnamon Apple Muffins with Orange & Pecans 271
Fresh Apple & Orange Muffins 272
Buttermilk Blueberry Muffins with Pecans 273

MUFFINS, SCONES, BISCUITS, WAFERS (Continued)

Butterscotch Pecan Muffins 274
New Orleans Cornbread Muffins with Currants 275
Cajun Honey Bran Muffins with Raisins & Pecans 276
Cajun Jalapeno & Cheese Biscuit Muffins 277
Cajun Banana Pecan Crusty Muffins 278
Black Forest Chocolate Cherry Cupcakes 279
Sour Cream Muffins with Chocolate Chips 280
Cranberry, Orange & Apple Muffins 281
Chewy Orange Raisin Muffins 282
Best Papaya Lemon Cream Cheese Muffins 283
Currant & Oatmeal Muffins with Orange 284
Sour Cream Pumpkin Muffins with Walnuts 285
Spiced Pumpkin Muffins with Orange 286
Honey Whole Wheat & Wheat Germ Muffins 287
Maple Oat Bran Muffins with Walnuts 288
Raisin Bran Muffins with Apple & Orange 289
Honey Whole Wheat Oatmeal Muffins with Apples 290
Feather Cream Drop Biscuits 291
Chive Biscuits 291
Bacon Biscuits 291
Sesame Biscuits 291
Herb Biscuits 291
Parmesan Biscuits 291
Poppyseed Biscuits 291
Yogurt & Pecan Breakfast Wafers 292
Victorian Cream Scones with Currants 293
Whole Wheat Scones with Currants & Dates 294
Blueberry Buttermilk Scones 295
Buttery Scones with Buttermilk & Raisins 296

To the tens of thousands of fans,
from every corner of the world,
who have written me the most
affectionate and endearing letters,
my love and appreciation.

Coffeecakes

with

Fruits

&

Vegetables

Coffeecakes with Fruits & Vegetables

Royal Sour Cream Apple Coffeecake 24

Sour Cream Apple Kuchen 25

Fresh Apple & Walnut Honey Cake 26

Majestic Apple Cake with Orange 27

Fresh Apple Spiced Cake with Walnuts 28

Easiest & Best Apple Cake with Pecans 29

Cinnamon Apple Cake with Raisins 30

Fresh Apple Sour Cream Cake 31

Spiced Applesauce Cake with Raisins 32

Spiced Banana Cake 33

Country Home Carrot & Raisin Cake 34

California Carrot Cake with Pineapple 35

Cooked Carrot Spice Cake 36

Easiest & Best Carrot Cake with Orange 37

Farmhouse Carrot Cake with Pineapple 38

French Clafouti with Bing Cherries 39

Black Cherry & Almond Cake with Streusel 40

Red Cherry Almond Cake with Almond Cream Glaze 41

Glazed Cranberry Cake with Orange 42

Cranberry Orange & Lemon Tea Cake 43

Daffodil Lemon Cake 44

Extra Tart Springtime Lemon Cake 45

Lemon Pound Cake with Lemon Creme Fraiche 46

Lemon Cream Cheese Coffeecake 47

Spicy Nectarine Ginger Cake 48

Fantastic Spiced Orange Cake 49

Buttery Orange Walnut Coffeecake 50

World's Best Orange & Lemon Sponge Cake 51

Peach & Walnut Cinnamon Coffeecake 52

Fresh Peach & Orange Cake with Streusel 53

Pear Cobbler with Orange & Pecans 54

Ginger Snap Pumpkin Cake with Raisins 55

Honey & Spice Pumpkin Cake 56

Royal Raspberry & Almond Cake 57

Old-Fashioned Zucchini Cake 58

From my Notebook:

Coffeecakes with Fruits & Vegetables

Coffeecakes made with fresh fruits and vegetables rank among the best for flavor and goodness. Each season brings the lush flavors of different fruits. The fresh fruits of summer ... succulent peaches, apricots, strawberries, raspberries ... are glorious in coffeecakes. There is no substitute for eating these in their purest form. However, there are a few excellent alternatives that can be used for baking.

Fresh **Apples** are available all year round, and any variety works well in baking. The recipes that follow were tested with Red or Golden Delicious, which are sweeter than the Pippins or Granny Smiths. However, during the summer months, you can substitute some of the marvellous summer fruits in season for the apples. As an example, if you were to prepare the Apple Kuchen (Page 25) for a summer luncheon or tea, then sliced peaches or papayas are a grand substitution.

Canned **Applesauce** works well in coffeecakes and the chunky-style is especially good.

Bananas should be very ripe for extra flavor. They should be mashed. If you puree them, their density will require at least 5 minutes extra baking time.

Cranberries are a winter fruit, but they freeze well and can be enjoyed at other times of the year. However, their taste better matches fall and winter baking.

Blueberries, Strawberries, Raspberries, similarly, can be purchased frozen ... yet, are a better choice for spring and summer baking. This, at best, is general, for there is a certain excitement eating foods out of season ... so let your taste be your guide.

Frozen Peaches are an especially fine substitution. They come peeled, pitted and sliced, so they can be used at a moment's notice.

Carrots and **Zucchini** are also available throughout the year. They should be peeled and grated. (Especially the zucchini. Green flecks in cakes are less than satisfactory for my taste. But if they do not bother your sensibilities, they can be left unpeeled.) Both carrots and zucchini can be grated in a food processor using the grating attachment. Carrots can be finely chopped in a food processor, using the steel blade. In absence of a processor, use the 3rd largest side of a hand grater. Grating in a blender is a total bother and is not recommended.

Royal Sour Cream Coffeecake with Apples, Orange & Walnuts

This is a majestic coffeecake, full of flavor and goodness, very delicious and the essence of simplicity to prepare. It will grace a brunch or luncheon buffet in grand taste.

    2 eggs
    1/2 cup butter, softened
    3/4 cup sour cream
  1 1/2 cups sugar
    3 tablespoons grated orange. (Use fruit, juice and peel.
        Remove any large pieces of membrane.)

  1 1/2 cups flour
    2 teaspoons baking powder
    1 cup chopped walnuts

    2 medium apples, peeled, cored and thinly sliced. (This can
        be done in a processor or on the slicing side of a
        four-sided grater.) (Use Pippin apples . . . as they
        render less juice.)
    2 teaspoons cinnamon

Beat together first 5 ingredients until blended. Combine and add flour, baking powder and walnuts and beat until dry ingredients are just blended. Do not overbeat. In a bowl, toss apples with cinnamon.

Spread half the batter in a greased 10-inch springform pan and place apples evenly over the batter. Top with remaining batter and spread to even.

Bake in a 350° oven for 45 minutes, or until a cake tester, inserted in center, comes out clean. (Tent loosely with foil after 30 minutes, if top is browning too quickly.) Allow to cool in pan for 20 minutes and then remove metal ring and allow to cool completely. When cool, drizzle top with Vanilla Cream Glaze and allow a little to drip down the sides. Serves 8 to 10.

Vanilla Cream Glaze:
    1 tablespoon cream
    1/2 teaspoon vanilla
    3/4 cup sifted powdered sugar

Stir together all the ingredients until blended. Add a little sugar or cream to make glaze a thick drizzling consistency.

Sour Cream Apple Kuchen with Raisins & Almonds

This is a little gem that I hope you use often. It is unorthodox, I agree, but the results are fantastic. It is a tender, very flavorful coffeecake. Even though it contains yeast, the yeast does not need to rise, thus qualifying it as a "quick" coffeecake. You can substitute different fruits in season, such as peaches or pears. Procedure remains the same.

1 package dry yeast
2 tablespoons warm water (105°)
1 teaspoon sugar

1/2 cup butter, softened
1/2 cup sugar
2 eggs
1/3 cup sour cream
1 tablespoon grated lemon
1 teaspoon almond extract

2 cups flour
1 tablespoon baking powder
1/2 cup yellow raisins
1/2 cup chopped toasted almonds

1/2 cup sugar
1 teaspoon cinnamon
2 apples, peeled, cored and thinly sliced (about 2 cups)

In a small bowl, stir together yeast, warm water and sugar, and allow to rest for 10 minutes or until yeast starts to foam. Meanwhile, beat together next 6 ingredients until nicely blended. Beat in yeast mixture. Beat in flour, baking powder, raisins and almonds until blended. Spread batter evenly in a greased 9x13-inch baking pan.

Toss together sugar, cinnamon and apples and place mixture evenly on top of the batter. Bake in a 350° oven for about 35 to 40 minutes, or until top is browned and a cake tester, inserted in center, comes out clean. Allow to cool in pan. Cut into squares to serve. Serves 12.

Fresh Apple & Walnut Honey Cake
with Apple Glaze

This cake is very dense, and I originally thought not to include it. But everyone loved it at the tasting . . . so here it is. I hope you enjoy it, although it is a bit heavy.

    3 eggs
    1/2 cup oil
    1/2 cup honey
    2 teaspoons vanilla

    2 cups flour
  1 1/2 cups sugar
    1 teaspoon baking powder
    1 teaspoon baking soda
    2 teaspoons cinnamon

    3 apples (about 3 cups) peeled, cored and thinly sliced
    2 cups walnuts, coarsely chopped

Beat together first 4 ingredients until blended. Combine and add the next 5 ingredients and beat until blended. Do not overmix. Stir in the apples and walnuts.

Pour mixture into a buttered 10-inch tube pan and bake at 350° for about 60 to 65 minutes, or until a cake tester, inserted in center, comes out clean. Allow to cool in pan. When cool, drizzle top with Apple Glaze and allow a little to drip down the sides. Serves 10.

Apple Glaze:
    1 tablespoon apple juice
    1/2 cup sifted powdered sugar
    2 tablespoons chopped toasted walnuts

Stir together all the ingredients until blended. Add a little sugar or apple juice to make glaze a drizzling consistency.

Majestic Apple Cake with Oranges, Walnuts & Cinnamon Topping

This is a regal cake that is very different from the traditional apple cakes. It is a marvellous nut cake with layers of cinnamony apples. It is also a good-sized cake and will amply serve 12.

2 cups sugar
1/4 cup orange juice
1/2 medium orange, grated (about 3 tablespoons)
1 cup oil
4 eggs
2 teaspoons vanilla

3 cups flour
3 teaspoons baking powder
1 cup chopped walnuts

2 cups grated apples
2 tablespoons sugar
2 teaspoons cinnamon

1 tablespoon cinnamon sugar

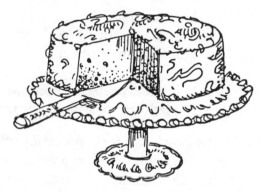

Beat together first 6 ingredients until blended. Add the next 3 ingredients and beat until blended. Do not overbeat.

Spoon 1/3 the batter into a greased 10-inch tube pan. Mix together apples, sugar and cinnamon, and place half this mixture over the batter. Cover this with 1/3 the batter, and then the remaining apple mixture. Top with remaining batter. Sprinkle top with cinnamon sugar.

Bake in a 350° oven for 1 hour. Reduce heat to 325° and continue baking for about 30 minutes, or until a cake tester, inserted in center, comes out clean. Cool in pan on a rack. When cool, remove from pan and place on your prettiest footed cake plate. Serves 12.

Fresh Apple Spiced Cake with Orange & Walnuts

This cake is fruity and moist and flavored with cinnamon and cloves. It can be prepared in minutes. When the apple and orange is being processed, leave a little texture in the fruit. Do not puree.

1 cup graham cracker crumbs
1 teaspoon baking powder
2 teaspoons cinnamon
1/8 teaspoon each ground nutmeg and ground cloves
6 eggs
1 cup sugar
2 cups chopped walnuts
1 teaspoon vanilla

1 apple, peeled, cored and cut into 8 slices
1/2 medium orange, cut into 4 pieces. (Do not peel.)

In the bowl of a food processor, place first 9 ingredients and blend mixture for 15 seconds. Add the apple and orange and blend for an additional 20 to 25 seconds, or until fruit is finely chopped.

Scrape batter into a greased 10-inch springform pan and bake at 350° for about 40 to 45 minutes, or until a cake tester, inserted in center, comes out clean. Allow cake to cool in pan, and then drizzle with Orange Walnut Glaze. Serves 8 to 10.

Orange Walnut Glaze:
1 cup sifted powdered sugar
1 1/2 tablespoons orange juice
1 tablespoon grated orange peel
4 tablespoons chopped walnuts

Stir together all the ingredients until blended, adding a little more powdered sugar to make glaze a drizzling consistency.

Note: — Cake can be prepared 1 day earlier and stored in the refrigerator. Allow to come to room temperature before serving.

Easiest and Best Apple Cake with Orange & Pecans & Creamy Glaze

This little gem is truly a wonder. Place a few ingredients in your food processor and Voila! a fruity, nutty torte that is just bursting with moistness and flavor.

   1/4 medium orange, cut into 4 pieces
     1 cup pecans
     1 large apple (peeled, cored and sliced)
     2 eggs
1 1/4 cups sugar
     2 teaspoons vanilla
   2/3 cup flour
     2 teaspoons baking powder

Combine all the ingredients in the bowl of a food processor and blend for 30 seconds. Scrape down the sides and continue blending for another 30 seconds or until fruit and pecans are finely chopped. Pour batter into a buttered 10-inch springform pan and bake in a 350° oven for 30 to 35 minutes, or until a cake tester, inserted in center, comes out clean. Allow to cool in pan.

When cool, swirl top with Creamy Raisin Glaze, in a decorative fashion and allowing some of the cake to show. Cut into wedges to serve. Serves 8.

Creamy Raisin Glaze:
     1 tablespoon cream
     1 cup sifted powdered sugar
     2 tablespoons finely chopped raisins
  1/2 teaspoon vanilla

Stir together all the ingredients until blended. Add a little cream or sifted powdered sugar, if necessary to make glaze a drizzling consistency.

Note: — Cake can be prepared 1 or 2 days earlier and stored in the refrigerator. Bring to room temperature to serve.

Cinnamon Apple Cake
with Raisins & Walnuts

This is a moist, spicy apple cake that is just lovely at teatime. The secret ingredient is mayonnaise. And it is a secret, for it imparts no taste at all.

        2 cups flour
  1 1/2 cups sugar
      2/3 cup mayonnaise
      1/4 cup sour cream
        2 eggs
        1 teaspoon baking soda
      1/2 teaspoon baking powder
  1 1/2 teaspoons cinnamon

        2 apples, peeled, cored and grated
      1/2 orange, grated. Use fruit juice and peel
      1/2 cup yellow raisins
        1 cup chopped walnuts

Beat together first 8 ingredients until blended. Do not overbeat. Stir in remaining ingredients until blended.

Pour batter into a greased 10-inch springform pan and bake in a 350° oven for about 50 minutes, or until a cake tester, inserted in center, comes out clean. Allow to cool in pan.

When cool, frost top with Orange Cream Cheese Frosting. Serves 10.

Orange Cream Cheese Frosting:
      1/4 cup butter (1/2 stick)
      1/4 pound (4 ounces) cream cheese
        1 teaspoon vanilla
        2 cups sifted powdered sugar
        2 tablespoons grated orange peel
        2 tablespoons finely chopped walnuts

Beat butter and cream cheese until blended. Beat in the remaining ingredients until blended. Will frost 1 10-inch cake.

Fresh Apple Sour Cream Cake with Buttermilk Glaze

Fresh apples, sour cream, cinnamon, raisins and walnuts all add to make this cake rich and flavorful. The Buttermilk Glaze adds the perfect tartness.

1 1/3 cups sugar
2/3 cup butter
3 eggs
1/2 cup sour cream

2 cups flour
2 teaspoons cinnamon
1 teaspoon baking powder
1/2 teaspoon baking soda

2 apples, peeled, cored and grated
2 cups chopped walnuts
3/4 cup yellow raisins
1 teaspoon vanilla

Beat together first 4 ingredients until blended. Combine and add the next 4 ingredients and stir until dry ingredients are nicely blended. Do not overmix. Stir in the apples, walnuts, raisins and vanilla.

Pour batter into a greased 10-inch tube pan and bake at 350° for 50 minutes to 1 hour, or until a cake tester, inserted in center, comes out clean. Allow to cool in pan. When cool, drizzle top decoratively with Buttermilk Glaze. Serves 10.

Buttermilk Glaze:
3/4 cup sifted powdered sugar
1 tablespoon buttermilk
1 teaspoon lemon juice
2 tablespoons chopped yellow raisins

Stir together all the ingredients, adding a little more sugar or buttermilk, to make glaze a drizzling consistency.

Spiced Applesauce Cake with Raisins & Walnuts

What a nice cake to serve in the fall between Halloween and Thanksgiving. It is truly delicious. Serve it with hot cider that has been sparkled with cinnamon and spice. Use cinnamon sticks as stirrers for a nice holiday touch.

    1/2 cup butter
      1 cup sugar
      1 egg
    1/4 cup sour cream

  1 3/4 cups flour
      1 teaspoon baking powder
      1 teaspoon baking soda
  1 1/2 teaspoons pumpkin pie spice
    1/2 cup yellow raisins
    1/2 cup currants
      1 cup chopped walnuts

      1 cup applesauce

Cream together butter and sugar. Beat in egg and sour cream until blended. Stir together the next 7 ingredients and add these alternately with the applesauce to the creamed mixture, beating only until blended.

Place batter into a well-greased 10-inch tube pan and bake at 350° for about 45 to 50 minutes or until a cake tester, inserted in center, comes out clean. Allow to cool in pan.

When cool, drizzle top with Orange Glaze and allow some to drizzle down the sides. Serves 10 to 12.

Orange Glaze:
      1 tablespoon orange juice
      1 teaspoon grated orange peel
      1 tablespoon finely chopped walnuts
    2/3 cup sifted powdered sugar

Stir together all the ingredients until blended.

Spiced Banana Cake with Cinnamon & Walnut Topping

This is another one of those cakes that calls for ingredients that are basic to your pantry. Therefore, it can be prepared at any time with the minimum amount of fuss. Notice that it calls for little butter, is moistened with water and banana and wonderfully flavored with spices.

    1/3 cup butter, softened
1 1/3 cups sugar
    2 eggs
  1/4 cup water

    2 large bananas, mashed

1 2/3 cups flour
    1 teaspoon baking powder
    1 teaspoon baking soda
    2 teaspoons cinnamon
  1/4 teaspoon nutmeg
  1/4 teaspoon ground cloves

    1 tablespoon cinnamon sugar
  1/2 cup coarsely chopped walnuts

Beat together first 4 ingredients until mixture is nicely blended. Stir in the bananas. Stir in the next 6 ingredients until blended. Spread batter into a greased 10-inch tube pan and sprinkle top with cinnamon sugar and walnuts. Press the walnuts lightly into the batter. Bake in a 325° oven for about 40 minutes, or until a cake tester, inserted in center, comes out clean. Allow to cool in pan. Serves 10.

Note: — Bananas should be coarsely mashed and not pureed.

Country Home Carrot & Raisin Cake with Cinnamon & Walnut Topping

As this cake does not contain pineapple, coconut, cream cheese or sour cream, it is a good cake to consider when you want a terrific-tasting cake made with a few staple ingredients. This cake is so moist and delicious, I know you will use this recipe often. This is not a traditional carrot cake, in that it uses only 1/4 cup butter, is moistened with water, and is made with the simplest everyday ingredients. Great to serve at anytime.

1/4 cup butter
1 1/2 cups sugar
2 large carrots, grated (about 1 1/2 cups)
1 1/3 cups water
2 teaspoons pumpkin pie spice
1 cup yellow raisins
3 tablespoons grated orange

1 egg, beaten

2 cups flour
2 teaspoons baking soda
1 teaspoon vanilla

1 tablespoon cinnamon sugar
1 cup chopped walnuts

In a saucepan, heat together first 7 ingredients and bring mixture to a boil. Remove from heat and refrigerate until cold. Beat in the egg until blended. Beat in the flour, baking soda and vanilla until blended.

Spread batter evenly into a greased 9x13-inch baking pan and sprinkle top with cinnamon sugar and walnuts. Press the walnuts gently into the batter. Bake in a 350° oven for 35 to 40 minutes, or until a cake tester, inserted in center, comes out clean. Allow to cool in pan and cut into squares to serve. Serves 12.

California Carrot Cake with Pineapple, Coconut & Walnuts

Some carrot cakes have pineapple or coconut or walnuts for additional excitement and interest. This carrot cake has all of these and it is very good, indeed. Cream Cheese Frosting is really the best frosting for this cake. This recipe produces 2 good-sized cakes. Use one and freeze the other.

        4 eggs
1 1/4 cups oil
        2 cups sugar
        2 teaspoons vanilla

        2 cups flour
        2 teaspoons baking powder
        1 teaspoon baking soda
     1/4 teaspoon salt
2 1/2 teaspoons cinnamon

2 1/2 cups grated carrots
        1 can (8 ounces) crushed pineapple, drained
     1/2 cup coconut flakes
        1 cup chopped walnuts

Beat together first 4 ingredients until blended. Beat in the next 5 ingredients until blended. Stir in the remaining ingredients.

Divide batter between 2 greased 9-inch tube pans and bake in a 350° oven for about 40 minutes, or until a cake tester, inserted in center, comes out clean. When cool, frost with Butter Cream Cheese Frosting. Each cake serves 8.

Butter Cream Cheese Frosting:
     1/2 cup butter, softened
        1 package (8 ounces) cream cheese
        1 teaspoon vanilla
        3 cups sifted powdered sugar

Beat butter and cream cheese until blended. Beat in remaining ingredients until blended.

Cooked Carrot Spice Cake with Walnuts & Raisins

This is a variation of the classic Carrot Bread, made with cooked carrots and vanilla yogurt. The Cream Cheese Frosting is traditional and the perfect accompaniment.

        2 eggs
        1 cup sugar
      1/3 cup oil
      1/3 cup vanilla yogurt
        2 teaspoons vanilla

        1 can (1 pound) julienned carrots (thoroughly drained)

    1 3/4 cups flour
    1 1/2 teaspoons baking powder
      1/2 teaspoon baking soda
        2 teaspoons pumpkin pie spice (or 1 1/2 teaspoons
           cinnamon, 1/4 teaspoon ground nutmeg and 1/4 teaspoon
           ground cloves)
        1 cup chopped walnuts
      1/2 cup yellow raisins

Beat together first 5 ingredients until blended. Beat in the carrots. Combine and add the remaining ingredients and stir until dry ingredients are blended. Do not overmix.

Spread batter into a greased 10-inch tube pan and bake in a 350° oven for about 40 to 45 minutes, or until a cake tester, inserted in center, comes out clean.

Allow to cool in pan. When cool, remove pan and frost with Cream Cheese Frosting. Serves 10.

Cream Cheese Frosting:
      1/4 pound cream cheese, softened
      1/4 cup butter, softened (1/2 stick)
        1 teaspoon vanilla
        2 cups sifted powdered sugar

Beat together all the ingredients until blended.

Easiest and Best Carrot Cake with Orange Pecan Frosting

This is an adaptation of my Carrot Torte, made especially easy using the food processor. No need to grate the carrots, chop the nuts or beat the eggs separately. I think you will like the fact that it can all be assembled in the food processor and prepared in a few minutes.

> 1 package (3 ounces) cream cheese
> 2 eggs
> 1 1/4 cups sugar
> 1 cup pecans or walnuts
> 1/2 cup oil
> 3 small carrots, scraped and cut into 1-inch slices
> 1 cup flour
> 1 teaspoon cinnamon
> 1 teaspoon baking powder
> 1/2 teaspoon baking soda
> 1 teaspoon vanilla

Combine all the ingredients in the bowl of a food processor and blend for 30 seconds. Scrape down the sides and continue blending for about 30 seconds, or until carrots are finely grated.

Place batter into a buttered 10-inch springform pan and bake in a 350° oven for about 35 to 40 minutes, or until a cake tester, inserted in center, comes out clean. Allow to cool in pan.

Frost top with Orange Pecan Frosting and cut into wedges to serve. Serves 8 to 10.

Orange Pecan Frosting:
> 1 tablespoon orange juice
> 1 tablespoon cream
> 1 tablespoon grated orange peel
> 2 tablespoons finely chopped pecans
> 1 1/2 cups sifted powdered sugar (or more as necessary)

In a bowl, combine all the ingredients and stir until blended. Add a little powdered sugar, if necessary, to make a thicker frosting.

Farmhouse Carrot Cake with Pineapple & Buttermilk Glaze

This is an old-fashioned cake with a very special touch. After baking, a delightful glaze made with buttermilk and honey and flavored with lemon is poured on the top. This makes the cake exceedingly moist and it will last for days in the refrigerator.

- 2 eggs
- 1/2 cup oil
- 1/2 cup buttermilk
- 1 1/3 cups sugar
- 2/3 cup crushed pineapple, drained
- 1 1/4 cups grated carrots
- 1 1/2 teaspoons vanilla

- 2 1/3 cups flour
- 1 teaspoon baking powder
- 1 teaspoon baking soda
- 2 teaspoons cinnamon
- 1/4 cup coconut flakes
- 1 cup chopped walnuts

Beat together first 7 ingredients until blended. Mix together the remaining ingredients and add, all at once, to the liquid ingredients. Beat until nicely blended.

Pour batter into a greased 10-inch springform pan and bake in a 350° oven for about 55 minutes, or until a cake tester, inserted in center comes out clean. Remove from oven and pour Lemon Buttermilk Glaze over the top and let it seep in. Serves 10 to 12.

Lemon Buttermilk Glaze:
- 1/3 cup sugar
- 1/4 teaspoon baking soda
- 3 tablespoons buttermilk
- 2 tablespoons butter
- 1 tablespoon honey
- 2 teaspoons grated lemon
- 1/4 teaspoon vanilla

In a 4-cup saucepan, simmer all the ingredients together for 4 minutes, stirring now and again. (Do not use a smaller pan as syrup could bubble over.)

French Clafouti with Bing Cherries & Almond Creme Fraiche

A traditional clafouti is not made with baking powder, and therefore, must be baked just before serving. It puffs up and settles quickly, much like a popover or Yorkshire pudding. The addition of the small amount of baking powder, gives this clafouti stability and as a result, it can be prepared in advance and heated a little, just before serving. This is nice to serve for brunch or lunch. Teatime is good, too.

1 1/2 cups pitted bing cherries, fresh or frozen

- 1 cup flour
- 1 teaspoon baking powder
- 1/2 cup sugar
- 1/2 cup butter, softened
- 2 eggs
- 1/2 cup sour cream
- 1/2 cup toasted chopped almonds
- 1 teaspoon almond extract

In a 10-inch quiche baker, place the cherries. Beat together the remaining ingredients until blended. Spread batter evenly over the cherries. Bake in a 350° oven for about 35 minutes, or until top is browned and a cake tester, inserted in center, comes out clean. Allow to cool in pan. Can be served at room temperature or warmed before serving.

To serve, cut into wedges and spoon a little Almond Creme Fraiche on top. Serves 8.

Almond Creme Fraiche:

- 1/2 cup sour cream
- 1/2 cup cream
- 2 tablespoons sugar
- 1/2 teaspoon almond extract
- 2 tablespoons almond meal (very finely ground almonds)

Stir together all the ingredients until blended. Allow mixture to stand at room temperature for 2 hours or until thickened. Refrigerate until serving time. This can be prepared 1 day earlier and stored in the refrigerator.

Black Cherry & Almond Cake
with Streusel Oat Topping

A hearty, country cake with a streusel topping made with flour and oats, that is crunchy and delicious.

1/2 cup butter
1 cup sugar
2 eggs
2/3 cup sour cream
1 cup pitted black cherries (or Bing cherries),
   fresh or frozen

1 cup flour
1/2 cup whole wheat flour
1/2 cup quick-cooking oats
2 teaspoons baking powder
1 teaspoon baking soda
1 cup chopped toasted almonds

Beat together first 5 ingredients until blended. Combine and add the remaining ingredients and stir until nicely blended. Do not overmix.

Place batter into a greased 10-inch springform pan and sprinkle top with Streusel Oat Topping. Bake in a 350° oven for about 40 minutes, or until a cake tester, inserted in center, comes out clean. Allow to cool in pan. When cool, remove from pan and cut into wedges to serve. Serves 10.

Streusel Oat Topping:
   1/4 cup butter
   1/4 cup sugar
   1/4 cup flour
   1/4 cup quick-cooking oats
   1/2 teaspoon cinnamon
       pinch of baking powder

Mix together all the ingredients until mixture is crumbly.

Red Cherry Almond Cake with Almond Cream Glaze

If you love cherries and almonds, this is a delicious cake to consider. The Almond Cream Glaze is the perfect balance of flavors.

- 1/2 cup butter
- 1 cup sugar
- 2 eggs
- 1/2 cup cream
- 1/2 orange, grated (about 3 tablespoons)
- 1 teaspoon almond extract

- 1 cup flour
- 2 teaspoons baking powder
- 1 cup almond meal (finely grated almonds that can be purchased in health food stores)
- 1 cup canned red sour cherries, drained and patted dry

Cream butter with sugar. Beat in eggs, cream, orange and almond extract, beating well after each addition. Stir together and beat in the flour, baking powder and almond meal. Stir in the sour cherries.

Spread batter into a greased 10-inch springform pan and bake in a 350° oven for about 40 minutes, or until a cake tester, inserted in center, comes out clean. Allow to cool in pan.

When cool drizzle top with Almond Cream Glaze and allow a little to drip down the sides. Decorate top with toasted almond halves, or a sprinkle of finely chopped toasted almonds. Serves 10.

Note: — In the absence of almond meal, you can substitute finely grated walnuts. The texture of the almonds or walnuts should resemble flour.

Almond Cream Glaze:
- 2 tablespoons cream
- 1/2 teaspoon almond extract
- 1 cup sifted powdered sugar

Stir together all the ingredients until blended.

Glazed Cranberry Cake with Orange & Walnuts

This cake is so deliciously tart and fruity that it will serve well after a hearty meal. It is a low cake, filled with tart cranberries, orange and walnuts. A dollup of whipped cream is really nice, but please... forego it, if you are counting...

    1 package (1 pound) fresh cranberries, picked over,
        rinsed and patted dry
1/2 cup sugar
  4 tablespoons melted butter

1/2 cup butter
3/4 cup sugar
  1 egg
1/2 cup milk
  2 tablespoons grated orange peel
  1 teaspoon vanilla

1 1/4 cups flour
  2 teaspoons baking powder
3/4 cup finely chopped walnuts

In a 10-inch springform pan, place cranberries evenly. Sprinkle with sugar and drizzle with melted butter.

Beat butter, sugar, egg, milk, orange peel and vanilla until blended. Beat in flour, baking powder and walnuts until blended. Spread batter evenly over the cranberries. Place pan on a larger baking pan (to catch any drippings) and bake in a 350° oven for about 45 minutes, or until top is browned and a cake tester, inserted in center, comes out clean. Allow to cool in pan.

When cool, remove metal ring and invert cake on a lovely serving platter. Carefully remove the bottom of the pan. Sprinkle top with a little powdered sugar just before serving. Serves 8.

Note: — *It is important to place springform on a cookie sheet or jelly roll pan to catch the drippings. You may also want to line the outside bottom of the springform pan.*

Cranberry Orange & Lemon Tea Cake with Orange Lemon Wash

This is a tart, fruity cake, very chunky and simply delicious. When cranberries are in season, buy extras, for they freeze well. And, then, you can enjoy this lovely cake, at other times during the year.

- **1** cup sugar
- **1/2** cup butter, softened
- **1/2** cup sour cream
- **1/4** cup orange juice
- **2** tablespoons grated orange
- **1** tablespoon grated lemon

- **2** cups flour
- **1** teaspoon baking powder
- **1** teaspoon baking soda
- **1** cup cranberries, chopped
- **1** cup chopped walnuts

Beat together first 6 ingredients until blended. Beat in the remaining ingredients until blended. Do not over beat. Spread batter evenly into a greased 10-inch tube pan and bake in a 325° oven for about 45 minutes, or until a cake tester, inserted in center, comes out clean.

While hot, brush top with Orange Lemon Wash until it is absorbed. Serves 10.

Orange Lemon Wash:
- **4** tablespoons sugar
- **1** tablespoon orange juice
- **1** tablespoon lemon juice

In a bowl, mix together all the ingredients, and stir occasionally, until sugar is dissolved. This will take about 30 minutes. To test, put a drop of syrup between your teeth and if sugar is not dissolved, you will feel the grit.

Note: — Cranberries can be easily chopped in a food processor using about 10 on/off impulses. They should be coarsely chopped.

Daffodil Cake with Lemon & Pecans and Cream Cheese Filling

This bread is like a Danish ring, with a layer of lemon nut cake and little puddles of cheesecake filling. It is fashioned after a similar cake we enjoyed in Italy, but the filling was made with Ricotta cheese and glaceed fruits.

      2 eggs
  2/3 cup sugar
  1/2 cup oil
  1/2 cup sour cream
      1 tablespoon grated lemon (use fruit, juice and peel)
      1 teaspoon vanilla

2 1/4 cups flour
      1 teaspoon baking powder
  1/2 teaspoon baking soda
      1 cup chopped toasted pecans

      1 tablespoon cinnamon sugar

Beat together first 6 ingredients until blended. Combine and add the next 4 ingredients and stir until dry ingredients are blended. Do not overmix.

Place half the batter into a greased 10-inch springform pan. Spoon Cream Cheese Filling over the batter and pour remaining batter evenly on top. Sprinkle top with cinnamon sugar.

Bake in a 350° oven for about 40 minutes or until top is golden brown and a cake tester, inserted in center, comes out clean. (As this cake forms a crust, you will have to test carefully.) Allow to cool in pan. Cut into wedges to serve. Serves 8 to 10.

Cream Cheese Filling:
      1 package (8 ounces) cream cheese
  1/2 cup sugar
      1 egg
      1 tablespoon grated lemon (use fruit juice and peel)

Beat together all the ingredients until blended.

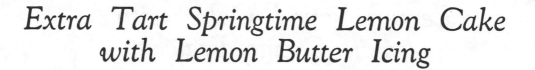

Extra Tart Springtime Lemon Cake
with Lemon Butter Icing

This is a basic lemon cake, tart and lemony, and dense as a poundcake. You can add 1 cup of blueberries as a lovely addition. Stir these in, at the end, with the flour. A lovely cake for a ladies lunch or tea.

        3/4 cup butter, softened
          2 cups sugar
          4 eggs
        3/4 cup sour cream
        1/2 cup milk
      1 1/2 lemons grated. Use fruit, juice and peel. Remove any
                large pieces of membrane

          3 cups flour
          2 teaspoons baking powder
          1 cup chopped pecans
          1 cup blueberries (optional)

Beat together first 6 ingredients until blended. Combine and add the remaining ingredients, and stir until blended. Do not overmix.

Spread batter into a greased 10-inch tube pan and bake in a 325° oven for about 1 hour, or until a cake tester, inserted in center, comes out clean. Allow to cool in pan.

When cool, brush top with Lemon Butter Icing. Serves 10 to 12.

Lemon Butter Icing:
        1 tablespoon butter, at room temperature
        1 tablespoon lemon juice
      3/4 cup sifted powdered sugar

Stir together all the ingredients until blended. Add a little more sugar or cream until icing is a brushing consistency. (This is a little thicker than a glaze.)

Note: — Cake can be decorated with small slivers of lemon zest. (The yellow part of the peel is called the "zest".)

Lemon Pound Cake with Lemon Creme Fraiche

When you bake this lovely cake in a 10-inch ring mold with a 4-cup capacity, you can fill the center with luscious strawberries or blueberries. Sprinkle the top with sifted powdered sugar and serve with a little bowl of Lemon Creme Fraiche on the side. Very delicious and very pretty for brunches or luncheons.

1/2 cup butter, softened
1/2 cup sugar

2 eggs
3 tablespoons grated lemon. Use fruit, juice and peel.
1 teaspoon vanilla

1 cup flour
1/2 teaspoon baking powder

Beat together butter and sugar until mixture is creamy. Beat in eggs, 1 at a time, beating well after each addition. Beat in lemon and vanilla. Combine and add flour and baking powder and beat until blended. Do not overbeat.

Spread batter into a greased and floured 10-inch ring mold with a 4-cup capacity and bake in a 350° oven for 30 minutes or until top is very lightly browned, and a cake tester, inserted in center, comes out clean. Allow to cool in pan for 5 minutes and then invert on a footed serving platter. Sprinkle top with sifted powdered sugar.

Serve with fresh fruit and a dollup of Lemon Cream Fraiche. (Please note that this is a very narrow ring, leaving a large inside circle for filling with fruit.) Serves 6.

Lemon Creme Fraiche:
1/2 cup sour cream
1/2 cup cream
2 tablespoons sugar
2 tablespoons grated lemon

Stir together all the ingredients until blended. Refrigerate for several hours. Overnight is good, too. Place in a lovely sauce boat and serve as an accompaniment to lemon cakes or lemon breads. Yields about 1 cup sauce.

Lemon Cream Cheese Coffeecake with Creamy Lemon Glaze

Not quite a poundcake, nor a spongecake, this is what I would call a "cakebread". (I've coined that word, and you are the first to know it.) It is light and tangy, not very sweet and a good choice for brunch or lunch. It can be assembled in minutes and is the essence of simplicity to prepare.

> 1 package (8 ounces) cream cheese, softened
> 1/2 cup (1 stick) butter, softened
>
> 1 cup sugar
> 2 eggs
> 1 lemon grated (about 3 tablespoons). Use fruit, juice and peel.
>
> 2 cups flour
> 1 tablespoon baking powder

Beat together cream cheese and butter until mixture is fluffy, about 2 minutes. Beat in sugar until blended. Beat in eggs, one at a time, until blended. Beat in lemon. Combine and add flour and baking powder and beat until blended. Do not overbeat.

Spread batter evenly into a greased 10-inch tube pan and bake in a 350° oven for about 35 minutes, or until top is browned and a cake tester, inserted in center, comes out clean. Allow to cool in pan.

When cool, remove from pan, drizzle top with Creamy Lemon Glaze and allow a little to drip down the sides. Serves 10.

Creamy Lemon Glaze:
> 1 tablespoon cream
> 2 teaspoons grated lemon peel
> 1/2 cup sifted powdered sugar

Stir together all the ingredients until blended.

Spicy Nectarine Ginger Cake with Sour Cream Glaze

Baked in a 12x8-inch fluted pan, makes this cake especially easy to serve on a buffet for brunch or lunch. Fruity and spicy, it is light and delicious. Peaches can be substituted for the nectarines.

    1 egg
1/4 cup butter, softened
3/4 cup sugar
1/4 cup sour cream
1/4 cup buttermilk
    1 cup finely chopped ripe and peeled nectarines

1 3/4 cups flour
    2 teaspoons baking powder
    1 teaspoon cinnamon
1/4 teaspoon ginger
1/8 teaspoon nutmeg
1/2 cup chopped pecans

  10 thin slices nectarine
   1 tablespoon cinnamon sugar

Beat together first 6 ingredients until blended. Combine and add the next 6 ingredients and stir until dry ingredients are just blended. Do not overmix.

Spread batter in a 12x8-inch greased fluted pan (with a removable bottom) and place nectarine slices decoratively on top. Sprinkle top with cinnamon sugar. Bake in a 350° oven for about 35 minutes, or until a cake tester, inserted in center, comes out clean. Allow to cool in pan.

When cool drizzle top with Sour Cream Glaze in a decorative fashion. Yields 24 2-inch squares.

Sour Cream Glaze:
    1 tablespoon sour cream
1/2 teaspoon lemon juice
1/2 cup sifted powdered sugar

Stir together all the ingredients until blended.

Fantastic Spiced Orange Cake with Orange Glaze

This is a very flavorful, super marvellous cake, flavored with orange and yogurt and spices. The walnuts and currants add a great balance of texture.

> 3 eggs
> 1 cup sugar
> 3/4 cup oil
> 1/2 cup unflavored yogurt
> 1 medium orange, cut into 8 pieces
>
> 2 1/2 cups flour
> 2 teaspoons baking powder
> 1 teaspoon baking soda
> 1 teaspoon cinnamon
> 1/4 teaspoon powdered cloves
> 1/4 teaspoon ground nutmeg
> 1 cup chopped walnuts
> 1/2 cup dried currants

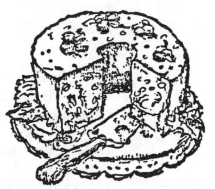

In the bowl of a food processor, place first 5 ingredients and blend until orange is very finely chopped, just short of pureed.

In the large bowl of an electric mixer, stir together the remaining ingredients. Add the orange mixture and beat until blended. Do not overbeat. Spread batter into a greased 10-inch tube pan and bake in a 350° oven for about 40 to 45 minutes, or until a cake tester, inserted in center, comes out clean. Allow to cool in pan.

When cool, drizzle top with Orange Glaze, allowing some to drip down the sides. Serves 10.

Orange Glaze:
> 1 tablespoon orange juice
> 1/2 cup sifted powdered sugar
> 2 teaspoons grated orange peel

Stir together orange juice and sugar until blended. Stir in the orange peel until blended.

Buttery Orange Walnut Coffee Cake with Cinnamon Walnut Topping

You will love the flavor and texture of this marvelous coffee cake. The cream cheese adds tremendous depth to this lovely creation.

    2 tablespoons butter
1/3 cup finely chopped walnuts

    1 cup butter, softened
    1 package (8 ounces) cream cheese
1 1/2 cups sugar

    4 eggs

    2 cups flour
    2 teaspoons baking powder
1/4 teaspoon salt

    2 tablespoons grated orange peel
    1 cup chopped walnuts
    1 teaspoon vanilla

Butter a 10-inch springform pan. Roll the 1/3 cup finely chopped walnuts in pan to evenly coat pan with nuts. Set aside.

Beat butter, cream cheese and sugar together until mixture is light and fluffy. Beat in eggs, one at a time, beating well after each addition. Beat in flour, baking powder and salt until blended. Beat in orange, walnuts and vanilla until blended.

Pour batter (it will be thick) into prepared pan and sprinkle top with Cinnamon Walnut Topping. Bake in a 300° oven for about 1 hour and 15 minutes or until a cake tester, inserted in center, comes out clean. Allow to cool in pan. Remove from pan and cut into wedges to serve. Serves 12.

Cinnamon Walnut Topping:
    2 tablespoons sugar
1/2 teaspoon cinnamon
1/4 cup finely chopped walnuts

Combine all the ingredients in a small bowl and stir until blended.

World's Best Orange & Lemon Sponge Cake

This is my very favorite sponge cake. I truly love it . . . . not only because of its marvellous taste and texture, but also, because it is amazingly easy to prepare. This cake is a base for many desserts and is a great recipe for your repertoire.

    6 eggs
    1 cup sugar

    1 cup flour, sifted
    1/2 medium orange, grated (about 4 tablespoons)
    2 tablespoons grated lemon peel
    2 teaspoons vanilla

In the large bowl of an electric mixer, beat eggs and sugar at high speed for about 10 minutes or until eggs have tripled in volume and are light and frothy.

On low speed, beat in flour only until blended. Fold in orange, lemon and vanilla. Pour batter into an ungreased 10-inch tube pan and bake in a 350° oven for about 40 to 45 minutes, or until a cake tester, inserted in center, comes out clean. Do not overbake. Remove from the oven, INVERT, and allow to cool. (If your tube pan does not have the three-little legs for inverting, you must invert cake over the neck of a large-size soda bottle.)

When cool, remove from pan and serve with fresh sliced strawberries and whipped cream. It can also be served with a faint sprinkling of sifted powdered sugar. Serves 10.

Note: — *Do not underbeat the eggs or cake will lose volume.*

     — *If your mixer does not have a very low and gentle setting, then fold in the flour by hand.*

Peach & Walnut Cinnamon Coffeecake
with Milky Glaze

This is a divine coffeecake, using the untraditional leavening of yeast and baking powder. The yeast imparts the wonderful bread quality while the baking powder assists in the rising. It is a fine tasting coffeecake, and I am certain you will enjoy it.

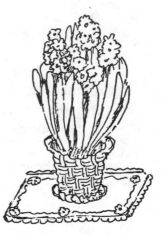

   1 package dry yeast
1/4 cup water
   1 teaspoon sugar

1/3 cup butter, softened
1/2 cup sugar
   1 teaspoon vanilla
   2 eggs

1 3/4 cups flour
   2 teaspoons baking powder

1/2 cup milk

Topping:
   3 peaches (fresh or frozen) pitted, peeled and sliced.
3/4 cup chopped walnuts
   4 tablespoons cinnamon sugar

In a small bowl, stir together yeast, water and sugar and allow to stand until mixture starts to foam and bubble. (This is called "proofing the yeast" and if it does not rise, it is inactive and should be discarded.)

In the large bowl of an electric mixer, beat together butter, sugar, vanilla and eggs until blended. Beat in the yeast mixture. Combine flour and baking powder and beat it in alternately with the milk. Spread batter in a greased 9x13-inch baking pan and place peaches in the batter in an attractive fashion. Sprinkle top with walnuts and cinnamon sugar, pressing the nuts lightly into the batter. Bake at 350° for 35 minutes, or until a cake tester, inserted in center, comes out clean. Allow to cool in pan. When cool, drizzle top with Milky Glaze. Serves 8 to 10.

Milky Glaze: Stir together 1 tablespoon milk and 1/2 cup sifted powdered sugar until blended. Stir in 1/4 teaspoon vanilla. Add a little sugar or milk to make glaze a drizzling consistency.

Fresh Peach & Orange Cake with Cinnamon Streusel Topping

This is like the old-fashioned crumb cakes we used to enjoy after a hard day at school. Only this one is sparkled with peaches, yogurt, and walnuts. This is one of the best tasting cakes and a lovely addition to a luncheon buffet.

2 eggs
1 carton (8 ounces) vanilla yogurt
1 cup sugar
1/2 cup butter
1 teaspoon vanilla

2 cups flour
2 teaspoons baking powder
1/2 teaspoon baking soda
1 cup finely chopped peaches
2 tablespoons grated orange peel

Beat together first 5 ingredients until blended. Combine and add the remaining ingredients and beat until blended. Spread batter into a greased 10-inch tube pan and sprinkle top with Cinnamon Streusel Topping. Bake in a 350° oven for about 50 minutes, or until a cake tester, inserted in center, comes out clean. Allow to cool in pan. When cool, remove from pan and place on the loveliest footed platter. Serves 8 to 10.

Cinnamon Streusel Topping:
2 tablespoons melted butter
1/3 cup sugar
3 tablespoons flour
1 teaspoon cinnamon

1/3 cup chopped walnuts

Stir together first 4 ingredients until mixture is blended and crumbly. Stir in the walnuts until blended.

Pear Cobbler with Cinnamon, Orange & Pecans

This is one of the most delicious desserts, filled with lots of fruit, flavored with orange and cinnamon, and topped with crunchy pecans. It is the essence of simplicity to prepare and wonderful for family dinners.

4 Bartlett pears, peeled, cored and sliced (about 1 1/2 pounds)
1/2 cup sugar
2 teaspoons cinnamon

2 eggs
1/2 cup oil
1 cup sugar
1 cup flour
1 teaspoon baking powder

2 tablespoons grated orange peel

1 cup chopped pecans
2 tablespoons cinnamon sugar

In a 9x13-inch baking pan, toss together pears, sugar and cinnamon, until fruit is evenly coated. Spread fruit evenly in pan.

Beat together next 5 ingredients until blended. Beat in the orange peel. Dribble batter over the pears, covering them evenly. Sprinkle top with pecans and cinnamon sugar. Pat the pecans lightly into the batter.

Bake in a 350° oven for 30 minutes, or until top is nicely browned. Allow to cool in pan. Cut into squares to serve and top with a little cream (optional) if you like. Serves 8.

Note: — *Can be served warm or at room temperature.*

— *Apples or peaches can be substituted.*

— *Enjoy!*

Ginger Snap Pumpkin Cake
with Raisins & Walnuts

This is a rather unusual pumpkin cake which is nice to serve around Thanksgiving. It is spicy and gingery and sparkled with walnuts and raisins. Serve this with giant mugs of hot cider.

      3 eggs
    3/4 cup sugar
    2/3 cup canned pumpkin puree

  2 1/4 cups ginger snap cookie crumbs
  1 1/2 teaspoons pumpkin pie spice
      1 cup chopped walnuts
    1/2 cup yellow raisins
      1 teaspoon vanilla

Beat eggs with sugar for about 3 minutes or until eggs are light and fluffy. Beat in the pumpkin until blended. Beat in the remaining ingredients until blended.

Spread batter into a buttered 9-inch pie pan and bake in a 350° oven for about 40 to 45 minutes, or until a cake tester, inserted in center, comes out clean. Allow to cool and then frost with Cognac Cream. Refrigerate for 4 to 6 hours. Overnight is good, too. Serves 8.

Cognac Cream:
      1 cup cream
      2 tablespoons sugar
    1/2 teaspoon vanilla
      1 tablespoon Cognac

Beat cream with sugar until soft peaks form. Add vanilla and Cognac and beat until cream is stiff.

Note: — Can be frozen, with or without the frosting.

Honey & Spice Pumpkin Cake with Raisins & Pecans

This is another variation of the traditional pumpkin cake, only this one is sparkled with grated orange, honey and buttermilk. It is a very spicy version that includes raisins and pecans.

    1/2 cup butter
      1 cup sugar
      2 eggs
    1/2 orange, grated (3 heaping tablespoons)
    3/4 cup buttermilk
    1/2 cup honey

      1 cup flour
      1 cup whole wheat flour
      1 teaspoon baking powder
      1 teaspoon baking soda
      3 teaspoons pumpkin pie spice
      1 cup yellow raisins
      1 cup chopped pecans

Cream butter with sugar. Beat in eggs, orange, buttermilk and honey, beating well after each addition. Stir together the remaining ingredients and add all at once, beating until blended. Do not overbeat.

Spread batter into a greased 10-inch tube pan and bake in a 325° oven for 45 minutes, or until a cake tester, inserted in center, comes out clean. Allow to cook in pan. When cool, sprinkle top with a little sifted powdered sugar. Serves 8 to 10.

Royal Raspberry & Almond Cake with Toasted Almond Glaze

Serving this at brunch or tea will bring rounds of applause and cries of "Bravo!" It has the subtle flavors of almond and raspberries and it is very moist.

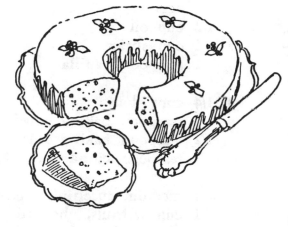

1/2 cup almond paste
1/3 cup oil
1 egg
1/2 cup sugar
1/2 cup buttermilk
1/2 cup sour cream
1 teaspoon almond extract

2 cups flour
1 tablespoon baking powder

3/4 cup raspberries

Beat together first 7 ingredients until blended. Combine and add flour and baking powder and stir until dry ingredients are just moistened. Gently fold in the raspberries.

Place batter into a greased 10-inch tube pan and bake in a 325° oven for 45 minutes, or until a cake tester, inserted in center comes out clean.

Allow to cool in pan. When cool, remove from pan and drizzle top with Toasted Almond Glaze, allowing a little to drip down the sides. Serves 8 to 10.

Toasted Almond Glaze:
1 tablespoon cream
1/4 teaspoon almond extract
3/4 cup sifted powdered sugar
3 tablespoons finely chopped toasted almonds

Stir together all the ingredients until blended.

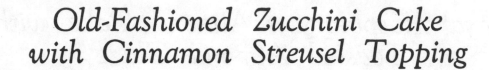

Old-Fashioned Zucchini Cake
with Cinnamon Streusel Topping

This old-fashioned zucchini cake is enhanced with raisins, walnuts and cinnamon. The Streusel topping is not traditional, but a really lovely addition.

    2 eggs
1/2 cup oil
    1 cup sugar
    1 teaspoon vanilla

1 1/4 cups flour
    1 teaspoon baking powder
1/2 teaspoon baking soda
    1 teaspoon cinnamon

    1 medium zucchini, peeled and grated (about 1 cup)
    1 cup walnuts, chopped
    1 cup yellow raisins

Beat together first 4 ingredients until blended. Add the next 4 ingredients, all at once, and stir until blended. Do not overmix. Stir in the zucchini, walnuts and raisins.

Spread mixture into a greased 10-inch tube pan and sprinkle top with Cinnamon Streusel Topping. Bake in a 350° oven for 45 to 50 minutes or until a cake tester, inserted in center, comes out clean. Allow to cool in pan. Serves 8 to 10.

Cinnamon Streusel Topping:
    3 tablespoons flour
1/2 teaspoon cinnamon
1/4 cup brown sugar
    pinch of baking powder
    1 tablespoon melted butter
    2 tablespoons finely chopped walnuts

Stir together all the ingredients until mixture is crumbly.

Other
Coffeecakes
with
Dried Fruit,
Nuts, Jams,
Spirits

Other Coffeecakes with Dried Fruits, Nuts, Jams

Sour Cream Almond Cake with Almond Glaze 62
Royal Apricot Cake with Vanilla Glaze 63
Apricot Pecan Yogurt Cake 64
Apricot Jam & Macaroon Cake 65
California Date Nut Cake 66
Old-Fashioned Marble Poundcake 67
Poppyseed Orange Cake 68
Old-Fashioned Spiced Prune & Walnut Cake 69
Bara Brith-Welsh Raisin Date Nut Cake 70
Buttery Scotch Shortcake with Raspberries 71
Strawberry Jam & Almond Cake 72
Golden Bourbon Fruit & Nut Cake 73
Bourbon & Eggnog Spiced Cake 74
Cappucino Poundcake 75
English Sherry Spice Cake 76
Sunny California Sour Cream Pineapple Cake 77
Old-Fashioned Spiced Honey Cake 78
Orange & Walnut Cake 79
Orange & Yogurt Cake with Cinnamon Streusel Swirl 80

Other Coffeecakes with
Dried Fruits, Nuts, Jams & Spirits

It's hard to believe that plums, grapes and apricots are the origins of prunes, raisins and dried apricots ... so different are they in appearance, taste and texture. Dried fruits are integral ingredients for coffeecakes, and are readily available at all times during the year.

Dried **Apricots** are tart and add an intense flavor to cakes and breads. It is one of my very favorites. **Almonds** are an excellent accompaniment.

Raisins, both dark and light, add a good deal of flavor and texture and mix well with fresh fruits or nuts.

Dried Fruits should be soft when used. If the fruit appears hard or extra-dry, it can be softened (or plumped) by soaking in hot water for 5 minutes; then drained and patted dry with paper towelling.

Walnuts and **Pecans** have a better flavor when toasted. **Almonds,** especially, should be toasted for fuller flavor. Nuts used for toppings should not be toasted.

Nuts should be scrupulously fresh. The slightest taint will ruin any cake beyond repair. Taste one or two nuts to make certain the batch is fresh.

Spices add a good deal of depth and character and fragrance to cakes. The most popular spices are cinnamon, nutmeg, ground cloves and ground ginger. Many cakes in this chapter can be transformed into a spice cake with the addition of 1 1/2 teaspoons cinnamon, 1/4 teaspoon nutmeg and 1/4 teaspoon ground cloves ... this will add your personal and individual touch to the recipe.

Liquors and **Liqueurs** act as flavorings and are also versatile. Golden Bourbon Fruit & Nut Cake can become Cognac Fruit & Nut Cake with the substitution of Cognac for the Bourbon. Sherry has such a delightful flavor, that I do not recommend a substitution.

Tucked away at the end of this chapter are 3 wonderful cakes made with a mix. Their excellence merits their inclusion.

Sour Cream Almond Cake with Almond Glaze

If you love almonds, this cake is a must. It is dense and compact and just full of flavor. This recipe is basic. Fresh blueberries or raspberries can be gently stirred into the batter as the last addition.

       4 **ounces almond paste, crumbled**
    1/2 **cup butter, softened**
       1 **cup sugar**
       2 **eggs**

    3/4 **cup sour cream**
       1 **teaspoon almond extract**

       2 **cups flour**
       1 **teaspoon baking powder**
       1 **teaspoon baking soda**
       1 **cup chopped toasted almonds**

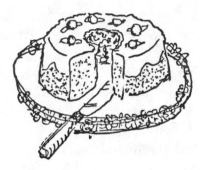

Cream together almond paste, butter and sugar until mixture is light. Beat in eggs until nicely blended. Beat in sour cream and almond extract until blended. Stir together and add the remaining ingredients and beat until blended. Do not overbeat.

Spread batter into a greased 10-inch tube pan and bake in a 350° oven for 35 to 40 minutes, or until top is browned and a cake tester, inserted in center, comes out clean. Allow to cool in pan.

When cool, drizzle top with Almond Glaze, and allow some to drip down the sides. Serves 8 to 10.

Almond Glaze:
  1 1/2 **tablespoons cream**
    1/2 **teaspoon almond extract**
    3/4 **cup sifted powdered sugar**

Stir together all the ingredients until blended. Add a little powdered sugar or cream to make glaze a thick drizzling consistency.

Royal Apricot Cake with Raisins, Walnuts & Vanilla Glaze

This is a dense cake, filled with apricots, raisins and walnuts. It is simply marvelous and gloriously delicious. The Vanilla Glaze is for dressing up a luncheon buffet, although a sprinkle of powdered sugar is just fine.

        1/2 cup butter
          4 ounces cream cheese
        3/4 cup sugar

          2 eggs
          2 teaspoons vanilla

          1 cup flour
          1 teaspoon baking powder
          1 cup chopped apricots (use soft dried apricots)
        1/2 cup chopped raisins
          1 cup chopped walnuts

Cream together butter, cream cheese and sugar until fluffy, about 2 minutes. Beat in eggs and vanilla until blended. In a bowl, mix together the remaining ingredients, and add to egg mixture. Beat until blended.

Place batter into a buttered and floured 9-inch kugelhopf pan that has been heavily greased and lightly floured. (A 9-inch tube pan can be substituted.) Bake in a 325° oven for about 50 minutes, or until top is browned and a cake tester, inserted in center, comes out clean.

Allow to cool in pan for 20 minutes and then invert, and continue cooling on a rack. When cool drizzle top with Vanilla Glaze in a decorative fashion. Serves 8.

Vanilla Glaze:
          1 tablespoon cream
        1/2 teaspoon vanilla
        1/2 cup sifted powdered sugar

Stir together all the ingredients until blended.

Note: — Apricots, raisins and walnuts can be chopped together in a processor.

Apricot Pecan Yogurt Cake with Vanilla Yogurt Glaze

This cake is enriched with a little extra butter, eggs and yogurt. It is absolutely delicious, sparkled with apricots, pecans and yellow raisins.

3/4 cup butter
1 cup sugar
3 eggs

3/4 cup vanilla yogurt
1/2 teaspoon vanilla

2 cups flour
2 teaspoons baking powder
1 cup finely chopped apricots
1 cup yellow raisins
1 cup chopped pecans

Cream butter and sugar until mixture is light, about 2 minutes. Beat in eggs, one at a time, beating well after each addition. Beat in yogurt and vanilla. Beat in the remaining ingredients until blended.

Spread batter into a greased 10-inch tube pan and bake at 350° for 40 to 45 minutes, or until a cake tester, inserted in center, comes out clean. Allow to cool in pan. When cool, brush top with Vanilla Yogurt Glaze and allow a little to drip down the sides. Serves 10.

Vanilla Yogurt Glaze:
2 tablespoons vanilla yogurt
3/4 cup sifted powdered sugar

Stir together yogurt and sugar until blended.

Note: — This glaze is on the sticky side, so don't think anything went wrong.

Apricot Jam & Macaroon Cake
with Walnuts & Raisins

This is a very unusual combination of ingredients, but it does produce a fine tasting cake with a chewy texture. Please use a good quality coconut macaroon cookie, and blend into crumbs in a food processor. The apricot jam makes it sticky and dense.

1/2 cup butter, softened
1 cup sugar
2 eggs
1/2 cup sour cream
1 teaspoon vanilla

2 cups flour
1 teaspoon baking powder
1 teaspoon baking soda

1/2 cup apricot jam
3/4 cup macaroon cookie crumbs
1 cup yellow raisins
1 cup chopped walnuts

Beat together first 5 ingredients until blended. Beat in flour, baking powder and soda until blended. Beat in the remaining ingredients, in order listed, until blended.

Spread mixture in a greased 9x13-inch baking pan and bake in a 350° oven for about 35 minutes or until a cake tester, inserted in center comes out clean. Allow to cool in pan.

When cool, top may be sprinkled with a little sifted powdered sugar, no more. Cut into squares to serve. Yields 2 dozen squares. Serves 12.

California Date Nut Cake
with Cream Cheese Frosting

There are certain cakes that are very Californian in character, and this is one of them. Use the beautiful, plump California dates and they do not need to be softened.

    1/2 cup butter (1 stick) softened
      1 cup sugar
      2 eggs
      1 cup orange juice
      1 teaspoon vanilla

1 1/2 cups flour
      1 teaspoon baking soda
    1/2 teaspoon baking powder
      1 teaspoon cinnamon
      1 cup finely chopped dates
      1 cup finely chopped walnuts

Beat together first 5 ingredients until blended. Beat in remaining ingredients until dry ingredients are nicely blended. Do not overmix.

Divide batter between 2 greased 10-inch springform pans and bake in a 350° oven for about 30 minutes or until a cake tester, inserted in center, comes out clean. Remove rings and cool on a rack.

With a sharp knife, remove layers and fill and frost with Cream Cheese Frosting. Serves 10.

Cream Cheese Frosting:
      1 package (8 ounces) cream cheese, softened
    1/2 cup butter, softened (1 stick)
      2 teaspoons vanilla
      3 cups sifted powdered sugar

Beat together cream cheese and butter until blended. Beat in vanilla and sugar until frosting is blended. Will fill and frost a 10-inch layer cake.

Old-Fashioned Marble Poundcake
with Vanilla Glaze

Many were the times when this delicious poundcake was waiting for us after school. Now, the marble is very dark and chocolaty. This is not a very high cake, so don't feel anything went wrong.

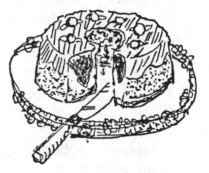

    1/2 cup butter
      1 cup sugar
      3 eggs

    1/2 cup sour cream
    1/2 cup cream
      2 teaspoons vanilla

      2 cups flour
      1 teaspoon baking powder
      1 teaspoon baking soda

      3 tablespoons cocoa
      3 tablespoons sifted powdered sugar

Cream butter with sugar until mixture is light and fluffy. Beat in eggs, one at a time, beating well after each addition. Beat in sour cream, cream and vanilla until blended.

Mix together flour, baking powder and soda and beat it in until blended. Spread 1/2 the batter in a greased 10-inch tube pan. Stir the cocoa and sifted powdered sugar into the remaining batter. Place large spoonsful of chocolate batter over the batter in the pan. With a knife, cut into the batter in a zig-zag fashion.

Bake in a 350° oven for about 40 to 45 minutes, or until a cake tester, inserted in center, comes out clean. Allow to cool in pan. When cool drizzle top with Vanilla Glaze. Serves 8 to 10.

Vanilla Glaze:
      1 tablespoon cream
    1/2 cup sifted powdered sugar
    1/2 teaspoon vanilla

Stir together all the ingredients until blended. Add a little sugar or cream to make glaze a drizzling consistency.

Poppyseed Orange Cake
with Orange Glaze

This is a very moist, delicately flavored coffeecake, that is lovely for a brunch buffet or afternoon tea. It has an excellent crumb, and is a lovely texture.

    3/4 cup oil
      1 medium orange, grated (about 6 tablespoons). Reserve 1
          tablespoon for glaze.
    1/2 cup milk
    1/2 cup sour cream
      2 eggs
      1 cup sugar

  2 1/2 cups flour
      1 tablespoon baking powder
      4 tablespoons poppy seeds

Beat together first 6 ingredients until blended. Stir together and add the remaining ingredients and beat until dry ingredients are nicely blended. Do not overbeat.

Spread batter evenly into a 10-inch tube pan and bake in a 350° oven for about 50 minutes, or until a cake tester, inserted in center, comes out clean. Allow to cool in pan. When cool, drizzle top with Orange Glaze, and allow a little to drip down the sides. Serves 8 to 10.

Orange Glaze:
      1 tablespoon grated orange. (Use fruit, juice and peel.)
    1/2 cup sifted powdered sugar

Stir together all the ingredients until blended. Add a little orange juice or powdered sugar to make glaze a drizzling consistency.

Old-Fashioned Spiced Prune & Walnut Cake

This delicious layer cake is filled with old-fashioned goodness. Spicy, filled with prunes and walnuts, and frosted with an old-fashioned fluffy frosting, makes this totally irresistible.

3 eggs
2 cups sugar
1 cup oil
1 cup sour cream

2 cups flour
1 teaspoon baking powder
1 teaspoon baking soda
1 teaspoon cinnamon
2 teaspoons pumpkin pie spice

1 cup finely chopped soft pitted prunes
1 cup finely chopped walnuts

Beat together first 4 ingredients until blended. Combine and add the next 5 ingredients and stir until dry ingredients are blended. Do not overmix. Stir in the prunes and walnuts.

Divide mixture between 2 greased 10-inch springform pans and bake in a 350° oven for 30 minutes or until a cake tester, inserted in center, comes out clean. Allow to cool in pan. When cool, remove from pan and fill and frost with Fluffy Vanilla Frosting. Serves 10 to 12.

Fluffy Vanilla Frosting:
2 egg whites
3/4 cup sugar
pinch of salt
pinch of cream of tartar
1 teaspoon vanilla

Place all the ingredients in the top of a double boiler and beat until whites are foamy. Place top over simmering water and beat with a rotary beater or electric hand mixer, until mixture stands in stiff peaks. Swirl frosting between cake layers and on the top and sides of cake. Will fill and frost a 10-inch cake.

Bara Brith
Welsh Raisin Date Nut Cake

This recipe is fashioned after a lovely cake we enjoyed, one morning, in a charming village in Wales. There are many versions of the Bara Brith, as many perhaps, as there are Welsh housewives. It is basically a spicy raisin cake, deep, dark and delicious. This cake is a bit unorthodox, but very moist and fruity.

    1 1/4 cups butter (2 1/2 sticks)
    1 1/4 cups brewed tea
        1 can (14 ounces) condensed milk
        1 cup yellow raisins
        1 cup black currants
        1 cup chopped dates

    1 1/4 cups flour
    1 1/4 cups whole wheat flour
        1 teaspoon baking powder
        1 teaspoon baking soda
        1 teaspoon cinnamon
      1/4 teaspoon nutmeg
      1/4 teaspoon ground cloves
        1 cup chopped walnuts

        2 tablespoons apricot jam

In a saucepan, heat together first 6 ingredients and allow mixture to simmer for a minute or 2, or until nicely blended and raisins are plumped. Allow to cool for 30 minutes. Mix together and stir in the next 8 ingredients until dry ingredients are just moistened. Do not overmix. Stir in the apricot jam.

Scrape batter into a greased 10-inch springform pan and bake in a 325° oven for about 1 hour 20 minutes or until a cake tester, inserted in center, comes out clean. (Tent pan loosely with foil if top is browning too rapidly.)

Allow to cool in pan, and then cover tightly with plastic wrap and store cake in the refrigerator.

Note: — This cake is not very sweet, more like a dark raisin bread.

Buttery Scotch Shortbread
with Raspberries & Cream

This is a good basic shortbread (actually like our shortcake). It is very buttery and just lovely with berries and cream. It could not be easier to prepare, and with ingredients always found in your cupboard. Good for spring and summer desserts.

- **1 cup butter**
- **1 cup sifted powdered sugar**

- **2 eggs**
- **2 cups flour**
- **1 teaspoon baking powder**
- **1/2 teaspoon vanilla**

- **1 pint raspberries (or strawberries)**

Cream butter with sugar until mixture is light and fluffy. Beat in eggs, beating well after each addition. Mix together flour and baking powder and beat in until blended. Beat in vanilla.

Spread batter into a greased 10-inch springform pan and bake in a 350° oven for about 30 minutes, or until top is browned and a cake tester, inserted in center, comes out clean. Allow to cool in pan.

When cool, remove from pan and spread top with Whipped Creme Fraiche and stud top with raspberries or strawberries. Serves 8 to 10.

Whipped Creme Fraiche:
- **3/4 cup cream**
- **2 tablespoons sifted powdered sugar**
- **1/2 teaspoon vanilla**

- **1/4 cup sour cream**

Beat cream with sugar and vanilla until cream is stiff. Beat in sour cream until blended.

Note: — It is not easy to test this cake, as the high butter content can leave the tester clean and the cake can still be undercooked. So, make certain that the top is golden brown, that the edges start to pull away slightly and that the center feels firm and dry.

Strawberry Jam & Almond Cake with Strawberry Glaze

Here's a real taste treat with the combination of strawberry jam and almonds. This is a luscious cake, very moist and tender. The Strawberry Glaze is an invitation of the good things to come.

        1/2 cup butter
        3/4 cup sugar
          2 eggs

        1/2 cup strawberry jam
        1/4 cup sour cream
          1 teaspoon almond extract

    1 1/2 cups flour
          1 teaspoon baking powder
        1/2 teaspoon baking soda
        1/2 cup chopped toasted almonds

Cream butter with sugar, until mixture is light. Beat in eggs until thoroughly blended. Beat in jam, sour cream and almond extract until blended. Combine and add the remaining ingredients and beat until mixture is blended. Do not overbeat.

Spread batter into a greased 10-inch tube pan and bake in a 350° oven for 35 to 40 minutes, or until a cake tester, inserted in center, comes out clean. Allow to cool in pan.

When cool, brush top with Strawberry Glaze and allow a little to drip down the sides. Serves 8 to 10.

Strawberry Glaze:
        2 tablespoons strawberry jam
        1 tablespoon cream
      2/3 cup sifted powdered sugar

Stir together all the ingredients until blended.

Golden Bourbon Fruit & Nut Cake with Bourbon Cream Glaze

This is a golden fruitcake that is one of my favorites. It is chock full of fruit and nuts. If you plan this for gift-giving, recipe can easily be doubled. Add a little more Bourbon, (about 2 tablespoons), if you like a stronger liquor flavor.

    3/4 cup butter
      1 cup sugar
      3 eggs

  1 1/2 cups flour
      1 teaspoon baking powder

    1/4 pound glaceed cherries, chopped
    1/4 pound glaceed mixed fruits
  1 1/2 cups chopped walnuts or pecans
      2 tablespoons Bourbon
      1 teaspoon vanilla

Cream butter with sugar until light and fluffy. Add eggs, one at a time, beating well after each addition. Beat in flour and baking powder until blended. Stir in the remaining ingredients until blended.

Divide batter between 4 greased mini-loaf foil pans, (6x3x2-inches) and bake in a 350° oven for 45 to 50 minutes, or until a cake tester, inserted in center, comes out clean. Allow to cool in pans for 15 minutes and then remove from pans and continue cooling on a rack.

When cool, drizzle tops with Bourbon Cream Glaze, and decorate with 2 or 3 glaceed cherries. Yields 4 mini-loaves.

Bourbon Cream Glaze:
      1 tablespoon Bourbon
      1 tablespoon cream
  1 1/4 cups sifted powdered sugar

Stir together all the ingredients until blended. Add a little more cream or sugar to make glaze a drizzling consistency.

Bourbon & Eggnog Spiced Cake with Cherries & Almonds

Oh! what a lovely cake to serve for family get-to-gethers during the time from Thanksgiving to the New Year. It is truly a holiday cake and serving it will feel like a celebration.

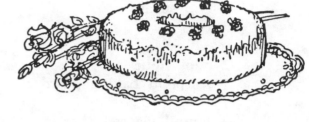

1 1/2 cups sugar
    1 cup butter
    2 eggs

    3/4 cup prepared egg nog
    1/4 cup Bourbon

2 1/4 cups flour
    1 teaspoon baking powder
    1 teaspoon baking soda
    1 teaspoon cinnamon
    1/2 teaspoon ground allspice
    1/4 teaspoon ground nutmeg
    3/4 cup chopped glaceed cherries
    3/4 cup chopped toasted almonds

Cream together sugar and butter until light and fluffy. Beat in eggs until blended. Beat in egg nog and Bourbon until blended. In a bowl, mix together the remaining ingredients and beat into egg mixture until nicely blended. Do not overbeat.

Spread batter evenly into a greased 10-inch tube pan and bake in a 350° oven for about 55 minutes, or until a cake tester, inserted in center, comes out clean. Allow to cool in pan.

When cool, remove from pan and drizzle top with Eggnog Cream Glaze. Decorate top with whole glaceed cherries and toasted slivered almonds. Serves 10 to 12.

Eggnog Cream Glaze:
    1 tablespoon cream
    1 tablespoon eggnog
    1 cup sifted powdered sugar

Stir together all the ingredients until blended.

Cappucino Pound Cake with Coffee Kahlua Cream

My favorite version of Cappucino is flavored with Creme de Cacao and Kahlua liqueurs. This delicious cake is fashioned after the famous coffee and the frosting carries through with this theme.

- 3/4 cup oil
- 1/2 cup honey
- 1 cup sugar
- 4 eggs
- 1/2 cup milk
- 1/2 cup sour cream
- 1 tablespoon Creme de Cacao (chocolate liqueur)
- 1 tablespoon Kahlua (coffee liqueur)

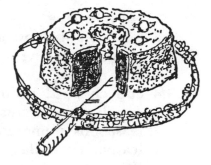

- 2 cups flour
- 1/2 cup cocoa
- 2 teaspoons baking powder
- 1 teaspoon baking soda
- 1 tablespoon instant coffee
- 2 teaspoons cinnamon
- 1/4 teaspoon ground nutmeg
- 1/4 teaspoon ground cloves

Beat together first 8 ingredients until thoroughly blended, about 4 minutes. Mix together and beat in the remaining ingredients until blended. Spread batter into a greased 10-inch tube pan and bake in a 325° oven for about 1 hour 10 minutes, or until a cake tester, inserted in center, comes out clean. Allow to cool in pan.

When cool, frost top with Coffee Kahlua Cream. Serves 8 to 10.

Coffee Kahlua Cream:
- 1 cup cream
- 1 teaspoon instant coffee
- 2 tablespoons sugar
- 1 tablespoon Kahlua

Beat cream with remaining ingredients until cream is stiff.

Note: — You can use either powdered instant coffee or freeze-dried crystals. The freeze-dried crystals will not incorporate as readily, but the little grains of coffee intensify the flavor, and is very good, indeed.

English Sherry Spice Cake with Sherry Glaze

This is an adaptation of the famous English Sherry Cake. It is a fine cake to serve around the holidays. It is not too sweet, yet very flavorful and satisfying.

1/2 cup butter, softened
1 cup brown sugar
1 egg
1/2 cup golden cream sherry
3 tablespoons grated orange

2 cups flour
2 teaspoons baking powder
1/2 teaspoon baking soda
3/4 cup raisins
3/4 cup chopped walnuts
3/4 cup black currants
2 teaspoons pumpkin pie spice
1 teaspoon vanilla

Beat together first 5 ingredients until blended. Combine and add the remaining ingredients and beat until blended. Do not overbeat.

Spread batter into a greased 10-inch tube pan and bake in a 325° oven for about 50 minutes, or until a cake tester, inserted in center, comes out clean. Allow to cool in pan. When cool, brush top with Sherry Glaze. Serves 10.

Sherry Glaze:
1 tablespoon golden cream sherry
1/2 cup sifted powdered sugar

Stir together sherry and sugar until blended.

Sunny California Sour Cream Pineapple Cake with Pineapple Glaze

If this cake didn't make such a hit, I probably would not have included it. It is so simple, I thought, you probably might snub it altogether. But the fact remains that some real coffeecake lovers thought it was wonderful . . . moist, delicious and velvety. So here it is, and I hope you enjoy it, too.

> 1 package (18 1/2 ounces) yellow cake mix (without pudding)
> 3 eggs
> 1/3 cup oil
> 1 cup crushed pineapple, with a little juice
> 1/2 cup sour cream

Beat together all the ingredients, for 4 minutes, at medium speed. Spread batter evenly into a greased 10-inch tube pan and bake in a 350° oven for 45 to 50 minutes, or until a cake tester, inserted in center, comes out clean. Allow to cool in pan.

When cool, remove from pan and brush top with Pineapple Glaze, and allow a little to drip down the sides. Serves 10.

Pineapple Glaze:
> 1 tablespoon crushed pineapple (a little juice and a little fruit)
> 1/2 cup sifted powdered sugar

Stir together pineapple and sugar until blended.

Note: — This cake is a good choice for a ladies luncheon, for it is very light and very delicious.

Old-Fashioned Spiced Honey Cake
with Raisins & Walnuts

What a nice cake to serve on a Sunday night when the family gets together. It's a delicious cake, not too sweet, and just bursting with goodness. It is made with all manner of good things ... whole wheat flour, honey and raisins.

 1/2 cup butter
  1 cup honey
  2 eggs
 1/2 cup milk
 1/2 cup sour cream
  2 teaspoons vanilla

 2 1/4 cups whole wheat pastry flour
 1 1/2 teaspoons baking powder
  1 teaspoon baking soda
  2 teaspoons cinnamon
 1/4 teaspoon ground nutmeg
 1/4 teaspoon ground cloves
 1/2 cup raisins

 1/2 cup chopped walnuts

Beat together first 6 ingredients until thoroughly blended, about 4 minutes. Mix together next 7 ingredients and beat in until blended. Spread batter into a greased 10-inch tube pan and sprinkle top with chopped nuts, pressing them lightly into the batter.

Bake in a 350° oven for about 40 to 45 minutes, or until a cake tester, inserted in center, comes out clean. Allow to cool in pan. When cool, remove from pan and cut into wedges to serve. Serves 8 to 10.

Orange & Walnut Cake with Cinnamon & Cream Glaze

This cake starts with humble ingredients, but ends up intensely delicious. The batter is sparkled with a deep flavor of orange and cinnamon. No one will guess that you started with a cake mix.

    1 package (18 1/2 ounces) yellow cake mix (without
        pudding)
    3 eggs
    1/3 cup oil
    1 cup sour cream
    1/3 cup water
    6 tablespoons grated orange (1 medium orange). Use fruit,
        juice and peel

    4 tablespoons cinnamon sugar
    3/4 cup chopped walnuts

Beat together first 6 ingredients, at medium speed, for 4 minutes. Spread half the batter into a lightly greased 10-inch tube pan. Sprinkle 3 tablespoons cinnamon sugar and 1/4 cup chopped walnuts over the batter. Cover with remaining batter. Sprinkle top with remaining cinnamon sugar and chopped walnuts. (Pat walnuts lightly into the batter.)

Bake in a 350° oven for about 50 minutes, or until a cake tester, inserted in center, comes out clean. Allow to cool in pan.

When cool remove from pan and drizzle top with Vanilla Cream Glaze. Yields 10 servings.

Vanilla Cream Glaze:
    1/2 cup sifted powdered sugar
    1 tablespoon cream
    1/4 teaspoon vanilla

Stir together all the ingredients until blended.

Orange & Yogurt Cake with Cinnamon Streusel Swirl & Walnuts

This is a super delicious cake, and is a good choice if you have some yellow cake mix around the house. It is fruity and moist and unbelievably good.

- 1 package yellow cake mix (18 1/2 ounces)
- 1/3 cup oil
- 1 cup unflavored yogurt
- 1 medium orange, grated (about 6 tablespoons)
- 3 eggs

Cinnamon Streusel:
- 2 tablespoons sugar
- 2 tablespoons flour
- 1 tablespoon butter
- 1/2 teaspoon cinnamon

1/2 cup chopped nuts

Beat together first 5 ingredients for 4 minutes or until batter is light. To make the streusel, mix together sugar, flour, butter and cinnamon until blended. Spread half the batter into a greased 10-inch tube pan. Sprinkle with Cinnamon Streusel and cover with remaining batter. With a knife or spatula, cut into batter at 2-inch intervals. Sprinkle top with walnuts and press them lightly into the batter.

Bake at 350° for about 45 to 50 minutes, or until top is browned and a cake tester, inserted in center, comes out clean. When cool, remove from pan and sprinkle top with sifted powdered sugar. Serves 8 to 10.

Cakes

with

Chocolate

&

Chocolate

Chips

Cakes with Chocolate & Chocolate Chips

Sour Cream & Chocolate Banana Cake 84
Chocolate Banana Cake 85
Chocolate Carrot Almond Cake 86
Swiss Chocolate Cake with Cherries 87
Chocolate Fudge Decadence with Rum & Raisins 88
Chocolate Chestnut Cake 89
Chocolate Chip Buttermilk Cake 90
Sour Cream Chocolate Chip Chocolate Cake 91
Chocolate Chip Chocolate Cake 92
Sour Cream Chocolate Fudge Cake 93
Sour Cream Poundcake with Chocolate Chips 94
Bittersweet Chocolate Fudge Cake 95
Mocha Chocolate Cake 96
Chocolate Pumpkin Pecan Cake 97
Chocolate Pumpkin Spiced Cake 98
Raspberry & Chocolate Chip Cake 99
Anniversary Chocolate & Raspberry Cake 100
Vanilla Poundcake with Chocolate Chips 101
Basic Chocolate Sponge Cake 102
Chocolate Velvet Cake 103
Chocolate Zucchini Cake 104

From my Notebook:

Cakes with Chocolate & Chocolate Chips

This chapter will clearly indicate how most cakes have a chocolate counter-part. Bananas, carrots, cherries, chestnuts, pumpkin, raspberries, zucchini, all are truly marvellous when used with chocolate.

Let me say, right at the start, that vegetables impart little taste to the cake, but they do add a wonderful moistness. Fruits add a delicious flavor and interesting texture.

The cakes in this chapter can be described as afternoon into evening cakes. They are lovely with afternoon tea and are grand desserts. Children will love them with milk, after school.

These are fine cakes to consider for birthdays and celebrations. But, as they are so easy to prepare, they do not have to be reserved for special occasions and can be enjoyed at any time. These cakes are not very sweet or cloying.

To make a cake "chocolate", substitute 6 tablespoons of cocoa for 6 tablespoons of the flour. For a more intense bittersweet chocolate flavor, substitute 1/2 cup of cocoa for 1/2 cup of the flour used in the recipe. So, using this formula, you can make Chocolate Applesauce Cake, Chocolate Gingerbread, Chocolate Date Cake, Chocolate Prune Cake, Chocolate Coconut Cake and a host of other combinations. Again, please first make the recipe as indicated, familiarize yourself with its personality, and then add your personal and individual touch.

If a recipe calls for chocolate, you can substitute 3 tablespoons cocoa and 1 tablespoon butter for each ounce of chocolate called for.

If you love a dark, dense chocolate fudge cake, I hope you try my Sour Cream Chocolate Fudge Cake (Page 93) which is truly a poem of flavor and texture. No one could ever guess (until you tell) that this divine cake was prepared in minutes.

Sour Cream & Chocolate Banana Cake with Chocolate Chips

Very moist and full of flavor is this lovely chocolate cake. It is sparkled with the mini-chocolate chips. The addition of chopped walnuts is optional in this cake, but it does provide a little texture.

        1/2 cup butter
          1 cup sugar
          2 eggs

        1/2 cup sour cream
          1 large banana, mashed
          1 teaspoon vanilla

    1 1/2 cups flour
          6 tablespoons cocoa
          1 teaspoon baking powder
        1/2 teaspoon baking soda
          1 cup (6 ounces) mini-morsel chocolate chips

Cream butter with sugar until mixture is light and creamy. Beat in eggs until nicely blended. Beat in sour cream, banana and vanilla until blended. Stir together and add the remaining ingredients and beat until batter is nicely blended, but do not overbeat.

Spread batter into a greased 10-inch tube pan and bake in a 350° oven for about 40 to 45 minutes, or until a cake tester, inserted in center, comes out clean. Allow to cool in pan.

When cool, remove from pan and sprinkle top with sifted powdered sugar. Serves 10.

Chocolate Banana Cake with Chocolate Chips & Walnuts

What a nice cake . . . light, moist and full of flavor. This can be frosted or served with just a sprinkling of powdered sugar.

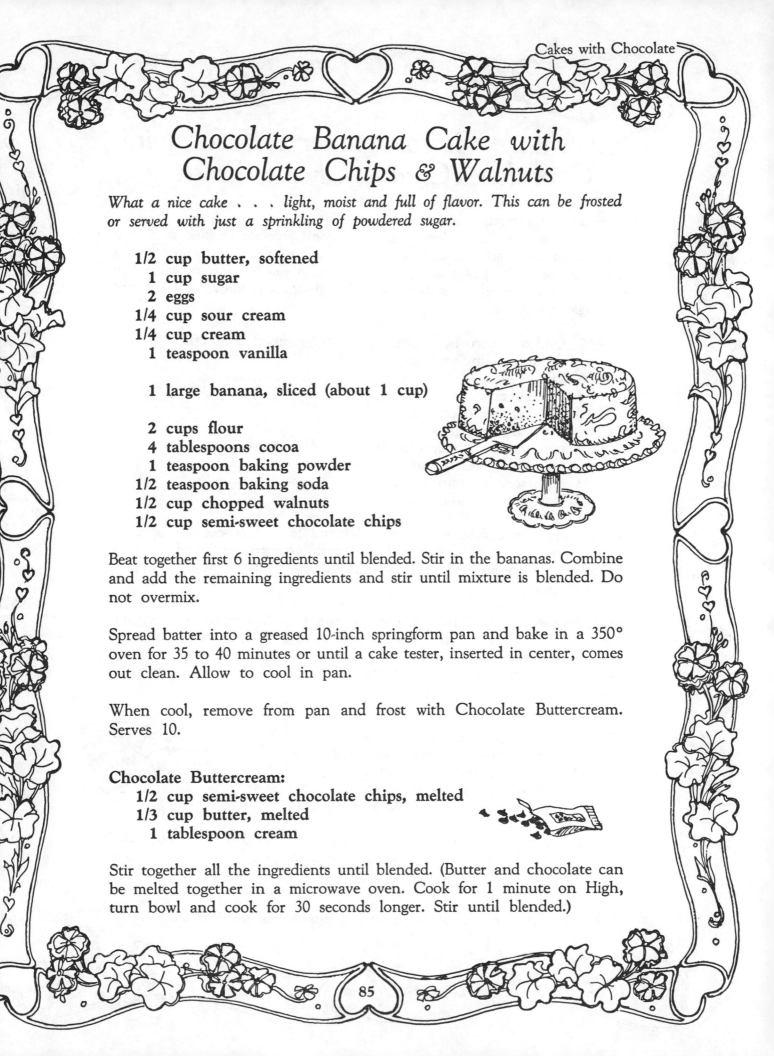

   1/2 cup butter, softened
     1 cup sugar
     2 eggs
   1/4 cup sour cream
   1/4 cup cream
     1 teaspoon vanilla

     1 large banana, sliced (about 1 cup)

     2 cups flour
     4 tablespoons cocoa
     1 teaspoon baking powder
   1/2 teaspoon baking soda
   1/2 cup chopped walnuts
   1/2 cup semi-sweet chocolate chips

Beat together first 6 ingredients until blended. Stir in the bananas. Combine and add the remaining ingredients and stir until mixture is blended. Do not overmix.

Spread batter into a greased 10-inch springform pan and bake in a 350° oven for 35 to 40 minutes or until a cake tester, inserted in center, comes out clean. Allow to cool in pan.

When cool, remove from pan and frost with Chocolate Buttercream. Serves 10.

Chocolate Buttercream:
   1/2 cup semi-sweet chocolate chips, melted
   1/3 cup butter, melted
     1 tablespoon cream

Stir together all the ingredients until blended. (Butter and chocolate can be melted together in a microwave oven. Cook for 1 minute on High, turn bowl and cook for 30 seconds longer. Stir until blended.)

Chocolate Carrot Almond Cake with Chocolate Cream Cheese Frosting

OH! what a glorious unusual cake, interesting in taste and texture. It is an adaptation of the classic Carrot Cake and the Chocolate Frosting is truly a great accompaniment. The almond meal can be purchased at most health food stores. Actually, it is almonds, finely grated to a fine meal consistency. You can grate the almonds in a nut grater, but the food processor will not give you right consistency.

> 2 medium carrots, about 4 ounces, scraped and cut
>   into 1-inch pieces
> 5 eggs
> 1 cup sugar
> 4 tablespoons cocoa
> 1 1/2 cups almond meal
> 1 cup vanilla wafer crumbs
> 1 teaspoon baking powder
> 1 teaspoon almond extract
> 1/2 teaspoon vanilla

Place carrots in a food processor and blend for a few seconds, or until carrots are coarsely chopped. Add the remaining ingredients and continue to blend until mixture is blended and carrots are very finely chopped, but not pureed.

Place batter into a 10-inch springform pan that has been buttered and lightly coated with vanilla wafer crumbs. Bake in a 350° oven for about 35 minutes or until a cake tester, inserted in center, comes out clean. Allow to cool in pan. When cool, spread Chocolate Cream Cheese Frosting on top and sides. Serves 8.

Chocolate Cream Cheese Frosting:
> 4 ounces cream cheese, softened
> 1 cup sifted powdered sugar
> 3 tablespoons sifted cocoa
> 1/2 teaspoon vanilla or almond extract

Beat cream cheese until fluffy. Sift in the sugar and cocoa and beat until blended. Beat in vanilla (or almond extract). Spread on top and sides of cake.

Note: — This is not a lot of frosting... just a thin delicious coating.

Swiss Chocolate Cake with Cherries & Almonds

This is a dark and delicious chocolate cake, studded with cherries and almonds. It is so full of flavor, that it should not be frosted.

1 can (1 pound) dark sweet pitted cherries, drained. Reserve juice.

3/4 cup butter
1 cup sugar
3 eggs
1/2 cup reserved cherry juice
1 teaspoon vanilla
1/2 teaspoon almond extract

2 cups flour
6 tablespoons cocoa
1 teaspoon baking powder
1 teaspoon baking soda
1/2 cup chopped almonds

18 blanched whole almonds

Drain the cherries and measure 1/2 cup of the juice. Cream butter and sugar. Beat in eggs until nicely blended. Beat in cherry juice, vanilla and almond extract until blended.

Combine and add the next 5 ingredients and beat until blended. Stir in the cherries. Spread batter evenly into a greased 10-inch springform pan and press almonds gently on top. Bake at 350° for about 40 minutes, or until a cake tester, inserted in center, comes out clean. Allow to cool in pan.

When cool, remove from pan and sprinkle top with sifted powdered sugar. Cut into wedges to serve. Serves 10.

Note: — To decorate top, place a doily over the cake. Sprinkle with sifted powdered sugar. Remove doily carefully and top will show a lovely, delicate pattern.

— This is a very moist cake, so please refrigerate. Bring to room temperature to serve.

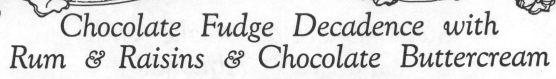

Chocolate Fudge Decadence with Rum & Raisins & Chocolate Buttercream

Rum and chocolate are a favorite blend of flavors. This is an adaptation of one of my preferred chocolate fantasies. The addition of rum and raisins adds a totally different character to this decadently rich and delicious cake.

       4 tablespoons rum
    1/2 cup dark raisins

       1 cup semi-sweet chocolate chips
    1/2 cup (1 stick) butter

       5 eggs, at room temperature
       1 cup sugar

  1 1/2 cups finely ground walnuts
    2/3 cup flour
    3/4 teaspoon baking powder

Soak raisins in rum. In the top of a double boiler, over hot, not boiling, water, melt chocolate with butter and stir to blend. Set aside to cool for 30 minutes.

Beat eggs with sugar until light and fluffy. Stir together walnuts, flour and baking powder and fold into egg mixture. Fold in the chocolate and raisin mixtures.

Spread batter into a greased 10-inch springform pan and bake in a 350° oven for 30 minutes, or until a cake tester, probed in center, comes out clean. Allow to cool in pan. Invert onto a lovely serving platter. Swirl top with Chocolate Rum Buttercream. Keep the portions small and serve 10 to 12.

Chocolate Rum Buttercream:
    1/2 cup butter (1 stick)
    3/4 cup semi-sweet chocolate chips, melted and cooled
       2 tablespoons rum
    1/2 teaspoon vanilla

Beat butter until light and creamy. Beat in chocolate until blended. Beat in rum and vanilla. Will frost 1 layer.

Chocolate Chestnut Cake with Hazelnuts & Chestnut Cream Glaze

This is an unusual coffeecake, with surprising and subtle shades of chestnut and chocolate. Everyone will ask what is different about this cake, but hardly anyone will guess this marvelous combination.

- 2 eggs
- 3/4 cup sour cream
- 3/4 cup sugar
- 1/2 cup canned sweetened chestnut puree
- 1/2 cup butter, softened
- 2 teaspoons vanilla

- 1/2 cup semi-sweet chocolate chips, melted

- 2 cups self-rising flour
- 1 teaspoon baking powder
- 1/2 cup chopped toasted hazelnuts
- 1/2 cup mini-morsel chocolate chips

Beat together first 6 ingredients until blended. Beat in the melted chocolate. Combine and add the remaining ingredients and beat until blended. Do not overmix.

Spread batter into a buttered and floured 9-inch kugelhopf pan and bake in a 350° oven for 45 to 50 minutes, or until a cake tester, inserted in center, comes out clean. Allow to cool in pan for 15 minutes, and then invert and continue cooling on a rack.

When cool, drizzle top decoratively with Chestnut Cream Glaze and allow it to drizzle down the grooves on the sides. Serves 8.

Chestnut Cream Glaze:
- 1/2 cup sifted powdered sugar
- 1 tablespoon cream
- 1/2 teaspoon vanilla
- 2 tablespoons chopped toasted hazelnuts
- 1 tablespoon canned sweetened chestnut puree

Stir together sugar, cream and vanilla until blended. Stir in hazelnuts and chestnut puree until blended.

Note: — *This can be baked in a 9-inch tube pan, but the kugelhopf pan is far more attractive for this cake.*

— *Hazelnuts can be toasted in a 350° oven for 10 to 15 minutes or until skins have loosened. Place between kitchen towels and rub to remove skins.*

Chocolate Chip Buttermilk Cake with Chocolate Sour Cream Frosting

This cake is simple, but by no means plain. It has good old-fashioned goodness. Just a nice, dark, dense chocolate cake, filled with chocolate chips and walnuts.

       3/4 cup butter (1 1/2 sticks)
     1 3/4 cups sugar
         3 eggs
         1 cup buttermilk
         2 teaspoons vanilla

         2 cups flour
         6 tablespoons cocoa
         1 teaspoon baking soda
         1 teaspoon baking powder
       3/4 cup semi-sweet chocolate chips
       3/4 cup chopped walnuts

Beat together first 5 ingredients until blended. Combine and add the remaining ingredients and beat until nicely blended. Do not overbeat. Spread batter into a greased 10-inch tube pan and bake in a 350° oven for about 45 minutes, or until a cake tester, inserted in center, comes out clean. Allow to cool in pan.

When cool, remove from pan and frost top and sides with Chocolate Sour Cream Frosting. Serves 10.

Chocolate Sour Cream Frosting:
       1/3 cup semi-sweet chocolate chips, melted
       1/4 cup butter, melted
         2 tablespoons sour cream
         1 cup sifted powdered sugar
         1 teaspoon vanilla

Beat together chocolate and butter until blended. Beat in sour cream and powdered sugar until blended. Beat in vanilla.

Sour Cream Chocolate Chip Chocolate Cake with Chocolate Mousse Frosting

There are few chocolate cakes that you can prepare that are easier or moister or fudgier than this one. The Chocolate Mousse Frosting is totally decadent. Keep the portions small, if you are able.

    1/2 cup butter, softened
1 1/2 cups sugar
    3 eggs
1 1/2 cups sour cream
    2 teaspoons vanilla

    2 cups flour
    6 tablespoons cocoa
    1 tablespoon baking powder
1/2 teaspoon baking soda
1/4 teaspoon salt (optional)
3/4 cup mini-morsel chocolate chips

Beat together first 5 ingredients until blended. Beat in the remaining ingredients until batter is nicely blended. Divide batter between two greased 10-inch springform pans and bake in a 350° oven for about 35 to 40 minutes, or until a cake tester, inserted in center, comes out clean. Do not overbake, or cake will not be moist. (The two layers can be baked together.)

Allow to cool in pans. When cool remove from pans and spread Chocolate Mousse Frosting between the layers and on the top and sides.

This can be stored in the refrigerator, but bring to room temperature before serving. Serves 10.

Chocolate Mousse Frosting:
1 1/3 cups semi-sweet chocolate chips (8 ounces)
    1 cup whipping cream
1/4 cup butter (1/2 stick), at room temperature
    3 egg yolks
1/2 teaspoon vanilla

Place chocolate chips in blender container. Heat cream to boiling point and pour into blender. Blend for about 1 minute, or until chocolate is melted. Beat in butter until blended. Beat in yolks and vanilla for about 30 seconds. Will fill and frost one 10-inch layer cake.

Chocolate Chip Chocolate Cake with Chocolate Buttercream

This luscious cake is a chocolate lover's dream. It is not overly sweet or cloying. It is dense, dark and delicious.

    3 eggs
    2 cups sugar
  3/4 cup oil
    1 cup sour cream
    2 teaspoons vanilla

    2 cups flour
  1/2 cup cocoa
1 1/2 teaspoons baking powder
    1 teaspoon baking soda
      pinch of salt

    1 cup semi-sweet chocolate chips (6 ounces)

Beat together first 5 ingredients until nicely blended. Beat in the next 5 ingredients until blended. Stir in the chocolate chips.

Divide batter between 2 greased 10-inch springform pans and bake in a 350° oven for 35 minutes, or until a cake tester, inserted in center, comes out clean. Do not overbake. Allow to cool in pan. When cool, remove from pans and fill and frost with Chocolate Buttercream. Serves 10 to 12.

Chocolate Buttercream:
  2/3 cup sifted powdered sugar
    1 egg

  3/4 cup semi-sweet chocolate chips, melted
  1/2 cup butter, at room temperature, cut into 4 pieces
    1 teaspoon vanilla

Beat together sugar and egg until mixture is thick and pale colored. Beat in the chocolate until blended. Beat in the butter, one piece at a time, until blended. Beat in the vanilla. Will fill and frost 1 10-inch cake.

Sour Cream Chocolate Fudge Cake with Chocolate Buttercream

The fact that this glorious chocolate cake takes just seconds to assemble will make you feel like a wizard with a magic wand. This is a marvelous fudgy chocolate cake and you will enjoy the simple but delicious Chocolate Buttercream.

    4 eggs
1 1/4 cups sugar
    1 cup chopped walnuts
  1/2 cup flour
    4 tablespoons cocoa
    1 teaspoon baking powder
  1/2 cup sour cream
    1 teaspoon vanilla

Place all the ingredients in a food processor and blend for 30 seconds, or until the nuts are finely chopped.

Pour batter into a 10-inch buttered springform pan and bake in a 350° oven for about 30 minutes, or until a cake tester, inserted in center, comes out clean. Allow to cool in pan.

When cool, swirl Chocolate Buttercream on the top, in a decorative fashion and frost the sides. This is a low cake, so don't think anything went wrong. Serves 8.

Chocolate Buttercream:
  1/2 cup semi-sweet chocolate chips, melted
  1/4 cup butter, melted
  1/2 teaspoon vanilla

In a bowl, stir together melted chocolate and melted butter until blended. Stir in vanilla. Yields 3/4 cup frosting.

Note: — If you own a microwave oven, chocolate and butter can be melted together by placing in a bowl and microwaving for 1 minute on high. Turn the bowl and microwave for an additional 30 seconds. Stir together until blended.

Sour Cream Pound Cake
with Chocolate Chips & Walnuts

What a lovely cake, tender and compact, that children love when they come home after a hard day at school. And the aroma of this cake, baking in your oven, will bring the neighbors to your door. The chocolate powder melts while baking, forming a rich, moist chocolate layer.

        1/2 cup butter
          1 cup sugar
          3 eggs
          1 cup sour cream
          1 teaspoon vanilla

          2 cups flour
          1 teaspoon baking powder
          1 teaspoon baking soda

Chocolate Walnut Filling

Beat together first 5 ingredients until blended. Beat in the next 3 ingredients until nicely blended, about 30 seconds. Spoon half the batter into a greased 10-inch tube pan. Sprinkle with the Chocolate Walnut Filling. Top with remaining batter.

Bake in a 350° oven for about 45 to 50 minutes, or until a cake tester, inserted in center, comes out clean. Allow to cool in pan. When cool, remove from pan and sprinkle top with sifted powdered sugar. Serves 10 to 12.

Chocolate Walnut Filling:
        1/2 cup semi-sweet mini-morsel chocolate chips
          6 tablespoons Nestle's Quik chocolate powder
          6 tablespoons finely chopped walnuts

Stir together all the ingredients until blended.

Bittersweet Chocolate Fudge Cake with Chocolate Fudge Frosting

This recipe is only for those who are addicted to chocolate . . . moist, bittersweet layers of chocolate cake (with chocolate chips), filled and frosted with dense chocolate fudge. Keep the portions small so you can enjoy this with a clear conscience.

   3/4 cup butter
1 1/2 cups sugar
    2 eggs
  1/2 cup sour cream
  1/2 cup milk
    1 tablespoon vanilla

1 3/4 cups flour
    2 teaspoons baking powder
  1/2 teaspoon baking soda
  1/2 cup sifted cocoa
    1 cup semi-sweet chocolate chips

Cream together butter and sugar until light, about 2 minutes. Beat in eggs until blended. Beat in sour cream, milk and vanilla, until blended.

In a bowl, mix together the remaining ingredients and add all at once to the egg mixture. Beat until blended.

Divide batter between 2 10-inch springform pans that have been lightly greased, and bake in a 350° oven for about 30 minutes, or until a cake tester, inserted in center, comes out clean Allow to cool in pans.

When cool, remove from pans and fill and frost with Chocolate Fudge Frosting. Serves 12 decadent chocolate lovers.

Chocolate Fudge Frosting:
  1/2 pound semi-sweet chocolate chips
    1 cup whipping cream
    4 egg yolks

Place chocolate in blender or food processor container. Bring cream to a boil and pour into blender. Blend for 1 minute. (Chocolate will melt.) Add yolks and beat for another 30 seconds. Allow to cool a little and then fill and frost cake.

Mocha Chocolate Cake with Mocha Mousse Frosting

This is a low, dense, deep and dark chocolate cake, with just a hint of coffee. The Mocha Mousse Frosting is the perfect accompaniment.

    1/2 cup butter
      1 cup sugar

      6 eggs
      1 teaspoon vanilla
      1 cup semi-sweet chocolate chips, melted and cooled

  1 3/4 cups finely grated walnuts
    1/2 cup vanilla wafer crumbs
    1/2 teaspoon baking powder
      1 teaspoon instant coffee

Cream butter with sugar until mixture is light and fluffy, about 4 minutes. Add eggs, one at a time, beating well after each addition. Beat in the vanilla and melted chocolate.

Combine the remaining ingredients and beat them in until just blended. Pour batter into a greased 10-inch springform pan and bake at 350° for about 45 minutes, or until a cake tester, inserted in center, comes out clean. Allow cake to cool in pan.

When cool, pour Mocha Mousse Frosting over the top and refrigerate until firm. Remove from refrigerator about 10 minutes before serving. Serves 10.

Mocha Mousse Frosting:
      1 cup semi-sweet chocolate chips
    1/2 cup cream
      1 teaspoon instant coffee
      1 tablespoon Kahlua liqueur

Place chocolate in blender container. Heat cream with instant coffee and bring to boiling point. Pour into blender and beat for 1 minute, or until chocolate is melted. Blend in liqueur. Allow to cool for a few minutes and pour over cooled cake.

Chocolate Pumpkin Pecan Cake
with Chocolate Glaze

Let me say at the outset, that the only evidence that this cake contains pumpkin, is in its very moist quality. Other than that, this is a grand chocolate cake, in every other way. Raisins can be substituted for the pecans which will give this cake a totally different character.

    1/2 cup butter
      1 cup sugar
      2 eggs
    3/4 cup canned pumpkin puree
    1/2 cup sour cream

  1 3/4 cups flour
      6 tablespoons cocoa
    1/2 teaspoon cinnamon
      2 teaspoons baking soda
      1 cup finely chopped pecans

Cream butter with sugar. Beat in eggs, buttermilk and sour cream until blended. Stir together and add the remaining ingredients and beat until nicely blended. Do not overbeat.

Spread batter into a greased 10-inch tube pan and bake in a 350° oven for about 40 minutes, or until a cake tester, inserted in center, comes out clean.

Allow cake to cool in pan. When cool, spread Chocolate Glaze on top and allow some to drip down the sides. Serves 8 to 10.

Chocolate Glaze:
      1 tablespoon butter, at room temperature
      1 tablespoon buttermilk
      1 tablespoon sifted cocoa
    1/2 teaspoon vanilla
  1 1/4 cups sifted powdered sugar

Stir together all the ingredients until blended. Add a little more sugar or buttermilk to make glaze a drizzling consistency.

Chocolate Pumpkin Spiced Cake with Chocolate Glaze

The pumpkin imparts very little taste to this very spicy chocolate cake. It does add a wonderful moistness. The crumb is very tender and in all, it is an interesting and rather different cake to serve for the holidays.

    1/2 cup butter, softened
      1 cup sugar

      2 eggs
      1 cup canned pumpkin puree

 1 1/2 cups flour
      1 teaspoon baking powder
      1 teaspoon baking soda
      6 tablespoons cocoa
      2 teaspoons pumpkin pie spice
      1 cup chopped walnuts
    1/2 cup chopped yellow raisins

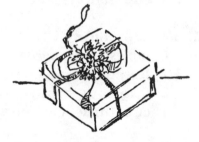

Beat together butter and sugar until mixture is light and creamy. Beat in the eggs and pumpkin puree until blended. Combine and add the remaining ingredients and beat until blended. Do not overbeat. Spread batter evenly into a greased 10-inch tube pan and bake in a 325° oven for about 35 minutes, or until a cake tester, inserted in center, comes out clean. Allow to cool in pan.

When cool, remove from pan and drizzle top with Chocolate Glaze. Serves 8 to 10.

Chocolate Glaze:
    1/2 cup semi-sweet chocolate chips
      2 tablespoons butter
        pinch of cinnamon

In the top of a double boiler, over hot, not simmering water, stir together chocolate, butter and cinnamon until blended.

Raspberry & Chocolate Chip Cake with Raspberry Cream Glaze

Raspberries and chocolate go together like love and marriage. This is a good choice to serve at teatime, or as a dessert for an informal dinner. This is a simple cake, but by no means plain.

2 eggs
1 cup sugar
1/3 cup oil
1/3 cup sour cream
1 teaspoon vanilla

1 cup raspberries, fresh or frozen

1 3/4 cups flour
4 tablespoons cocoa
1 teaspoon baking powder
1/2 teaspoon baking soda
1 cup semi-sweet chocolate chips (mini-morsels can be substituted)

Beat together first 5 ingredients until blended. Stir in the raspberries. Combine and add the remaining ingredients and stir until dry ingredients are just blended. Do not overmix.

Spread batter into a greased 10-inch tube pan and bake in a 350° oven for about 40 minutes, or until a cake tester, inserted in center, comes out clean. Allow to cool in pan.

When cool, remove from pan and brush top with Raspberry Cream Glaze and allow a little to drip down the sides. A few fresh raspberries will decorate the top nicely. Serves 10.

Raspberry Cream Glaze:
1 tablespoon cream
1 tablespoon seedless raspberry jam
1/2 cup sifted powdered sugar

Stir together all the ingredients until blended. Add a little sugar or cream to make glaze a drizzling consistency.

Note: — As with most desserts made with fresh fruit, I recommend storing cake in refrigerator. Bring to room temperature before serving.

— Cake should be prepared and served on the same day.

Anniversary Chocolate & Raspberry Cake with Chocolate Glaze

This is a very glamorous cake that just feels like a special occasion. Make it for someone who loves chocolate and raspberries (it could be you).

    1/2 cup butter
1 1/4 cups sugar
    3 eggs
    1 cup sour cream
    2 teaspoons vanilla

1 1/2 cups flour
    6 tablespoons cocoa
    2 teaspoons baking powder
1/2 teaspoon baking soda
1/2 cup mini-morsel chocolate chips

3/4 cup raspberries

Cream together butter and sugar until light and creamy. Beat in eggs until blended. Beat in sour cream and vanilla until blended. Combine and add the remaining ingredients and beat until blended. Stir in the raspberries.

Spread batter evenly into a greased 10-inch springform pan and bake in a 325° oven for about 55 minutes, or until a cake tester, inserted in center, comes out clean. Allow to cool in pan.

When cool, remove from pan and spread top and sides with Chocolate Glaze. Serves 10.

Chocolate Glaze:
    1 cup semi-sweet chocolate chips, melted
    2 tablespoons butter
    2 tablespoons light corn syrup

Melt chocolate. Heat together butter and corn syrup until bubbly, and stir into chocolate until blended. Allow to cool for 10 minutes or until slightly thickened.

Vanilla Poundcake with Chocolate Chips & Pecans & Vanilla Glaze

If you enjoy a very dense cake, strong with the flavor of vanilla, filled with chocolate and pecans, this is a nice cake to consider. It is dense and compact and a wonderful accompaniment with coffee or tea.

    3/4 cup butter, softened (1 1/2 sticks)
      6 ounces cream cheese
1 1/4 cups sugar

      2 eggs
1/2 cup vanilla yogurt
      2 teaspoons vanilla

      2 cups flour
      1 teaspoon baking powder
1/2 teaspoon baking soda

      1 cup (6 ounces) semi-sweet mini-morsel chocolate chips
      1 cup chopped pecans

Beat together butter, cream cheese and sugar until mixture is thoroughly blended. Beat in the eggs, yogurt and vanilla until blended. In a bowl, stir together the dry ingredients and add, all at once, beating until blended. Stir in the chocolate and pecans.

Spread batter evenly into a 10-inch springform pan and bake in a 350° oven for about 50 minutes, or until a cake tester, prodded in center, comes out clean. (This cake forms a crust, which will clean the tester. So you must open a little hole to insure proper testing.) Allow cake to cool in pan. When cool, drizzle top with Vanilla Glaze. Serves 8 to 10.

Vanilla Glaze:
      1 tablespoon cream
1/4 teaspoon vanilla
1/2 cup sifted powdered sugar

Stir together all the ingredients until blended. Add a little more sugar or cream until glaze is a drizzling consistency.

Basic Chocolate Sponge Cake
with Chocolate Whipped Cream

Everyone should have a good basic chocolate sponge cake in their repertoire. This is a particularly good one, for it can be varied in so many ways. For a simple dessert, it can be sprinkled with a little sifted powdered sugar ... for a glamorous dessert, a scrumptious chocolate buttercream is lovely. It can be glazed with marmalade or jam (apricot is especially good). And for very special occasions, it can be glazed and frosted. This can be served with fruit purees, ice cream, or a little hot fudge sauce.

    6 eggs
    1 cup sugar
    1 teaspoon vanilla

    2/3 cup flour
    1/2 cup cocoa
    1/2 teaspoon cinnamon

Beat eggs with sugar and vanilla until mixture is light and fluffy, about 5 to 6 minutes, at high speed. Mix together flour, cocoa and cinnamon and carefully fold into egg mixture until blended.

Spread batter into an ungreased 10-inch tube pan and bake in a 350° oven for about 35 minutes, or until a cake tester, inserted in center, comes out clean. Invert pan, and allow cake to cool. When cool, remove from pan and frost with Chocolate Whipped Cream. Serves 8 to 10.

Chocolate Whipped Cream:
    1 cup cream
    3 ounces chocolate syrup
    1/2 teaspoon vanilla

Beat together all the ingredients until cream is stiff.

Note: — *Be certain your 10-inch tube pan has inversion legs. If not, then cake must be cooled over the neck of a bottle.*

— *For a totally different presentation, the cooled sponge cake can be glazed with a thin layer (about 4 tablespoons) of apricot jam that has been heated for about 2 minutes or until bubbly.*

Chocolate Velvet Cake with Chocolate Buttercream

This cake is a breeze to whip up, yet the results are truly special. Chocoholics rejoice, for this triple chocolate cake is a chocolate lover's dream.

        1 cup butter (2 sticks)
        2 cups sugar

        5 eggs
        2 teaspoons vanilla
        1 cup sour cream

       10 tablespoons cocoa
  1 1/4 cups flour
        1 teaspoon baking powder
        1 teaspoon baking soda
      1/4 teaspoon salt

  1 1/2 cups grated walnuts
        1 cup semi-sweet mini-morsel chocolate chips

Cream butter with sugar until light and fluffy. Beat in eggs, one at a time, beating well after each addition. Beat in the sour cream until blended.

Mix together the next 5 ingredients and add these to the egg mixture. Beat until nicely blended. Beat in the nuts and chocolate.

Divide batter between 2 greased 10-inch springform pans and bake in a 325° oven for about 45 minutes or until a cake tester, inserted in center, comes out clean. Allow to cool in pan. When cool, remove layers and fill and frost with Chocolate Buttercream. Sprinkle top with shaved chocolate. Serves 10 to 12.

Chocolate Buttercream:
        1 cup butter, softened
        1 cup sifted powdered sugar
        3 tablespoons sifted cocoa
        1 teaspoon vanilla

Beat butter until light and creamy. Beat in the remaining ingredients until thoroughly blended. Will fill and frost a 10-inch cake.

Chocolate Zucchini Cake with Chocolate Cream Frosting

The only evidence of zucchini in this cake is the wonderful moistness it imparts. This cake requires no frosting ... a sprinkling of powdered sugar will do. But if you like to dress it up for a special dessert, this Chocolate Cream Frosting is very light and a good choice.

      3/4 cup butter
1 1/2 cups sugar

      3 eggs
  1/2 cup milk
      2 tablespoons grated orange
      1 tablespoon vanilla

2 1/2 cups flour
      6 tablespoons cocoa
      3 teaspoons baking powder
      1 teaspoon baking soda
      1 teaspoon cinnamon

      2 cups peeled and grated zucchini
      1 cup chopped walnuts

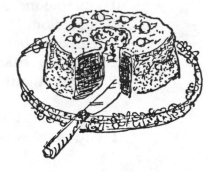

Cream together butter and sugar. Beat in eggs, one at a time, beating well after each addition. Beat in milk, orange and vanilla until blended.

Stir together and beat in the next 5 ingredients until blended. Beat in the zucchini and walnuts. Spread batter in a greased 10-inch tube pan and bake in a 350° oven for about 50 minutes, or until a cake tester, inserted in center, comes out clean.

Allow to cool in pan. When cool, swirl top with Chocolate Cream Frosting. Serves 8 to 10.

Chocolate Cream Frosting:
      2 tablespoons cream
  1/2 cup sifted powdered sugar
      2 tablespoons cocoa
  1/2 teaspoon vanilla
  1/4 teaspoon cinnamon

Stir together all the ingredients until blended. Add a little cream or sugar to make frosting a creamy consistency.

Dessert
Tortes

Dessert Tortes

Almond Torte with Chocolate Chip Crust   108
Almond Torte with Glazed Strawberries   109
Chocolate Almond Torte   110
Fresh Apple & Orange Pecan Torte   111
Easiest & Best Carrot & Pecan Torte   112
Chocolate Torte with Apricot   113
Chocolate Chip Graham Torte   114
Gateau au Chocolate   115
Easiest & Best Torte au Chocolate   116
Grand Duke's Pecan Torte with Apricot Jam   117
Hungarian Pecan Torte   118
Hungarian Chocolate Torte   119
Easiest & Best Macaroon Torte   120
Easiest & Best Walnut Torte   121
Coffee & Chocolate Walnut Torte   122
Yogurt Chocolate Fudge Torte   123
Viennese Nut Torte   124

Dessert Tortes

Gather ye round my friends, for this chapter will reveal a few simplicities of the century. These tortes are the grand dames of the Torte Kingdom. They are the most elegant and divine-tasting confections. And most impressive of all, they can be prepared in minutes with minimum effort. These are excellent choices for the "happy ending" of a dinner party or when you entertain with "just desserts." While preparation is simple, the results will truly amaze you.

Imagine, placing a few ingredients in a food processor and Viola! a majestic torte with a marvellous taste and an incredible texture. These are cakes to impress the most discriminating palates.

Traditional tortes are made by separating eggs, grating nuts, beating the yolks and whites separately, carefully folding both together. Hopefully, the whites aren't overbeaten and dry ... and folding was not done with a heavy hand, thus deflating the finished cake. Results are superb, indeed ... if all went well, that is. I have included 2 such tortes (Pages 116 and 117) for those who have a little more time.

My tortes are not temperamental primadonnas, and they eliminate all these time-consuming steps. The secret is the balance of ingredients which will impart the proper moistness ... little flour, lots of nuts (which act as flour when ground) ... and, of course, the processor does all the work for you. Technique is practically foolproof. Please do not make any substitutions in these recipes

Included in this chapter is one of my absolute favorite cakes, Fresh Apple & Orange Pecan Torte which is a symphony of flavors and textures. I do hope you will have the opportunity to try it soon.

Almond Torte with Chocolate Chip Crust and Chocolate Buttercream

Oh! what a cake. If you love almonds and chocolate, this will be a little treasure you will use often. It is wonderfully simple to prepare, as all the ingredients are beaten together in one operation. The torte is a dense layer of almond dough, sandwiched together by a chocolate crust and chocolate buttercream topping. The chocolate chips form a delicious chocolate crust... like a mystery pie.

        5 eggs
    1/2 cup butter, at room temperature
  1 1/4 cups sugar
    1/2 cup flour
        1 teaspoon baking powder
        2 cups sliced almonds
        1 teaspoon almond extract

        1 cup semi-sweet mini-morsel chocolate chips (or 1 cup coarsely chopped semi-sweet chocolate chips)

In the bowl of a food processor, place first 7 ingredients, and blend mixture for 1 minute. Scrape down the sides and continue beating for 3 minutes, or until almonds are finely ground. Stir in the chocolate chips.

Scrape batter into a greased 10-inch springform pan and bake in a 350° oven for about 30 to 35 minutes or until top is browned and a cake tester, inserted in center, comes out clean. Allow to cool in pan.

When cool, swirl Chocolate Buttercream on the top in a decorative fashion and allow some of it to drip down the sides. Serves 10.

Chocolate Buttercream:
    1/2 cup semi-sweet chocolate chips
      3 tablespoons butter
    1/4 teaspoon vanilla

Place all the ingredients in the top of a double boiler, over hot, not simmering water, and stir until chocolate is melted and mixture is blended.

Almond Torte with Glazed Strawberries & Grand Marnier

This is a lovely summer dessert, not too rich, but filled with flavor. It is a nice change from a strawberry pie, which I am not diminishing . . . it is one of my very favorites. The torte has the subtle flavor of almonds which is sensational with the fresh strawberries.

 1 cup blanched almonds (5 ounces)
3/4 cup sugar

 4 eggs
2/3 cup macaroon cookie crumbs
1/4 cup butter (1/2 stick), softened
 1 teaspoon baking powder
 1 teaspoon vanilla
1/2 teaspoon almond extract

In a food processor, process almonds and sugar until almonds are pulverized. Add the remaining ingredients and process mixture for 30 seconds. Pour batter into a buttered 10-inch springform pan and bake at 350° for 35 minutes, or until top is golden and a cake tester, inserted in center, comes out clean. Allow torte to cool in pan.

When torte is cool, spoon Strawberry & Grand Marnier Glaze over the top. Decorate with whole glazed strawberries. To serve, cut into wedges. A dollup of whipped cream is a nice addition, but not a "must". Serves 8 to 10.

Strawberries & Grand Marnier Glaze:
3/4 cup currant jelly
 2 tablespoons Grand Marnier Liqueur

 1 pint fresh strawberries, hulled and left whole
 1 pint fresh strawberries, hulled and sliced

In a saucepan, heat currant jelly until melted. Stir in Grand Marnier until blended. Dip whole strawberries in glaze and set aside. Add sliced strawberries to the glaze and mix until nicely coated.

Note: — If you do not own a food processor, almonds must be ground with a nut grater. Batter must then be beaten for 4 minutes at high speed.

Chocolate Almond Torte with Chocolate Rum Buttercream

Here's a beautiful cake that combines the wonderful tastes of chocolate and almonds. It is an elegant cake and can be served on special occasions.

5 eggs
1 cup sugar
1 teaspoon vanilla
1 tablespoon rum

1/2 cup flour
1/2 cup cornstarch
1/2 cup ground almonds (or almond meal, purchased at
    health food stores)
5 tablespoons cocoa
1/2 teaspoon baking powder
1/2 cup (1 stick) butter, melted and cooled

Beat eggs with sugar, vanilla and rum until eggs are very light and fluffy, about 8 minutes. Meanwhile, sift together flour, cornstarch, almonds, cocoa and baking powder. Gently beat flour mixture into the beaten eggs until blended. Gently beat in the melted butter. (You can fold flour and butter in by hand, if you do not have a very low setting on your mixer.)

Pour batter in a greased 10-inch springform pan and bake in a 350° oven for 30 minutes, or until a cake tester, inserted in center, comes out clean. Allow to cool in pan. When cool, frost with Chocolate Rum Buttercream. Serves 8.

Chocolate Rum Buttercream:
    2/3 cup semi-sweet chocolate chips
    6 tablespoons butter, at room temperature
    1 tablespoon rum

Melt chocolate over hot, not boiling water. Beat in the butter, 1 tablespoon at a time, until mixture is smooth and velvety. Beat in the rum. Pour frosting over cooled cake and refrigerate. Bring to room temperature to serve.

Fresh Apple & Orange Pecan Torte with Lemon Orange Glaze

Here's one of the finest tasting of the fresh fruit cakes. It is particularly moist and flavorful. Pecans with apples and orange and a hint of lemon are a wonderful blend of flavors.

        6 eggs
        1 cup sugar

1 1/2 cups finely grated pecans
        1 cup vanilla wafer crumbs
        1 teaspoon baking powder

        1 large apple, peeled, cored and grated
    1/2 medium orange, grated (about 4 tablespoons peel, fruit
            and juice)
    1/4 lemon grated (about 1 tablespoon peel, fruit and juice)

In the large bowl of an electric mixer, beat eggs with sugar for 5 minutes or until eggs are very light and creamy.

Toss pecans, crumbs and baking powder until blended and fold into egg mixture. Fold in the remaining ingredients, just until blended.

Pour batter into a buttered 10-inch springform pan and spread to even. Bake in a 350° oven for 45 minutes or until a cake tester, inserted in center, comes out clean. Allow cake to cool and then drizzle with Lemon Orange Glaze. Serves 8.

Lemon Orange Glaze:
        1 cup sifted powdered sugar
        1 tablespoon orange juice
        2 teaspoons lemon juice
        1 tablespoon grated orange peel
        2 tablespoons chopped pecans

Stir together all the ingredients until blended. Add a little orange juice or sugar to make glaze a drizzling consistency.

Easiest & Best Carrot & Pecan Torte with Orange Syrup

This little gem has magnificent texture, and is redolent with the fragrance of cinnamon and orange. With the aid of a food processor, it is the essence of simplicity to prepare.

    4 eggs
    1 cup sugar
    2 cups pecans
    2 medium carrots, cut into 1-inch pieces
       peel of 1 orange, using just the orange part (zest) and
          not the white part (pith)

    1 cup flour
    1 teaspoon baking powder
    2 teaspoons cinnamon

In the bowl of a food processor, place first 5 ingredients and blend until mixture is very finely chopped, just short of pureed. Add the remaining ingredients and mix until blended, about 7 seconds.

Spread batter into a greased 10-inch springform pan and bake in a 350° oven for about 30 minutes, or until a cake tester, inserted in center, comes out clean. Remove from the oven and spoon Orange Syrup over the hot torte. It will slowly absorb, and form the thinnest glaze on top.

Allow to cool in pan and cut into wedges to serve. Serves 10.

Orange Syrup:
    3 tablespoons orange juice
    1/2 cup sifted powdered sugar

Stir together the orange juice and sugar until blended.

Chocolate Torte with Apricot & Cocoa Buttercream

These simple little ingredients, produce the finest tasting chocolate cake. This is one of my favorites. Make certain that the grated walnuts are the consistency of flour. You must use the old-fashioned nut grater for this. In absence of one, grind the walnuts in a food processor with 1/3 cup sugar, taken from the 1 cup used in this recipe.

4 eggs
1 cup sugar

1 teaspoon vanilla
3 tablespoons flour
1 cup finely grated walnuts
2 tablespoons cocoa
1 teaspoon baking powder

1/3 cup chopped walnuts
1/2 cup heated apricot jam

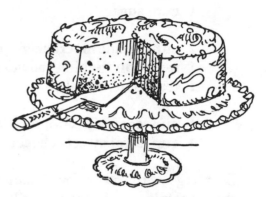

Beat eggs with sugar until eggs are light and creamy, about 2 minutes. With mixer on lowest speed, beat in the next 5 ingredients until just blended. Do not overbeat. Fold in chopped walnuts.

Pour batter into a greased 10-inch springform pan and bake in a 350° oven for 20 to 25 minutes, or until a cake tester, inserted in center, comes out clean. Do not overbake. (Cake will rise and settle a bit. This is normal.) Allow to cool in pan.

Drizzle warm apricot jam evenly over the cake. Spread top and sides with Cocoa Buttercream Frosting. Serves 8.

Cocoa Buttercream:
    1 cup butter (2 sticks) at room temperature
3/4 cup sifted powdered sugar
    3 tablespoons sifted cocoa
    1 teaspoon vanilla

Beat butter until light and creamy. Beat in the remaining ingredients until thoroughly blended.

Chocolate Chip Graham Torte with Whipped Cream Chantilly

This is one of the finest tasting tortes that could not be easier to prepare. It is one of the children's favorites and is a treat with a glass of milk or coffee or tea.

3 eggs
1 cup sugar

2 cups graham cracker crumbs
1 teaspoon baking powder
1 teaspoon vanilla

1 cup coarsely chopped walnuts
1 cup semi-sweet chocolate chips

Beat eggs with sugar for 2 minutes or until eggs are lightened. Stir in the remaining ingredients until blended.

Pour mixture into a 9-inch greased pie plate and bake at 350° for 30 minutes. Allow torte to cool. When cool, frost top with Whipped Cream Chantilly and refrigerate for at least 6 hours. Overnight is better. Decorate top with finely grated chocolate and cut into wedges to serve. Serves 8.

Whipped Cream Chantilly:
3/4 cup cream
1 tablespoon sugar
1/2 teaspoon vanilla

Beat cream until foamy. Add sugar and vanilla and continue beating until cream is stiff.

Gateau Au Chocolate with Chocolate Mousse Frosting

There are chocolate cakes and chocolate tortes and chocolate gateaus, but this is one of the best ... very moist and fudgy. The Chocolate Mousse Frosting is exceedingly easy to prepare. Consider this dessert when you need a "grand finale" for an impressive dinner.

    1/2 cup butter, melted
      1 package (6 ounces) semi-sweet chocolate chips, melted

      3 eggs
    2/3 cup sugar

      1 cup finely grated walnuts
    1/2 teaspoon baking powder
      6 tablespoons flour
      2 tablespoons Creme de Cacao liqueur

Stir together melted chocolate and melted butter until blended. Set aside.

Beat eggs with sugar until mixture is light and fluffy, about 4 minutes. Combine walnuts, baking powder and flour and stir together. Gradually beat into egg mixture, at low speed. Beat in the liqueur and chocolate mixture.

Pour batter into a 10-inch springform pan and bake in a 325° oven for 25 to 30 minutes. (Top will appear dry, but cake will be moist inside.) Allow to cool in pan. When cool, remove metal ring and pour Chocolate Mousse Frosting over the top. Spread evenly on top and sides. Allow to set at room temperature. (Refrigerating this cake will make the frosting too firm.) Serves 12.

Chocolate Mousse Frosting:
    2/3 cup semi-sweet chocolate chips
    1/2 cup cream
      1 tablespoon Creme de Cacao liqueur

Place chocolate chips in a blender or food processor container. Heat cream to boiling and pour over the chocolate. Beat until chocolate is melted, about 30 seconds. Beat in liqueur until blended. Slowly pour frosting over the cake and spread evenly. Will frost 1 10-inch cake.

Easiest & Best Torte Au Chocolate with Chocolate Buttercream Frosting

This cake is just a little bit more work, but worth every bit of it. The little more work I refer to, is separating the eggs, which, when I think about it, is hardly worth mentioning. Again the trusty processor, makes preparation time just minutes.

      6 egg yolks, at room temperature
      1 cup sugar
      1 teaspoon vanilla
 1 1/2 cups walnuts or pecans
   1/4 cup vanilla wafer crumbs
   1/3 cup butter (3/4 stick) melted
      1 cup semi-sweet chocolate chips, melted

      6 egg whites, at room temperature
   1/4 cup sugar

In the bowl of a food processor, place first 7 ingredients and blend until nuts are finely chopped.

In the large bowl of an electric mixer, beat whites until foamy. Continue beating, gradually adding the sugar, until whites are stiff and glossy.

Fold whites* into chocolate mixture, until blended. Pour batter into a 10-inch buttered springform pan, and bake in a 350° oven for 40 minutes, or until a cake tester, inserted in center, comes out clean. Allow to cool in pan. When cool, frost top with Chocolate Buttercream Frosting, allowing some of the frosting to dribble down the sides. Cut into wedges to serve. Serves 10.

Chocolate Buttercream Frosting:
   1/2 cup butter, at room temperature
   2/3 cup semi-sweet chocolate chips, melted
     1 teaspoon vanilla

Stir softened butter into melted chocolate chips until blended. Stir in the vanilla. Will frost 1 10-inch single layer.

Note: — *To facilitate folding whites into chocolate, follow this procedure. First place 1/4 the whites into the chocolate mixture to lighten it a bit. Then on the lowest speed of an electric mixer, gradually beat the chocolate into the whites. It's a bit unorthodox, but it works.*

Grand Duke's Pecan Torte with Chocolate & Apricot Jam

This is a fine dessert and well worth the extra preparation time. It is moist and delicious and the combination of chocolate and apricots is marvelous.

6 egg whites
1/3 cup sugar

1/2 cup butter
2/3 cup sugar
6 egg yolks

1 cup grated pecans. (These must be finely grated on a nut grater and not ground in the food processor. The grated pecans should be as fine as flour and not oily.)
1/2 cup macaroon cookie crumbs

3/4 cup apricot jam
3 ounces semi-sweet chocolate chips, melted

Beat egg whites until foamy. Slowly add the sugar, while you continue beating, until whites are stiff. Set aside

Cream butter with sugar. Beat in egg yolks until blended. Beat in grated pecans and cookie crumbs. (Batter will be stiff.) Loosen batter by stirring in 1/3 of the egg whites. Fold in the remaining egg whites until blended.

Divide batter between 2 buttered 10-inch springform pans and bake at 350° for 20 minutes. Allow to cool in pan.

With a sharp knife, remove layers from baking pan. Spread about 6 tablespoons apricot jam on the first layer. Top with second layer. Spread remaining jam on top layer. Now, swirl melted chocolate on the top, in a decorative fashion, allowing some of the apricot jam to show through.

To serve, cut into wedges and serve with pride. Serves 10.

Hungarian Pecan Torte
with Apricot & Walnut Glaze

This is one of my very preferred cakes. It is one of the most versatile of tortes, and can be served with strawberries and whipped cream; glazed strawberries; apricot jam and chocolate. The combinations and possibilities are endless. The Apricot Jam & Walnut Glaze is just lovely when you serve this torte as a breakfast or brunch cake.

          4 eggs
    1 1/4 cups walnuts
          1 cup sugar
          1 teaspoon vanilla
      1/2 cup vanilla wafer cookie crumbs
    1 1/2 teaspoons baking powder

Place all the ingredients in the bowl of a food processor and blend mixture for 30 seconds. Scrape down the sides and blend for another 30 seconds, or until nuts are finely ground.

Pour batter in a greased 10-inch springform pan and bake in a 350° oven for about 20 to 23 minutes, or until a cake tester, inserted in center, comes out clean. Allow to cool in pan.

When cool, brush top with Apricot & Walnut Glaze and slice into wedges to serve. Serves 8 to 10.

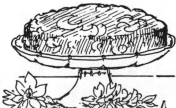

Apricot & Walnut Glaze:
      1/2 cup apricot jam
        2 tablespoons lemon juice
      1/4 cup finely chopped toasted walnuts

Combine all the ingredients in a saucepan, and heat mixture, stirring, until blended. Brush hot glaze over cooled torte.

Note: — *If you are planning to serve this at tea time, then decorate top with toasted walnut halves and glaceed cherries.*

Hungarian Chocolate Torte with Apricot Jam & Fudge Frosting

Two very thin, dense layers of chocolate cake, filled with apricot jam and topped with Fudge Frosting, makes this the perfect cake to serve when you invite friends for dessert and coffee. This cake is one of my very favorites. It is dense, moist and very delicious.

1/2 cup butter (1 stick), melted
1 cup semi-sweet chocolate chips (6 ounces), melted

5 eggs
1 1/2 cups sugar
2 1/2 cups chopped pecans
3/4 cup vanilla wafer crumbs
1 teaspoon baking powder
1/2 cup sour cream
1 teaspoon vanilla

1/2 cup apricot jam

Stir together butter and chocolate until blended. In the bowl of a large capacity food processor, place next 7 ingredients and blend for 30 seconds. Scrape down the sides and blend for another 30 seconds, or until pecans are very finely chopped. Add chocolate mixture and process until thoroughly blended.

Divide batter between 2 greased 10-inch springform pans and bake in a 325° oven for about 30 to 35 minutes, or until a cake tester, inserted in center, comes out clean. Allow to cool in pan.

When cool, remove from pan. Spread apricot jam between the layers and frost top and sides with Fudge Frosting. Cut into small portions to serve. Serves 12.

Fudge Frosting:
2/3 cup semi-sweet chocolate chips, melted
4 tablespoons butter, melted
1 cup sifted powdered sugar
1 teaspoon vanilla
2 tablespoons cream

Beat together chocolate and butter until blended. Beat in sugar and vanilla until blended. Beat in cream until blended. Allow frosting to cool a little until it is a spreading consistency.

Easiest & Best Macaroon Torte with Whipped Creme de Kahlua

3 egg whites
3/4 cup sugar

1 1/4 cups macaroon cookie crumbs
1 cup chopped walnuts
3/4 cup semi-sweet chocolate chips
1 teaspoon vanilla

Beat whites until foamy. Continue beating, slowly adding the sugar, until whites are very thick and syrupy. Beat in the remaining ingredients.

Scrape batter into a 9-inch buttered pie plate, and bake in a 350° oven for 30 minutes, or until top is beginning to take on color. Allow to cool in pan.

Frost top with Whipped Creme de Kahlua and refrigerate torte for at least 4 hours. Overnight is good too. Sprinkle top with a faint shake of cocoa or powdered chocolate. Cut into wedges to serve. Serves 8.

Whipped Creme de Kahlua:
3/4 cup cream
1 tablespoon sugar

2 tablespoons Creme de Kahlua

Beat cream with sugar until stiff. Beat in Creme de Kahlua until blended. Will frost 1 9-inch pie.

Note: — Can be prepared 1 or 2 days before serving.

— Can be frozen, frosted or unfrosted.

— Top can be swirled with a drizzle of chocolate syrup.

P.S. This is one of my family's favorite tortes.

Easiest & Best Walnut Torte with Raspberry Jam & Lemon Glaze

This is another one of those delicious tortes, combined with wonderful tastes of raspberry and lemon. If you are planning a gala luncheon, this is a good one to consider.

       4 eggs
       1 cup sugar
 1 1/2 cups chopped walnuts
       6 tablespoons flour
       1 teaspoon baking powder
       1 teaspoon vanilla

 3/4 cup seedless red raspberry jam, heated

Place first 6 ingredients in the bowl of a food processor and blend for 30 seconds. Scrape down the sides and blend for another 30 seconds or until nuts are very finely chopped. They should retain a small amount of texture.

Pour batter into a greased 10-inch springform pan and bake in a 350° oven for 25 to 28 minutes or until a cake tester, inserted in center, comes out clean. (Do not overbake, or cake will not be moist.) Allow to cool for 20 minutes, and then spread raspberry jam evenly over the top. Allow to cool completely.

Drizzle Lemon Glaze over the jam and in a decorative swirling pattern and allow some of the raspberry jam to show through. Run a little glaze down the sides. When glaze is set (about 1 hour), cut into wedges to serve. Serves 8.

Lemon Glaze:
       1 tablespoon lemon juice
 3/4 cup sifted powdered sugar

Stir together all the ingredients until blended. Add a little lemon juice or powdered sugar until glaze is a drizzling consistency.

Coffee & Chocolate Walnut Torte with Mocha Buttercream

If you love the taste of coffee with chocolate, this lovely cake will surely please. It is intensely flavored with coffee and chocolate and the Mocha Buttercream Frosting is in perfect balance. Please note that it only uses 2 tablespoons of flour, resulting in a very light and moist cake.

        4 eggs
      3/4 cup sugar
    1 1/3 cups chopped walnuts
        4 tablespoons instant coffee
        2 tablespoons flour
        1 teaspoon baking powder
        1 teaspoon vanilla

1/2 cup semi-sweet mini-morsel chocolate chips

In the bowl of a food processor, blend together first 7 ingredients for 30 seconds. Scrape down the sides and blend again for 30 seconds. Stir in the chocolate chips.

Pour batter into a 10x2-inch greased cake pan with a removable bottom and bake in a 350° oven for 25 minutes, or until a cake tester, inserted in center comes out clean. Allow to cool in pan.

When cool, remove metal ring and invert cake on a serving platter. Remove metal bottom. Spread Mocha Buttercream Frosting over the top and allow a little to drip down the sides. Serves 8.

Mocha Buttercream Frosting:
    1/4 cup butter, melted
    2/3 cup semi-sweet chocolate chips, melted
      1 tablespoon instant coffee
    1/2 teaspoon vanilla

Stir together all the ingredients until blended. (Chocolate and butter can be melted together in the top of a double boiler, over hot, not simmering water.)

Note: — If you own a 10x2-inch fluted pan with a removable bottom, the finished cake will have a more attractive border.

Yogurt Chocolate Fudge Torte with Chocolate Yogurt Frosting

This lovely cake is on the bittersweet side, with the tangy quality of yogurt. The frosting follows this theme, and is the perfect complement. It is exceedingly moist and quite dense, so a little goes a long way.

    2/3 cup flour
      5 tablespoons cocoa
      1 teaspoon baking powder
      5 eggs
1 1/2 cups sugar
1 1/4 cups chopped walnuts
    2/3 cup vanilla flavored yogurt

Place all the ingredients in food processor bowl and blend for 30 seconds. Scrape down the sides and process for another 30 seconds.

Pour batter into a greased 10-inch springform pan and bake at 350° for about 35 to 40 minutes or until a cake tester, inserted in center, comes out clean. Do not overbake. Allow to cool in pan.

Remove metal ring from pan and swirl Chocolate Yogurt Frosting on the top, allowing some to drip down the sides. Beautiful and delicious. Serves 8 to 10.

Chocolate Yogurt Frosting:
    1/2 cup semi-sweet chocolate chips, melted
    1/3 cup vanilla flavored yogurt

In a bowl, stir together melted chocolate with 2 tablespoons yogurt, until yogurt is incorporated and mixture is smooth. Add another 2 tablespoons yogurt and mix until smooth. Add remaining yogurt and mix until smooth. Yields about 3/4 cup frosting and will frost 1 10-inch cake.

Note: — *Chocolate should be melted in the top of a double boiler over hot, not simmering, water. Or melt it in the microwave oven for 1 1/4 minutes on high. Do not add all of the yogurt at one time as it has a high liquid content, and it could stiffen the chocolate.*

Viennese Nut Torte with Apricot & Chocolate Buttercream

This is one of my favorite nut cakes. Traditional Viennese Tortes are made with separated eggs and very little flour. This recipe uses little flour, but the eggs need not be separated. And the whole process, including the grinding of the nuts, can be prepared in one step.

          6 eggs
   1 1/2 cups sugar
       2/3 cup flour
   1 1/2 teaspoons baking powder
          1 teaspoon vanilla
          2 cups walnuts

   1/2 cup apricot jam, heated

Place first 6 ingredients in a food processor and blend until the nuts are very finely chopped, about 1 minute.

Pour batter into a greased 10-inch springform pan and bake in a 350° oven for 35 to 40 minutes, or until top is browned and a cake tester, inserted in center, comes out clean. Allow to cool for 20 minutes, and then spread the heated apricot jam over the top. Allow to cool thoroughly.

When cool, drizzle top with Chocolate Buttercream Frosting. Swirl it around decoratively, allowing some of the jam to show. Serves 10.

Chocolate Buttercream:
   1/2 cup semi-sweet chocolate chips, melted (3 ounces)
   1/4 cup melted butter
       1 teaspoon vanilla

Stir together all the ingredients until blended.

Note: — *If your own a microwave oven, butter and chocolate can be melted together. Microwave for 1 1/2 minutes on High. Stir mixture together until blended.*

Quick Breads

with

Fruits

&

Vegetables

Quick Breads with Fruits & Vegetables

Apple Orange Raisin Bread 128
Upside Down Honey Bran Bread 129
Spiced Applesauce Bread with Currants 130
Fresh Apricot & Cottage Cheese Bread 131
Old-Fashioned Banana Chocolate Chip Bread 132
Sour Cream Banana Bread 133
Whole Wheat Banana & Chocolate Chip Bread 134
Banana & Orange Raisin Bran Bread 135
Whole Wheat & Oatmeal Blueberry Bread 136
Spiced Carrot & Orange Bread 137
Pineapple Cranberry Bread 138
Holiday Cranberry Almond Bread 139
Sour Cream Lemon Tea Bread 140
Extra Tart Lemon Nut Bread 141
Sour Cream Orange & Pecan Bread 142
Orange Tea Bread 143
Honey Bran Bread with Peaches 144
Fresh Peach & Almond Bread 145
Orange Peach Bread 146
Peach & Orange Yogurt Bread 147
Honey Whole Wheat Pineapple Bread 148
Pineapple & Orange Bran Bread 149
Pineapple Raisin Bran Bread 150
Pineapple Orange & Coconut Bread 151
The Best Pumpkin Bread 152
Orange & Raisin Pumpkin Bread 153
Whole Wheat Pumpkin Pecan Bread 154
Spicy Pumpkin Bread 155
Raspberry & Pecan Lemon Bread 156
Rhubarb Oatmeal Bread 157
Strawberry Pecan Bread 158
Strawberry Yogurt Banana Bread 159
Strawberry Banana Bread 160
Cinnamon Zucchini Bread 161
Spiced Zucchini Walnut Bread 162

From my Notebook:

Quick Breads with Fruits & Vegetables

Let me say, right at the start, that the major difference between a coffeecake, or a tea bread, or a quick bread is the shape of the baking pan. True, quick breads are a teensy bit denser, but if they are baked in a tube pan, they serve rather well as coffeecakes. After all, coffeecakes do have a little more character and body. That's why I call them "Cakebreads".

In this chapter, you will find a wide-range of marvellous breads. They were chosen specifically to illustrate either a technique (like the Upside Down Bread) or a specific ingredient (such as cottage cheese, or yogurt or bran or oatmeal.)

Here you will find complex breads that combine multiple flavors and textures ... such as Banana & Orange Raisin Bran Bread or Whole Wheat & Oatmeal Blueberry Bread. These were all chosen for their outstanding taste and texture and balance.

Included are Lemon Breads, especially light for ladies luncheons ... Cranberry and Pumpkin Breads, excellent for the holidays between Thanksgiving and Christmas and wonderful breads to give as gifts from your kitchen. Here you will find summer breads and winter breads ... health breads with whole wheat, bran and oatmeal.

Please refer to Page 23, for additional pointers on fruits and vegetables.

You will notice that so many of the breads are baked in smaller pans. I have mentioned it earlier, in the introduction, but it bears repeating. Smaller breads never look like leftovers and you can immediately freeze those you do not plan to use. You might send one over to a neighbor ... much nicer than a few slices cut from a larger bread. Of course, if you are planning for a large number, then the larger loaves are just fine.

Apple Orange Raisin Bread with Lemon Glaze

Using the food processor simplifies preparing this loaf. In absence of one, apple and orange must be grated and raisins and pecans must be chopped.

    1 apple peeled cored and sliced
  1/2 medium orange, cut into 6 pieces
    1 cup yellow raisins
    1 cup pecans
    2 eggs
  1/2 cup oil
  1/2 cup orange juice
1 1/4 cups sugar
    1 teaspoon vanilla

    3 cups flour
    2 teaspoons baking powder
    1 teaspoon baking soda

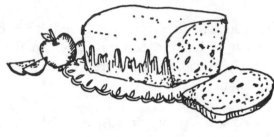

Place first 9 ingredients in the bowl of a food processor and blend for 30 seconds. Scrape down the sides and continue blending until fruit and nuts are finely chopped (not pureed), about 30 seconds.

In a large bowl, stir together the remaining ingredients. Add fruit and nut mixture to the bowl and stir until the dry ingredients are just moistened. Do not overmix.

Divide batter between 5 greased mini-loaf pans (6x3x2-inches), place pans on a cookie sheet and bake in a 350° oven for 30 minutes or until a cake tester, inserted in center, comes out clean. Cool in pans for 15 minutes and then remove from pans and continue cooling on a rack. When cool, drizzle top with Lemon Glaze. Yields 5 mini-loaves.

Lemon Glaze:
    1 tablespoon lemon juice
  3/4 cup sifted powdered sugar

Stir together all the ingredients until blended.

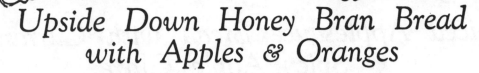

Upside Down Honey Bran Bread
with Apples & Oranges

There are few breads you can make that are more delicious than this one. This is truly a "cakebread" and excellent at any time from breakfast to tea.

Honey Walnut Coating:

- 1/4 cup honey
- 1/2 cup brown sugar
- 1/3 cup butter, melted
- 1/4 cup chopped pecans

Stir together all the ingredients until blended. Divide mixture between 2 greased 9x5-inch loaf pans or 3 greased 10-inch deerback loaf tins.

- 1 cup sugar
- 1 egg
- 1/2 cup sour cream
- 1/2 cup buttermilk
- 1/3 cup oil
- 1/3 cup honey
- 1 medium apple, very thinly sliced
- 1/2 orange, grated (about 3 tablespoons). Use fruit, juice and peel.
- 2 teaspoons vanilla

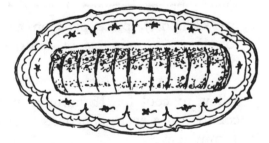

- 2 cups flour
- 3/4 cup all-bran cereal
- 1 teaspoon baking powder
- 1 teaspoon baking soda
- 3/4 cup yellow raisins
- 2 teaspoons cinnamon
- 1/2 cup chopped pecans

Beat together first 9 ingredients until blended. Combine and add the next 7 ingredients and stir until dry ingredients are blended. Do not overmix.

Divide batter between the prepared pans and bake in a 350° oven for about 1 hour (for the 9x5-inch loaves) or 50 minutes (for the deerback loaves), or until a cake tester, inserted in center, comes out clean. Allow to cool in pans for 15 minutes and then invert breads onto a serving platter. Yields 2 or 3 loaves.

Spiced Applesauce Bread with Currants & Spicy Apple Glaze

What a wonderful bread to serve with hot apple cider on a frosty night when you gather around with family and friends.

1/2 cup oil
1 cup sugar
1 1/2 cups applesauce

2 1/4 cups flour
2 teaspoons baking powder
1 teaspoon baking soda
2 teaspoons cinnamon
3/4 teaspoon ground nutmeg
1/4 teaspoon ground cloves

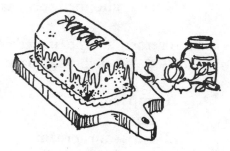

1 cup chopped walnuts
1 cup dried currants

Beat together first 3 ingredients until blended. Combine and add the next 6 ingredients and stir until dry ingredients are just moistened. Do not overmix. Stir in walnuts and currants.

Divide batter between 4 greased and lightly floured mini-loaf foil pans (6x3x2-inches), place pans on a cookie sheet, and bake in a 325° oven for 45 to 50 minutes or until a cake tester, inserted in center, comes out clean.

Allow to cool for 15 minutes and then remove from pans and continue cooling on a rack. When cool, brush tops with Spicy Apple Glaze. Yields 4 mini-loaves.

Spicy Apple Glaze:
2 tablespoons warm apple juice
1/2 teaspoon cinnamon
1/8 teaspoon ground cloves

1 cup sifted powdered sugar

Heat apple juice and spices in a metal measuring cup set over simmering water. In a bowl, sift powdered sugar and stir in apple juice mixture until blended.

Fresh Apricot & Cottage Cheese Bread with Creamy Glaze

When you are planning a picnic on a rolling meadow, in the middle of the summer, plan to take along this delightful, moist and fruity loaf.

    2 eggs
  1/2 cup butter, softened
  3/4 cup brown sugar
  1/2 cup sugar
1 1/2 cups small curd cottage cheese
    2 tablespoons grated orange peel
    1 tablespoon grated lemon peel

2 1/2 cups flour
    1 tablespoon baking powder
    1 teaspoon baking soda
    1 cup chopped walnuts
    1 cup chopped, peeled apricots (fresh or frozen)

Beat together first 7 ingredients until blended. Combine and add the next 5 ingredients and stir until dry ingredients are just moistened. Do not overmix.

Divide batter between 5 greased and lightly floured mini-loaf foil pans (6x3x2-inches), place pans on a cookie sheet, and bake in a 325° oven for 45 to 50 minutes or until a cake tester, inserted in center, comes out clean.

Allow to cool for 15 minutes and then remove from pans and continue cooling on a rack. When cool, drizzle top with Creamy Glaze. Yields 5 mini-loaves.

Creamy Glaze:
    2 tablespoons cream
    1 tablespoon chopped apricots
    1 cup sifted powdered sugar

Stir together all the ingredients until blended.

Old-Fashioned Banana Chocolate Chip Bread

This is one of the very best breads. Stirring the soda with sour cream is an old-fashioned technique, and it does produce a very moist, delicious loaf.

1/4 cup sour cream
1 teaspoon baking soda

1/2 cup butter, softened
1 1/4 cups sugar

2 eggs

1 1/2 cups flour
  pinch of salt
1 cup coarsely mashed bananas (about 2 small bananas)
1 cup (6 ounces) semi-sweet chocolate chips
1 teaspoon vanilla

Stir together the sour cream and soda and set aside. Cream butter with sugar until light and fluffy. Add eggs, one at a time, beating well after each addition. Beat in sour cream mixture. Stir in the remaining ingredients until dry ingredients are just blended. Do not overmix.

Divide mixture between 3 greased mini-loaf pans (6x3x2-inches) and bake in a 350° oven for about 40 minutes, or until a cake tester, inserted in center, comes out clean. Allow to cool in pans for 15 minutes and then, remove from pans and continue cooling on a rack. Yields 3 mini-loaves.

Note: — *Do not finely mash the bananas where they become liquidy. If you do, the breads will take forever to bake and will become overly crisp.*

Sour Cream Banana Bread with Chocolate Glaze

Oh, what a bread! This is one of Joey's favorites. Joey is the chocolate "rara avis" in our family. We are all chocolate fanatics, but I must confess, he is the one that hears the chocolate drummer.

   1/2 cup butter, at room temperature
1 1/4 cups sugar
   2 eggs
   1/2 cup sour cream
   1 teaspoon vanilla
   1 cup mashed ripe bananas (about 2 medium-sized)

1 3/4 cups flour
   1 teaspoon baking soda
   1 teaspoon baking powder
      pinch of salt
   1/2 cup (3 ounces) semi-sweet chocolate chips
   3/4 cup chopped walnuts

Beat together first 6 ingredients until blended. Stir in the remaining ingredients until dry ingredients are just moistened. Do not overmix.

Divide batter between 4 greased and lightly floured mini-loaf foil pans (6x3x2-inches), place pans on a cookie sheet, and bake in a 325° oven for 45 to 50 minutes, or until a cake tester, inserted in center, comes out clean.

Allow to cool in pans for 15 minutes and then remove from pans and continue cooling on a rack. When cool, drizzle top with Chocolate Glaze (optional, but very good, indeed). Yields 4 mini-loaves.

Chocolate Glaze:
   1/2 cup semi-sweet chocolate chips, melted
   3 tablespoons butter, melted

Stir together chocolate and butter until well blended.

Whole Wheat Banana & Chocolate Chip Bread with Creamy Glaze

1/2 cup butter, softened
1 cup sugar
2 eggs
1/2 cup sour cream
2 large bananas, mashed
1 teaspoon vanilla

1 cup flour
1 cup whole wheat flour
2 teaspoons baking powder
1 teaspoon baking soda
1/2 cup chopped walnuts
1/2 cup semi-sweet chocolate chips

Beat together first 6 ingredients until blended. Add the remaining ingredients and stir until dry ingredients are just moistened. Do not overmix.

Divide batter between 4 greased and lightly floured mini-loaf pans (6x3x2-inches), place pans on a cookie sheet, and bake in a 325° oven for 40 to 45 minutes, or until a cake tester, inserted in center, comes out clean.

Allow to cool for 15 minutes and then remove from pans and continue cooling on a rack. When cool, drizzle Creamy Glaze on the tops and in a decorative fashion. Yields 4 mini-loaves.

Creamy Glaze:
2 tablespoons cream
1/2 teaspoon chocolate extract
1 1/4 cups sifted powdered sugar

Stir together all the ingredients until blended.

Banana, Orange & Raisin Bran Bread

Bananas and orange couple well in this fragrant, moist loaf. Bran and raisins round out this delicious breakfast bread.

  1/2 cup butter, softened
    1 cup sugar
    2 eggs
    1 cup buttermilk
  3/4 cup 100% all-bran cereal
    1   orange, grated, (1/2 cup). Use fruit, juice and peel.
    1 medium banana, mashed

1 1/2 cups flour
    1 cup whole wheat flour
    2 teaspoons baking powder
    1 teaspoon baking soda
    1 cup yellow raisins
    2 teaspoons cinnamon
  1/4 teaspoon nutmeg
  1/4 teaspoon powdered cloves

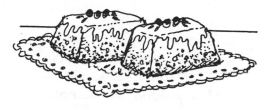

Beat together first 7 ingredients until blended. Combine and add the remaining ingredients and stir until blended. Do not overmix.

Divide batter between 4 greased mini-loaf pans (6x3x2-inches) and bake in a 350° oven for about 40 minutes or until a cake tester, inserted in center, comes out clean. Allow to cool in pan for 15 minutes, and then remove from pans and continue cooling on a rack. Yields 4 mini-loaves.

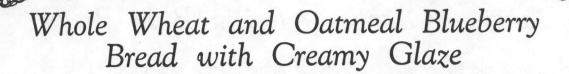

Whole Wheat and Oatmeal Blueberry Bread with Creamy Glaze

This is a sturdy, hearty loaf made with oats, whole wheat and buttermilk . . . good things, that are good for you too. Lots of blueberries and pecans round out this bread. The Creamy Glaze is nice for gift-giving.

1 cup quick-cooking oats
1 cup buttermilk
1/2 cup brown sugar
1/2 cup sugar
1 egg
6 tablespoons oil

1 cup flour
3/4 cup whole wheat flour
1 teaspoon baking powder
1 teaspoon baking soda
1 teaspoon cinnamon

1 cup blueberries, fresh or frozen
1 cup chopped toasted pecans

Beat together first 6 ingredients until blended. Combine and add the next 5 ingredients and stir until dry ingredients are just moistened. Do not overmix. Fold in the blueberries and pecans.

Divide batter between 4 greased mini-loaf pans (6x3x2-inches) and bake at 325° for 45 to 50 minutes or until a cake tester, inserted in center, comes out clean.

Allow to cool for 15 minutes and then remove from pans and continue cooling on a rack. When cool, brush tops with Creamy Glaze. Yields 4 mini-loaves.

Creamy Glaze:
  1 tablespoon cream
  1/2 teaspoon vanilla
  1/2 cup sifted powdered sugar

Stir together all the ingredients until blended.

Spiced Carrot & Orange Bread with Raisin Orange Glaze

This is a very moist, buttery, spiced bread that can be enjoyed all year 'round, but is especially nice around the winter holidays. It is rather decorative and good for holiday giving.

      3/4 cup butter (1 1/2 sticks)
        1 cup sugar
        3 eggs
  1 1/2 cups finely grated carrots
      1/2 orange, grated (about 3 tablespoons)
  1 1/2 cups chopped walnuts

        2 cups flour
        1 teaspoon baking powder
        1 teaspoon baking soda
        3 teaspoons pumpkin pie spice

Beat together first 6 ingredients until blended. Combine and add the next 4 ingredients and stir until dry ingredients are just moistened. Do not overmix.

Divide batter between 5 greased mini-loaf foil pans (6x3x2-inches), place pans on a cookie sheet, and bake in a 325° oven for 45 to 50 minutes, or until a cake tester, inserted in center, comes out clean.

Allow to cool for 15 minutes and then remove from pans and continue cooling on a rack. When cool, drizzle top with Raisin Orange Glaze. Yields 5 mini-loaves.

Raisin Orange Glaze:
        2 tablespoons orange juice
        1 cup sifted powdered sugar
        2 tablespoons finely chopped yellow raisins
        1 tablespoon grated orange peel

Stir together all the ingredients until blended.

Pineapple Cranberry Bread with Whole Wheat & Oats

The use of canned cranberry sauce and pineapple makes this bread especially convenient all year round. Whole wheat flour and oats add a good deal of solid character. This bread is especially moist and spicy.

    1/2 cup butter, softened
      1 cup sugar
    1/2 cup brown sugar
      2 eggs

      1 cup crushed pineapple (with a little juice)
    3/4 cup whole-berry cranberry sauce, broken up

      1 cup flour
      1 cup whole wheat flour
      1 cup quick-cooking oats
      1 teaspoon baking powder
      1 teaspoon baking soda
      2 teaspoons cinnamon
    1/2 teaspoon grated nutmeg
    1/2 teaspoon powdered cloves
      1 cup chopped walnuts

Beat together first 4 ingredients until blended. Stir in pineapple and cranberry sauce. Combine and add the remaining ingredients and stir until dry ingredients are blended. Do not overmix.

Divide batter between 4 mini-loaf foil pans and bake in a 350° oven for 40 to 45 minutes, or until a cake tester, inserted in center, comes out clean. Allow to cool in pans for 15 minutes, and then remove from pans and continue cooling on a rack. When cool brush tops with Pineapple Glaze. Yields 4 mini-loaves.

Pineapple Glaze:
    1 1/2 tablespoons pineapple juice
      3/4 cup sifted powdered sugar

Stir together all the ingredients until blended.

Holiday Cranberry Almond Bread with Orange Glaze

This is one of the best breads, very moist, bursting with flavor, and just lovely to serve at any time during the holidays. And if you are looking for a gift from your kitchen, this is a good bread to consider. As always, the glaze is optional, but does add a festive touch to the bread.

3/4 cup milk mixed with 1 tablespoon lemon juice

1/2 cup oil
  1 cup sugar
  2 eggs
  3 tablespoons grated orange
      (about 1/2 medium orange, grated)
  1 teaspoon vanilla
  1 teaspoon almond extract

2 1/2 cups flour
  2 teaspoons baking powder
  1 teaspoon baking soda
  1 cup chopped toasted almonds
  2 cups cranberries, chopped

In the large bowl of an electric mixer, stir together milk and lemon juice, until milk is slightly thickened, about 1 minute. Add the next 6 ingredients and beat until blended. Add the remaining ingredients and beat until blended. Do not overbeat.

Divide batter between 5 mini-loaf foil pans that have been greased and lightly floured. Place pans on a cookie sheet and bake in a 325° oven for about 45 to 50 minutes, or until a cake tester, inserted in center, comes out clean. Allow to cool for 15 minutes, and then remove from pans and continue cooling on a rack. When cool, drizzle tops in a decorative fashion, with Orange Glaze. Yields 5 mini-loaves.

Orange Glaze:
  1 tablespoon orange juice
  1/2 cup sifted powdered sugar
  2 teaspoons grated orange peel
  1 tablespoon chopped toasted almonds

Stir together all the ingredients until blended.

Note: — Combining milk and lemon juice produces what is called "sour milk." Old milk that has gone sour is never to be substituted.

Sour Cream Lemon Tea Bread with Lemon Glaze

This is a grand bread to serve when you are having the ladies for tea. Good for brunch, too. It is delicate, light and deliciously tart.

      1/2 cup butter, softened
    1 1/4 cups sugar
        2 eggs
      1/2 cup sour cream
        1 small lemon, grated, about 3 tablespoons. (Use fruit, juice
              and peel. Remove any large pieces of membrane.)

        2 cups flour
        2 teaspoons baking powder
      3/4 cup chopped pecans

Beat together first 5 ingredients until blended. Combine and add the next 3 ingredients and stir until dry ingredients are just moistened. Do not overmix.

Divide batter between 4 greased and lightly floured mini-loaf pans (6x3x2-inches), place pans on a cookie sheet, and bake in a 325° oven for about 45 to 50 minutes, or until a cake tester, inserted in center, comes out clean. Allow to cool in pans for 15 minutes and then remove from pans and continue cooling on a rack. When cool, drizzle top in a decorative fashion, with Lemon Glaze. Yields 4 mini-loaves.

Lemon Glaze:
        2 tablespoons lemon juice
        1 cup sifted powdered sugar

Stir together lemon juice and sugar until blended.

Extra Tart Lemon Nut Bread with Lemon Glaze

This delicious lemon bread is just lovely for a spring luncheon. It is especially tart and moist.

    1/2 cup butter, melted
1 1/4 cups sugar
    3 tablespoons grated lemon
    2 eggs
1/2 cup milk

    2 cups flour
    1 teaspoon baking powder
1/4 teaspoon salt

    1 cup finely chopped walnuts

Beat together first 5 ingredients until blended. Combine and beat in flour, baking powder and salt until blended. Do not overbeat. Stir in the walnuts.

Divide batter between 2 greased 8x4-inch loaf pans and bake at 350° for 1 hour, or until a cake tester, inserted in center, comes out clean. Leave loaves in pans and drizzle Lemon Glaze over the warm breads. Store in the refrigerator overnight, to allow flavors to set. Yields 2 loaves.

Lemon Glaze:
    4 tablespoons lemon juice
1/2 cup sugar

In a bowl, stir together lemon juice and sugar until sugar is dissolved. (Start this first, to allow plenty of time for the sugar to dissolve.)

Sour Cream Orange & Pecan Bread with Creamy Orange Glaze

If you are looking for a specialty from your kitchen for holiday gift-giving, you will do well to consider this lovely nut bread. Fragrant and flavorful, with the flavor of orange and the bountiful amount of pecans, makes it a taste treat for all nut lovers.

        1/2 cup butter, softened
        3/4 cup sugar
          2 eggs
        1/3 cup sour cream
        1/4 cup orange juice
          1 medium orange, grated (about 6 tablespoons). Use fruit, juice and peel. Remove any large pieces of membrane.

    1 3/4 cups flour
    1 1/2 teaspoons baking powder
    1 1/2 cups chopped pecans

Beat together first 6 ingredients until blended. Combine and add the remaining ingredients and stir until dry ingredients are just moistened. Do not overmix.

Divide batter between 3 greased mini-loaf foil pans (6x3x2-inches), place pans on a cookie sheet, and bake in a 325° oven for 45 to 50 minutes, or until a cake tester, inserted in center, comes out clean.

Allow to cool for 15 minutes and then remove from pans and continue cooling on a rack. When cool, brush tops with Creamy Orange Glaze. Yields 3 mini-loaves.

Creamy Orange Glaze:
        2 tablespoons cream
      3/4 cup sifted powdered sugar
        1 tablespoon grated orange peel

Stir together all the ingredients until blended.

Orange Tea Bread with Walnuts & Raisins & Orange Glaze

This dense bread, filled with orange, walnuts and raisins is just lovely for breakfast, brunch or teatime. The Orange Glaze is very festive and adds a delicious touch.

    1 egg
3/4 cup sugar
    1 cup sour cream
1/4 cup milk
    1 small orange, grated (about 6 tablespoons). Use fruit, juice
         and peel. Remove any large pieces of membrane.
    1 cup yellow raisins
    1 cup chopped walnuts
    1 teaspoon vanilla

    2 cups flour
    2 teaspoons baking powder

Beat together first 8 ingredients until blended. Add the flour and baking powder, and stir until dry ingredients are just moistened. Do not overmix.

Divide batter between 2 greased foil pans (4x8-inches), place pans on a cookie sheet and bake in a 350° oven for about 1 hour, or until a cake tester, inserted in center, comes out clean.

Allow to cool in pans for 15 minutes and then remove from pans and continue cooling on a rack. When cool, drizzle tops with Orange Glaze. Yields 2 loaves.

Orange Glaze:
    2 tablespoons orange juice
    1 tablespoon grated orange peel
1 1/4 cups sifted powdered sugar
    2 tablespoons finely chopped walnuts

Stir together all the ingredients until blended.

Honey Bran Bread with Peaches & Orange Honey Glaze

This bread is filled with all manner of good things... that are good for you, too.

- 1/3 cup butter, softened
- 2 eggs
- 3/4 cup sugar
- 1/3 cup honey
- 1/2 cup milk
- 1/2 cup sour cream
- 1/2 orange, grated. (Use fruit, juice and peel. Remove any large pieces of membrane.)
- .1 cup peeled and chopped peaches (fresh or frozen)

- 2 1/2 cups flour
- 1/2 cup all-bran cereal
- 2 teaspoons baking powder
- 1 teaspoon baking soda
- 1 teaspoon cinnamon
- 1 cup yellow raisins
- 3/4 cup chopped walnuts

Beat together first 8 ingredients until blended. Combine and add the next 7 ingredients and stir until dry ingredients are just moistened. Do not overmix.

Divide batter between 4 greased and lightly floured mini-loaf foil pans (6x3x2-inches), place pans on a cookie sheet, and bake in a 325° oven for 45 to 50 minutes or until a cake tester, inserted in center, comes out clean.

Allow to cool for 15 minutes and then remove from pans and continue cooling on a rack. When cool, brush tops with Honey Orange Glaze. Yields 4 mini-loaves.

Honey Orange Glaze:
- 1 tablespoon orange juice
- 1 teaspoon orange honey
- 3/4 cup sifted powdered sugar

Stir together all the ingredients until blended.

Fresh Peach & Almond Bread with Cinnamon Almond Topping

We always knew it was spring when Mom baked these delightful loaves. And we also knew that summer vacation was really close by. But now, with the lovely frozen peaches, you can enjoy this bread at any time during the year.

    1/2 cup butter, softened
    1/2 cup sugar
    1/2 cup brown sugar
      1 egg
    1/2 cup sour cream
    1/2 teaspoon almond extract

1 1/2 cups flour
    2 teaspoons baking powder
    1 teaspoon cinnamon
    1 cup chopped peaches, fresh or frozen
    1/2 cup chopped toasted almonds

Beat together first 6 ingredients until blended. Stir in the remaining ingredients until dry ingredients are just moistened. Do not overmix.

Divide batter between 4 greased and lightly floured mini-loaf foil pans (6x3x2-inches) and sprinkle tops with Cinnamon Almond Topping. Place pans on a cookie sheet and bake in a 325° oven for about 45 to 50 minutes, or until a cake tester, inserted in center, comes out clean.

Allow to cool in pans for 15 minutes and then remove from pans and continue cooling on a rack. Yields 4 mini-loaves.

Cinnamon Almond Topping:
    1/4 cup sugar
    1/2 teaspoon cinnamon
    1/2 cup finely chopped, toasted almonds

Stir together all the ingredients until blended.

Orange Peach Bread with Peach Nut Glaze

This simple little bread is one of the best... exceedingly moist and fruity and totally irresistible.

    2 eggs
    1/3 cup butter, softened
    3/4 cup sugar
    1 cup chopped canned peaches, with a little of the syrup
    1/2 orange, grated. (Use fruit, juice and peel. Remove any
            large pieces of membrane.)

    2 cups flour
    1 teaspoon baking powder
    1 teaspoon baking soda
    1 cup chopped walnuts

Beat together first 5 ingredients until blended. Combine and add the next 4 ingredients and stir until dry ingredients are just moistened. Do not overmix.

Divide batter between 4 greased and lightly floured mini-loaf foil pans (6x3x2-inches), place pans on a cookie sheet, and bake in a 325° oven for 45 to 50 minutes or until a cake tester, inserted in center, comes out clean.

Allow to cool for 15 minutes and then remove from pans and continue cooling on a rack. When cool, brush tops with Peach Nut Glaze. Yields 4 mini-loaves.

Peach Nut Glaze:
    2 tablespoons peach syrup (from canned peaches, above)
    2 tablespoons finely chopped canned peaches
    2 tablespoons chopped walnuts
    1 cup sifted powdered sugar

Stir together all the ingredients until blended.

Peach & Orange Yogurt Bread

In the summer when peaches are in full bloom, remember this little gem. An excellent bread to serve with chilled fruit soups or salads.

    1/3 cup butter, softened
    2/3 cup sugar
      1 egg
      1 orange, grated (about 6 tablespoons). Use fruit, juice and
            peel. Remove any large pieces of membrane.
    3/4 cup chopped peaches, fresh or frozen
    1/3 cup unflavored yogurt
      1 teaspoon vanilla

      2 cups flour
      2 teaspoons baking powder
      1 teaspoon baking soda
      1 teaspoon cinnamon
    1/2 cup chopped yellow raisins
    1/2 cup chopped walnuts

      4 tablespoons peach jam, heated

Beat together first 7 ingredients until blended. Add the next 6 ingredients and stir until dry ingredients are just moistened. Do not overmix.

Divide batter between 3 greased and lightly floured mini-loaf foil pans (6x3x2-inches), place pans on a cookie sheet, and bake in a 325° oven for about 45 to 50 minutes or until a cake tester, inserted in center, comes out clean.

Allow to cool in pans for 15 minutes and then remove from pans and continue cooling on a rack. When cool, brush tops with heated peach jam. Yields 3 mini-loaves.

Honey Whole Wheat Pineapple Bread with Walnuts & Cinnamon

This is another sturdy loaf filled with so many good things. Honey and whole wheat, spiced with cinnamon and moistened with pineapple. A good choice for breakfast or tea time.

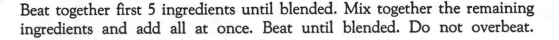

    2 eggs
1/2 cup oil
  1 cup honey
1 1/2 cups crushed pineapple (with a little juice)
1/2 teaspoon vanilla

1 1/3 cups whole wheat flour
1 1/3 cups flour
  2 teaspoons baking powder
  1 teaspoon baking soda
  2 teaspoons cinnamon
  1 cup chopped walnuts

Beat together first 5 ingredients until blended. Mix together the remaining ingredients and add all at once. Beat until blended. Do not overbeat.

Divide batter between 5 greased mini-loaf pan (6x3x2-inches) and bake in a 350° oven for about 40 to 45 minutes, or until a cake tester, inserted in center, comes out clean. Allow to cool in pans for 10 minutes, and then remove from pans and continue cooling on a rack. Serve warm with a little honey. Yields 5 mini-loaves.

Pineapple & Orange Bran Bread

If you are looking for a fruity breakfast bread, this is a good one to consider. It is filled with all manner of good things . . . bran, whole wheat flour, orange, pineapple and walnuts. This recipe produces a fine muffin, as well.

   1 cup milk
3/4 cup 100% all-bran cereal
   2 eggs
   1 cup sugar
1/2 cup oil
1/2 cup crushed pineapple
1/2 orange, grated (about 3 tablespoons)

1 1/2 cups flour
   1 cup whole wheat flour
   2 teaspoons baking powder
   1 teaspoon baking soda
   2 teaspoons cinnamon
   1 cup chopped walnuts

Beat together first 7 ingredients until blended. Combine and add the remaining ingredients and stir until blended. Do not overmix.

Divide batter between 4 greased mini-loaf pans (6x3x2-inches) and bake in a 350° oven for about 40 minutes or until a cake tester inserted in center, comes out clean. Allow to cool in pan for 15 minutes, and then remove from pans and continue cooling on a rack. Yields 4 mini-loaves.

Note: — *If you plan to bake this recipe into muffins, then divide batter between 18 paper-lined muffin cups and bake these at 350° for 30 minutes, or until muffins test done.*

Pineapple Raisin Bran Bread with Raisin Walnut Glaze

This marvellously moist bread has good solid character. Serve it with sweet butter and honey and summon a little restraint so as not to overeat.

- 1/2 cup butter, softened
- 1 egg
- 1 cup sugar
- 1/4 cup sour cream
- 1 cup canned crushed pineapple, drained

- 1 1/2 cups flour
- 1 cup all-bran cereal
- 2 teaspoons baking powder
- 1 teaspoon baking soda
- 1/2 cup yellow raisins
- 1/2 cup chopped walnuts

Beat together first 5 ingredients until blended. Combine and add the next 6 ingredients and stir until dry ingredients are just moistened. Do not overmix.

Divide batter between 4 greased and lightly floured mini-loaf foil pans (6x3x2-inches), place pans on a cookie sheet, and bake in a 325° oven for 45 to 50 minutes or until a cake tester, inserted in center, comes out clean.

Allow to cool for 15 minutes and then remove from pans and continue cooling on a rack. When cool, brush tops with Raisin Walnut Glaze. Yields 4 mini-loaves.

Raisin Walnut Glaze:
- 2 tablespoons cream
- 2 tablespoons chopped yellow raisins
- 2 tablespoons chopped walnuts
- 1 cup sifted powdered sugar

Stir together all the ingredients until blended.

Pineapple, Orange & Coconut Bread with Pineapple Glaze

This little bread is tropical in feeling and nice to serve at a luau. But, of course, it can be enjoyed at any time of the year, as it is prepared with readily available ingredients.

>   2 eggs
> 1/3 cup butter, softened
> 3/4 cup sugar
>   1 cup unsweetened crushed pineapple, with syrup
> 1/2 orange, grated. (Use fruit, juice and peel. Remove any
>   large pieces of membrane.)
>
>   2 cups flour
>   1 teaspoon baking powder
>   1 teaspoon baking soda
>   1 cup chopped walnuts
> 1/2 cup coconut flakes

Beat together first 5 ingredients until blended. Combine and add the next 5 ingredients and stir until dry ingredients are just moistened. Do not overmix.

Divide batter between 4 greased and lightly floured foil mini-loaf pans (6x3x2-inches), place pans on a cookie sheet, and bake in a 325° oven for 45 to 50 minutes or until a cake tester, inserted in center, comes out clean.

Allow to cool for 15 minutes and then remove from pans and continue cooling on a rack. When cool, brush tops with Pineapple Glaze. Yields 4 mini-loaves.

Pineapple Glaze:
>   2 tablespoons crushed pineapple with a little of the syrup
>   2 tablespoons coconut flakes
>   1 tablespoon chopped walnuts
> 3/4 cup sifted powdered sugar

Stir together all the ingredients until blended.

The Best Pumpkin Bread with Apples & Oranges

There are pumpkin breads and pumpkin breads... and then some. This is one of the best... deeply flavorful and rich with the subtle addition of apples and orange. How many Thanksgivings I recall, with happy memories of this bread baking in the oven and the fragrance that filled every nook and cranny in our home.

        2 cups sugar
        2 eggs
        1 cup canned pumpkin puree
    1/2 cup oil

    2 1/2 cups flour
    1 1/2 teaspoons baking soda
    1 1/2 teaspoons pumpkin pie spice
        1 teaspoon cinnamon
    1/2 orange, grated. (Use fruit, juice and peel. Remove any
            large pieces of membrane.)
        1 apple, peeled, cored and grated
    1/2 cup yellow raisins
    1/2 cup chopped walnuts

Beat together first 4 ingredients until blended. Stir in the remaining ingredients until dry ingredients are just moistened. Do not overmix.

Divide batter between 4 greased and lightly floured mini-loaf pans (6x3x2-inches), place pans on a cookie sheet and bake in a 325° oven for 45 to 50 minutes, or until a cake tester, inserted in center, comes out clean.

Allow to cool for 15 minutes and then remove from pans and continue cooling on a rack. When cool, brush tops with orange honey and sprinkle with a few chopped toasted walnuts. Yields 4 mini-loaves.

Orange & Raisin Pumpkin Bread
with Orange Honey Butter

Very spicy and deeply flavored with orange is this country loaf. The Orange Honey Butter can be placed in a pretty crock for holiday gift giving.

    1/4 cup butter, softened (1/2 stick)
1 1/8 cups sugar
    2 eggs
    1/3 cup orange juice
    3 tablespoons grated orange
    1 cup canned pumpkin puree

    2 cups flour
    2 teaspoons baking powder
    1/2 teaspoon baking soda
    2 teaspoons pumpkin pie spice
    1 teaspoon cinnamon
    1/4 teaspoon salt

    1 cup yellow raisins
    1 cup chopped walnuts

Beat together first 6 ingredients until blended. Stir in the remaining ingredients until dry ingredients are just blended. Do not overmix.

Divide mixture between 2 greased 8x4-inch loaf pans and bake in a 350° oven for about 50 minutes, or until a cake tester, inserted in center, comes out clean. Allow to cool in pans for 15 minutes and then remove from pans and continue cooling on a rack. Serve with Orange Honey Butter for special occasions. Yields 2 loaves.

Orange Honey Butter:
    1/2 cup butter
    1/3 cup orange honey
    1 tablespoon grated orange peel

Beat butter until light and creamy. Beat in honey and peel until blended. Place in a pretty bowl or crock, cover with plastic wrap and store in the refrigerator. Remove from the refrigerator about 20 minutes before serving.

Whole Wheat Pumpkin Pecan Bread with Orange Pecan Glaze

Thanksgiving and pumpkin breads go together like love and marriage. I do believe you will love this bread, for it is moist and fruity. The Orange Pecan Glaze is in perfect balance.

> 2 eggs
> 1/3 cup butter, melted
> 1 cup sugar
> 1 cup pumpkin puree
> 1/2 cup sour cream
> 1 small orange, grated (about 6 tablespoons). Use fruit, juice and peel. Remove any large pieces of membrane.

> 1 1/4 cups flour
> 1 cup whole wheat flour
> 2 teaspoons baking powder
> 1 teaspoon baking soda
> 1 tablespoon pumpkin pie spice
> 1/2 cup currants
> 1/2 cup chopped pecans

Beat together first 6 ingredients until blended. Combine and add the next 7 ingredients and stir until dry ingredients are just moistened.

Divide batter between 5 greased and lightly floured mini-loaf foil pans (6x3x2-inches), place pans on a cookie sheet, and bake in a 325° oven for 45 to 50 minutes, or until a cake tester, inserted in center, comes out clean.

Allow to cool for 15 minutes and then remove from pans and continue cooling on a rack. When cool, spoon Orange Pecan Glaze on top, and allow a little to drip down the sides. Yields 5 mini-loaves.

Orange Pecan Glaze:
> 2 tablespoons orange juice
> 1 tablespoon grated orange
> 3 tablespoons finely chopped pecans
> 3/4 cup sifted powdered sugar

Stir together all the ingredients until blended.

Spicy Pumpkin Bread with Dates, Nuts & Raisins

This is another holiday treat, good with coffee, tea or hot cider. It can be frozen with excellent results. If you are tempted to slice it straight from the freezer, please be sure to defrost it before you eat it.

    1 cup canned pumpkin
1/2 cup butter, softened
1 1/4 cups sugar
    2 eggs
1/3 cup sour cream
    1 teaspoon vanilla

1 1/2 cups flour
    1 teaspoon baking soda
1/2 teaspoon baking powder
    2 teaspoons pumpkin pie spice
1/2 cup chopped walnuts
1/2 cup yellow raisins
1/2 cup chopped dates

Beat together first 6 ingredients until blended. Combine and add the remaining ingredients and stir until dry ingredients are just moistened. Do not overmix.

Divide batter between 3 greased mini-loaf foil pans, 6x3x2-inches, place pans on a cookie sheet, and bake in a 350° oven for 35 to 40 minutes, or until a cake tester, inserted in center, comes out clean.

Allow to cool in pan for 15 minutes and then remove from pans and continue cooling on a rack. Serve with sweet whipped butter. Yields 3 mini-loaves.

Raspberry & Pecan Lemon Bread with Lemon Cream Glaze

This little bread is like a hope chest filled with all manner of good things. Lush raspberries, pecans and the subtle tang of lemon, all add to this impressive loaf.

      1/2 cup oil
  1 1/4 cups sugar
      1 egg
    3/4 cup sour cream
    3/4 cup buttermilk
      2 tablespoons grated lemon. (Use fruit, juice and peel. Remove any large pieces of membrane.)
      1 teaspoon vanilla

      3 cups flour
      1 tablespoon baking powder
      1 teaspoon baking soda

  1 1/2 cups chopped pecans
      1 cup raspberries (fresh or frozen)

Beat together first 7 ingredients until blended. Combine and add the next 3 ingredients and stir until dry ingredients are just moistened. Gently fold in the pecans and raspberries. Do not overmix.

Divide batter between 5 greased and lightly floured mini-loaf foil pans (6x3x2-inches), place pans on a cookie sheet, and bake in a 325° oven for 45 to 50 minutes or until a cake tester, inserted in center, comes out clean.

Allow to cool for 15 minutes and then remove from pans and continue cooling on a rack. When cool. brush tops with Lemon Cream Glaze. Yields 5 mini-loaves.

Lemon Cream Glaze:
      1 tablespoon cream
      1 teaspoon lemon juice
    3/4 cup sifted powdered sugar

Stir together all the ingredients until blended.

Rhubarb Oatmeal Bread with Ricotta & Walnuts & Cinnamon Topping

The Ricotta cheese in this loaf adds a nice texture to the crumb. It's a tart and tangy loaf, and just marvelous with sweet whipped butter. The oatmeal adds just the right amount of texture and the Cinnamon Topping is not a "must," but very good, indeed.

1 1/2 cups frozen chopped rhubarb
1/2 cup orange juice

1 cup quick-cooking oats

1/2 cup oil
1 1/4 cups sugar
1/2 cup Ricotta cheese
1/4 cup milk
2 teaspoons vanilla

1 1/2 cups flour
2 teaspoons baking powder
1 teaspoon baking soda
1 cup chopped walnuts

In a saucepan, cook together rhubarb and orange juice, for about 8 minutes or until rhubarb is tender. Stir in the oats. Place mixture in the large bowl of an electric mixer and beat in the oil, sugar, Ricotta cheese, milk and vanilla. Combine and add the remaining ingredients and stir until dry ingredients are just moistened. Do not overmix.

Divide batter between 5 greased mini-loaf pans, 6x3x2-inches, and place pans on a cookie sheet. Sprinkle tops with Cinnamon Topping and bake in a 350° oven for 45 to 50 minutes, or until a cake tester, inserted in center, comes out clean.

Allow to cool in pans for 15 minutes, and then remove pans and continue cooling on a rack. Yields 5 mini-loaves.

Cinnamon Topping:
2 tablespoons melted butter
2/3 cup brown sugar
2 teaspoons cinnamon

Stir together all the ingredients until blended.

Strawberry Pecan Bread
with Lemon Cream Glaze

The flavors of strawberry and lemon make this a perfect bread to serve at a Spring or Summer luncheon. Do not mash the strawberries to a pulp, but rather chop them coarsely. As with all breads made with fresh fruit, please store these in the refrigerator, and allow to come to room temperature before serving.

    1 cup sugar
    1/2 cup sour cream
    2 eggs
    1/3 cup oil
    1 teaspoon vanilla

    1 cup coarsely mashed strawberries, fresh or frozen

    2 cups flour
    2 teaspoons baking powder
    1 teaspoon baking soda
    1 tablespoon grated lemon peel
    1 cup chopped pecans

Beat together first 5 ingredients until blended. Stir in the strawberries. Combine and add the next 5 ingredients and stir until dry ingredients are just moistened. Do not overmix.

Divide batter between 4 greased mini-loaf foil pans (6x3x2-inches) and bake in a 325° oven for 45 to 50 minutes or until a cake tester, inserted in center, comes out clean.

Allow to cool for 15 minutes and then remove from pans and continue cooling on a rack. When cool, brush tops with Lemon Glaze. Yields 4 mini-loaves.

Lemon Glaze:
    1 cup sifted powdered sugar
    1 teaspoon lemon juice
    1/2 teaspoon grated lemon peel
    1 tablespoon cream

Combine all the ingredients and stir until blended.

Strawberry Yogurt Banana Bread with Strawberry Yogurt Glaze

This is a nice bread to serve on Valentine's Day, baked in a heart-shaped mold and glazed with a lovely strawberry glaze. This will produce 2 small hearts. Very moist and truly delicious.

      1/2 cup butter, softened
        1 cup sugar
        2 eggs
      2/3 cup strawberry yogurt
        1 teaspoon vanilla
        1 medium banana, mashed

  1 3/4 cups flour
        1 teaspoon baking powder
        1 teaspoon baking soda

      1/2 cup sliced strawberries
      1/2 cup chopped walnuts

Beat together first 6 ingredients until blended. Combine and add the next 3 ingredients and stir until dry ingredients are just moistened. Stir in the strawberries and walnuts. Do not overmix.

Divide batter between 2 greased heart molds (3-cup capacity) and bake in a 350° oven for 40 minutes, or until a cake tester, inserted in center, comes out clean.

Allow to cool in pan for 15 minutes and then remove from pans and continue cooling on a rack. When cool, brush tops with Strawberry Yogurt Glaze. Yields 2 small hearts and about 8 servings.

Strawberry Yogurt Glaze:
        2 tablespoons strawberry yogurt
      1/2 cup sifted powdered sugar

Stir together all the ingredients until blended.

Strawberry Banana Bread

This lovely bread is totally irresistible. It is just bursting with flavor and goodness with the combination of strawberries, banana and orange.

> 2 eggs
> 1 cup sugar
> 1 ripe banana coarsely chopped (do not puree.)
> 3/4 cup coarsely chopped strawberries (fresh or frozen)
> 1/2 cup oil
> 3 tablespoons grated orange. (Use fruit, juice and peel. Remove any large pieces of membrane.)

> 2 cups flour
> 1 teaspoon baking powder
> 1 teaspoon baking soda
> 1 teaspoon cinnamon
> 1/4 teaspoon nutmeg
> 1/4 teaspoon ground cloves
> 1 cup chopped walnuts

Beat together first 6 ingredients until blended. Combine and add the next 7 ingredients and stir until dry ingredients are just moistened. Do not overmix.

Divide batter between 4 greased and lightly floured mini-loaf foil pans (6x3x2-inches); place pans on a cookie sheet, and bake in a 325° oven for 45 to 50 minutes or until a cake tester, inserted in center, comes out clean.

Allow to cool for 15 minutes and then remove from pans and continue cooling on a rack. Yields 4 mini-loaves.

Cinnamon Zucchini Bread with Honey Orange Cream Cheese

It is not mandatory to peel the zucchini. But the green flecks diminish the appearance, for my taste. However, peeled or unpeeled, the delicious taste remains the same.

    1 cup grated and peeled zucchini
    1 cup sugar
  1/2 orange, grated. Use fruit, juice and peel.
    2 eggs
  1/2 cup butter, softened
    1 teaspoon vanilla

1 1/2 cups flour
    1 teaspoon baking powder
    1 teaspoon baking soda
    2 teaspoons cinnamon
    1 cup yellow raisins

Beat together first 6 ingredients until blended. Combine and add the remaining ingredients and stir until dry ingredients are just moistened. Do not overmix.

Place batter into a 9x5-inch greased loaf pan and bake in a 350° oven for 50 to 55 minutes, or until a cake tester, inserted in center, comes out clean.

Allow to cool for 15 minutes, and then remove from pan and continue cooling on a rack. Serve with Honey Orange Cream Cheese for a special occasion. Yields 1 large loaf.

Honey Orange Cream Cheese:
    1 package (8 ounces) cream cheese
  1/3 cup orange honey
    1 tablespoon grated orange peel
    1 tablespoon frozen orange juice concentrate

Beat cream cheese until light and fluffy. Beat in the remaining ingredients until blended. Place mixture into a pretty bowl or crock and refrigerate until serving time.

Spiced Zucchini Walnut Bread
with Sour Cream Glaze

This is a very moist zucchini bread that is on the spicy side. Sour cream, walnuts and cinnamon all add to make this bread immensely flavorful and delicious.

        3 eggs
    1/2 cup oil
        1 cup sugar
    1/2 cup sour cream
  1 1/2 cups zucchini, peeled and grated
        1 teaspoon vanilla

        1 cup flour
        1 cup whole wheat flour
        2 teaspoons baking powder
        1 teaspoon baking soda
    1/4 teaspoon salt
  1 1/2 teaspoons cinnamon
    1/4 teaspoon nutmeg
    1/4 teaspoon ground cloves
        1 cup chopped walnuts

Beat together first 6 ingredients until blended Add the remaining ingredients and stir until dry ingredients are just moistened. Do not overmix.

Divide batter between 4 greased mini-loaf foil pans (6x3x2-inches) and bake in a 325° oven for 45 to 50 minutes, or until a cake tester inserted in center, comes out clean.

Allow to cool for 15 minutes and then remove from pans and continue cooling on a rack. When cool, brush tops with Sour Cream Glaze.

Sour Cream Glaze:
    2 tablespoons sour cream
    1 cup sifted powdered sugar
1/2 teaspoon vanilla

Stir together all the ingredients until blended.

Quick Breads

with

Dried Fruits, Nuts, Spirits, Spices

Quick Breads with Dried Fruits, Nuts, Spirits

Honey Almond Bread 166
Mississippi Mud Pie Bread 167
Apricot & Orange Almond Bread 168
Apricot Jam & Almond Bread 169
Christmas Eggnog Cherry Bread 170
Buttermilk Chocolate Bread 171
Cafe Creme Chocolate Nut Bread 172
Two-Minute Cinnamon Swirl Bread 173
Cinnamon Cottage Cheese Bread 174
Old-Fashioned Date Nut Bread 175
Orange Date Nut Bread 176
Date Nut Orange Bread 177
Fig & Honey Pecan Bread 178
California Fruit & Nut Bread 179
Sticky Honey Gingerbread 180
Farmhouse Spiced Raisin Gingerbread 181
Oatmeal Bread with Orange & Prunes 182
Orange Marmalade Bread 183
Peanut Butter & Jam Bread 184
Danish Prune Bread 185
Old-Fashioned Honey Prune Walnut Bread 186
Sour Cream Walnut Tea Bread 187
Country Walnut & Raisin Bread 188
Honey-Spiced Walnut Bread 189
Wheat Germ Bread with Apricots 190
Bourbon Fruit & Nut Bread 191
Spiced Raisin & Walnut Sherry Bread 192
Holiday Brandy Fruit & Pecan Bread 193
St. Patrick's Day Bread 194
Christmas Sherry Fruit & Nut Bread 195
Health Bread with Yogurt, Oatmeal & Whole Wheat 196
Whole Wheat & Buttermilk Prune Bread 197
Molasses & Buttermilk Bran Bread 198
Whole Wheat & Oat Bran Bread with Dates 199
Irish Breakfast Soda Bread 200

Quick Breads with Dried Fruits, Nuts, Spirits, Spices

This chapter is a continuation of a variety of breads using ingredients other than fruits and vegetables. It includes those wonderful, flavorful dried fruits, which add tartness and chewy texture to the finished breads. Breads with dates, apricots, prunes, figs, raisins, glaceed fruits, and spices are all found here. Breads, sweetened with honey, molasses, marmalade, and jam ... holiday breads with fruits, nuts, spirits and eggnog are here for your pleasure.

This is probably a good time to repeat that the breads in this chapter have a wonderful potential for mixing and matching. Apricots, dates, prunes can be interchanged. So can walnuts and pecans. Raisins can be added to any number of nut breads producing a loaf with a different character.

Breads in this chapter can be converted to whole wheat breads. This is easily done by substituting 1/2 of the white flour with 1/2 whole wheat pastry flour. So, if a recipe calls for 2 cups of flour, it can be prepared with 1 cup of white flour and 1 cup of whole wheat pastry flour. If you use whole wheat flour that is stone-ground or milled, use about 1 tablespoon less whole wheat flour, as it is a little bulkier.

Yogurt can be substituted for sour cream, and the reverse is true, as well. Buttermilk and sour milk can substitute for each other.

These breads make wonderful gifts from your kitchen. Wrap them in brightly colored cellophane, with a spray of pretty bows, made with shiny ribbons. Remember a gift from your kitchen is like a hug and a squeeze. It says, "I like you." in just another way.

Honey Almond Bread with Apricots & Sour Cream Glaze

Apricots and almonds are another one of those marvellous combinations. Add honey and lemon and I promise you, this is delicious, in the fullest sense of the word.

 1/2 cup butter, softened
 2/3 cup sugar
 1/3 cup honey
 1/3 cup sour cream
  2 eggs
  1 teaspoon vanilla

1 1/2 cups flour
  2 teaspoons baking powder
 3/4 cup soft dried apricots, finely chopped. (If apricots are
    very dry, soften them in orange juice and drain.)
 1/2 cup chopped toasted almonds
  1 tablespoon grated lemon peel

Beat together first 6 ingredients until blended. Combine and add the next 5 ingredients and stir until dry ingredients are just moistened. Do not overmix.

Divide batter between 3 greased and lightly floured mini-loaf foil pans (6x3x2-inches), place pans on a cookie sheet, and bake in a 325° oven for 45 to 50 minutes or until a cake tester, inserted in center, comes out clean.

Allow to cool for 15 minutes and then remove from pans and continue cooling on a rack. When cool, brush tops with Sour Cream Glaze. Yields 3 mini-loaves.

Sour Cream Glaze:
  2 tablespoons sour cream
 1/2 teaspoon vanilla
  1 cup sifted powdered sugar

Stir together all the ingredients until blended.

Mississippi Mud Pie Bread with Chocolate & Almonds

This charming little bread is fashioned after the Mississippi Mud Pie, which is really a cake, and not a pie. Serve it for brunch or at tea time. In spite of the chocolate, this bread is not very sweet.

   2 eggs
1/2 cup butter, softened
3/4 cup sugar
1/2 cup milk
1/2 cup sour cream

3/4 cup semi-sweet chocolate chips, melted
   1 teaspoon vanilla

   2 cups flour
   1 teaspoon baking powder
   1 teaspoon baking soda
   4 teaspoons instant coffee
1/2 cup chopped toasted almonds

Beat together first 5 ingredients until blended. Beat in the melted chocolate and vanilla. Combine and add the remaining ingredients and stir until dry ingredients are just moistened. Do not overmix.

Divide batter between 4 greased mini-loaf pans (6x3x2-inches) and bake in a 325° oven for about 40 to 45 minutes, or until a cake tester, inserted in center, comes out clean.

Allow to cool in pan for 15 minutes, then remove from pans and continue cooling on a rack. When cool, brush tops with Chocolate Coffee Glaze. Yields 4 mini-loaves.

Chocolate Coffee Glaze:
1/2 cup semi-sweet chocolate chips, melted
   3 tablespoons butter, melted
   1 teaspoon instant coffee
   3 tablespoons chopped toasted almonds

Stir together all the ingredients until blended.

Apricot & Orange Almond Bread with Apricot Glaze

Apricots are one of my favorite dried fruits and this is one of my favorite breads. It is filled with so many delicious ingredients and the result is truly a delight.

    1/3 cup butter, softened
      1 cup sugar
      2 eggs
    1/2 cup milk
    1/2 cup sour cream
      1 small orange, grated (about 6 tablespoons). Use fruit, juice
          and peel. Remove any large pieces of membrane.
      1 cup chopped dried apricots (soaked in boiling water for
          10 minutes and thoroughly drained)

  1 1/2 cups flour
      1 cup whole wheat flour
      1 tablespoon baking powder
      1 teaspoon cinnamon
    1/2 cup chopped toasted almonds
    1/2 cup yellow raisins

Beat together first 7 ingredients until blended. Combine and add the next 6 ingredients and stir until dry ingredients are just moistened. Do not overmix.

Divide batter between 4 greased and lightly floured mini-loaf foil pans (6x3x2-inches), place pans on cookie sheet and bake in a 325° oven for 45 to 50 minutes or until a cake tester, inserted in center, comes out clean.

Allow to cool for 15 minutes and then remove from pans and continue cooling on a rack. When cool, brush tops with Apricot Almond Glaze. Yields 4 mini-loaves.

Apricot Almond Glaze:
    1/3 cup apricot jam
      1 tablespoon lemon juice
      1 tablespoon chopped yellow raisins
      2 tablespoons chopped toasted almonds

Heat together all the ingredients and stir until blended.

Apricot Jam & Almond Bread with Almond Crumb Topping

This bread is a special delight and just bursting with good taste. The Almond Crumb Topping adds a wonderful texture. This is a good choice for breakfast or brunch.

  1/4 cup butter, softened
  1/3 cup sugar
    1 egg
  1/3 cup sour cream
  1/3 cup apricot jam
    1 teaspoon vanilla

1 1/4 cups flour
    1 teaspoon baking powder
  1/2 cup chopped toasted almonds

Beat together first 6 ingredients until blended. Combine and add the remaining ingredients and stir until dry ingredients are just blended. Do not overmix.

Place batter into an 8x4-inch greased foil pan and place pan on a cookie sheet. Sprinkle top with Almond Crumb Topping and bake in a 325° oven for about 1 hour, or until a cake tester, inserted in center, comes out clean. (Tent pan loosely with foil if top is browning too rapidly.)

Allow to cool in pan for 15 minutes and then remove from pan and continue cooling on a rack. Yields 1 loaf.

Almond Crumb Topping:
    2 tablespoons sugar
    2 tablespoons melted butter
    2 tablespoons chopped almonds
    3 tablespoons flour

Stir together all the ingredients until blended. Mixture will be crumbly.

Christmas Eggnog Cherry Bread with Eggnog Glaze

Very moist and fragrant, this is a wonderful bread to serve during the Christmas holidays. Serve it with coffee, tea or hot cider. Decorate the top with 1 or 2 glaceed cherries and then drizzle with glaze, if you are planning these for gift-giving.

1 1/3 cups sugar
1/2 cup butter, softened
2 eggs
1 1/2 cups prepared eggnog

3 cups flour
1 tablespoon baking powder
1 teaspoon cinnamon
1/4 teaspoon ground nutmeg
1 cup chopped walnuts
1 cup chopped glaceed cherries

Beat together first 4 ingredients until blended. Combine and add the next 6 ingredients and stir until dry ingredients are just moistened. Do not overmix.

Divide batter between 5 greased and lightly floured mini-loaf foil pans (6x3x2-inches) and bake in a 325° oven for 45 to 50 minutes or until a cake tester, inserted in center, comes out clean.

Allow to cool for 15 minutes and then remove from pans and continue cooling on a rack. When cool, drizzle tops with Eggnog Glaze and allow a little to drip down the sides. Yields 5 mini-loaves.

Eggnog Glaze:
1/3 cup sifted powdered sugar
pinch of cinnamon
pinch of nutmeg
1 tablespoon prepared eggnog

Stir together all the ingredients until blended.

Buttermilk Chocolate Bread with Pecans & Creamy Cherry Glaze

Cherries and chocolate are a long-time favorite combination. This is an especially nice bread to serve around the winter holidays.

        1/2 cup butter, softened
          1 cup sugar
          2 eggs
        1/2 cup buttermilk
          1 teaspoon vanilla

        1/2 cup (3 ounces) semi-sweet chocolate chips, melted

      2 1/4 cups flour
          1 teaspoon baking powder
          1 teaspoon baking soda
             pinch of salt (optional)

          1 cup chopped pecans
        1/2 cup chopped glaceed cherries

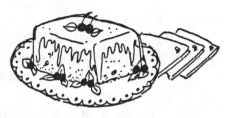

Beat together first 5 ingredients until blended. Beat in the melted chocolate. Combine and add the next 4 ingredients and stir until dry ingredients are just moistened. Do not overmix. Stir in pecans and cherries.

Divide batter between 3 greased and lightly floured mini-loaf foil pans (6x3x2-inches), place pans on a cookie sheet, and bake in a 325° oven for 45 to 50 minutes, or until a cake tester, inserted in center, comes out clean. Allow to cool for 15 minutes and then remove from pans and continue cooling on a rack.

When cool, drizzle tops with Creamy Cherry Glaze. Yields 3 mini-loaves.

Creamy Cherry Glaze:
  1 1/2 tablespoons cream
      2 tablespoons finely chopped glaceed cherries
    3/4 cup sifted powdered sugar

Stir together all the ingredients until blended.

Cafe Creme Chocolate Nut Bread with Coffee Cream Glaze

If the flavors of chocolate and coffee are your special delight, you will love this bread. The flavor of coffee is intense and the chocolate chips add the perfect touch.

1 egg
1/2 cup butter, softened
1/2 cup brown sugar
1/2 cup sugar
3 teaspoons instant coffee
2/3 cup sour cream
1 teaspoon vanilla

2 cups flour
1 tablespoon baking powder
1/2 cup semi-sweet chocolate chips
1/2 cup chopped walnuts

Beat together first 7 ingredients until blended. Combine and add the next 4 ingredients and stir until dry ingredients are just moistened. Do not overmix.

Divide batter between 4 greased and lightly floured mini-loaf pans (6x3x2-inches), place pans on a cookie sheet, and bake in a 325° oven for 45 to 50 minutes, or until a cake tester, inserted in center, comes out clean.

Allow to cool for 15 minutes and then remove from pans and continue cooling on a rack. When cool, brush tops with Coffee Cream Glaze. Yields 4 mini-loaves.

Coffee Cream Glaze:
2 tablespoons cream
1 teaspoon instant coffee
1 cup sifted powdered sugar

Stir together all the ingredients until blended. (Please note that the instant coffee will not dissolve. This intensifies flavor.)

2-Minute Cinnamon Swirl Bread with Honey & Raisins

If you are looking for a little gem for breakfast or brunch or as a snack with coffee, you would do well to consider this loaf. It is fragrant and moist in spite of the fact that it contains no butter.

    1 egg
    3/4 cup sugar
    1/2 cup milk
    1/2 cup sour cream
    1/4 cup honey

  2 1/4 cups self-rising flour
    1 teaspoon baking soda
    1/2 cup chopped walnuts
    1/2 cup yellow raisins

    8 tablespoons cinnamon sugar

Beat together first 5 ingredients until blended. Add the next 4 ingredients and stir until dry ingredients are just moistened. Do not overmix.

Divide half the batter between 4 greased mini-loaf pans (6x3x2-inches) and sprinkle 1 tablespoon cinnamon sugar on each. Top with remaining batter and sprinkle remaining cinnamon sugar on top. Place pans on a cookie sheet and bake in a 325° oven for about 45 minutes or until a cake tester, inserted in center, comes out clean.

Allow to cool in pans for 15 minutes and then remove from pans and continue cooling on a rack. Yields 4 mini-loaves.

Cinnamon Sugar:
    1/2 cup sugar
    2 teaspoons cinnamon

Stir together all the ingredients until blended.

Cinnamon Cottage Cheese Bread with Raisins, Oranges & Walnuts

This is a lovely breakfast bread, not sweet, very moist and nicely flavored with cinnamon and orange.

    1   egg
    1/4 cup butter
    1/3 cup sugar
    1   cup small curd, lo-fat cottage cheese
    1/2 orange, grated. Use fruit, juice and peel.

    1   cup flour
    1   teaspoon baking powder
    1/2 teaspoon baking soda
    1   teaspoon cinnamon
    1/2 cup yellow raisins
    1/2 cup chopped walnuts

    1/2 teaspoon cinnamon
    1   tablespoon sugar

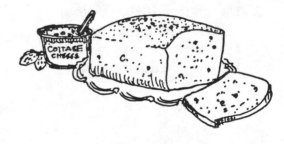

Beat together first 5 ingredients until blended. Combine and add the next 6 ingredients and stir until dry ingredients are just moistened. Do not overmix.

Scrape batter into a greased 8x4-inch foil loaf pan, and sprinkle top with mixture of cinnamon and sugar. Place pan on a cookie sheet and bake in a 350° oven for 40 to 45 minutes, or until a cake tester, inserted in center, comes out clean.

Allow to cool for 15 minutes, and then remove pan and continue cooling on a rack. Serve with cream cheese and jam and a few sliced strawberries. Yields 1 loaf.

Old-Fashioned Date Nut Bread with Walnut Glaze

This is a traditional Date Nut Bread with the addition of the orange flavor. The Walnut Glaze adds a nice touch and dresses up this dark, delicious loaf.

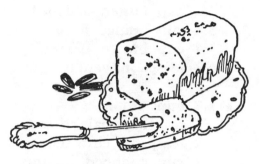

  2 eggs
3/4 cup orange juice
  6 tablespoons melted butter
3/4 cup sugar
  1 teaspoon vanilla

1 3/4 cups flour
  2 teaspoons baking powder
1/2 teaspoon baking soda
  1 cup chopped pitted dates
  1 cup chopped walnuts

Beat together first 5 ingredients until blended. Add the remaining ingredients and stir until dry ingredients are just moistened. Do not overmix.

Scrape batter into a greased and lightly floured 8x4-inch loaf pan, place pan on a cookie sheet, and bake in a 350° oven for about 50 minutes to 1 hour, or until a cake tester, inserted in center, comes out clean.

Allow to cool in pan for 15 minutes and then remove pan and continue cooling on a rack. When cool, drizzle top with Walnut Glaze. Yields 1 8x4-inch loaf.

Walnut Glaze:
  1 tablespoon cream
  2 tablespoons finely chopped walnuts
1/2 cup sifted powdered sugar

Stir together all the ingredients until blended.

Orange Date Nut Bread with Orange Glaze

This is a lovely bread for a ladies' brunch or lunch buffet. It is, also, a good choice for an afternoon tea. Dates should be soft and plump and cut into large pieces, adding a rich date flavor.

1/2 cup butter, softened
3/4 cup orange juice
1 cup brown sugar
1 teaspoon vanilla

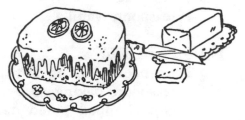

1 1/2 cups flour
1 teaspoon baking soda
1 teaspoon cinnamon
1 cup chopped walnuts
1 cup coarsely chopped soft pitted dates
2 tablespoons grated orange peel

Beat together first 4 ingredients until blended. Combine and add the remaining ingredients and stir until dry ingredients are just moistened. Do not overmix.

Divide mixture between 3 greased mini-loaf foil pans, 6x3x2-inches, place pans on a cookie sheet, and bake at 350° for about 40 minutes, or until a cake tester, inserted in center, comes out clean.

Allow to cool in pan for 15 minutes and then remove pans and continue cooling on a rack. When cool, drizzle top with Orange Glaze, and allow a little to drip down the sides. Yields 3 mini-loaves.

Orange Glaze:
1 tablespoon orange juice
1 teaspoon grated orange peel
2/3 cup sifted powdered sugar

Stir together all the ingredients until blended.

Date Nut Orange Bread with Orange Marmalade Butter

Dates and orange are a wonderful combination of flavors. This is a kind of sticky bread, not too sweet and very delicious.

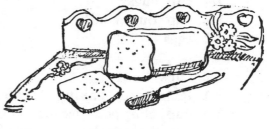

2 eggs
1/2 cup sugar
1/2 cup honey
2/3 cup orange juice
6 tablespoons melted butter
1 teaspoon vanilla

2 cups flour
2 teaspoons baking powder
1/2 teaspoon baking soda
1 cup chopped dates
3/4 cup chopped walnuts

Beat together first 6 ingredients until blended. Add the remaining ingredients, all at once, and stir until they are just moistened. Do not overmix.

Pour mixture into a greased 8x4x3-inch pan and bake in a 350° oven for about 50 minutes to 1 hour or until a cake tester, inserted in center, comes out clean. Allow to cool in pan for 10 minutes and then remove from pan and continue cooling on a rack. Serve with Orange Marmalade Butter as a breakfast treat. Yields 1 loaf.

Orange Marmalade Butter:
1/2 cup butter, softened
1/4 cup orange marmalade
2 tablespoons finely chopped walnuts

Beat butter until light and fluffy. Beat in the remaining ingredients until blended.

Fig & Honey Pecan Bread with Orange Honey Glaze

This is a nice homey loaf with the crunch of dried figs and pecans. It is a lovely winter bread and the honey and pecan topping dresses it up for gift-giving.

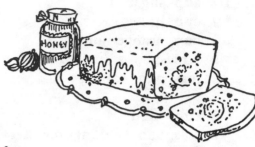

1/3 cup butter, softened
1/2 cup honey
1/4 cup sugar
1/2 cup buttermilk
2 eggs

2 cups flour
1 tablespoon baking powder
3/4 cup chopped pecans
1 cup finely chopped dried figs
1 tablespoon grated orange peel

Beat together first 5 ingredients until blended. Combine and add the next 5 ingredients and stir until dry ingredients are just moistened. Do not overmix.

Divide batter between 4 greased and lightly floured mini-loaf foil pans (6x3x2-inches), place pans on a cookie sheet, and bake in a 325° oven for 45 to 50 minutes, or until a cake tester, inserted in center, comes out clean.

Allow to cool for 15 minutes and then remove from pans and continue cooling on a rack. When cool, spoon and brush tops with Orange Honey Glaze. Yields 4 mini-loaves.

Orange Honey Glaze:
3 tablespoons honey
1 tablespoon grated orange peel
2 tablespoons finely chopped pecans

In a 1-cup measuring cup, stir together all the ingredients and place in a skillet with simmering water, until honey is thinned and easily spread.

California Fruit & Nut Bread with Vanilla Cream Glaze

Everyone who has tasted this delightful loaf ends up purring like a kitten. It is a taste treat, I promise you.

1 cup diced, mixed dried fruit. (These are sometimes called Fruit Bits.)
1 cup hot orange juice

2 eggs
1/3 cup butter
1 cup sugar
1 teaspoon vanilla

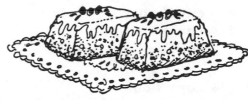

1 cup flour
1 cup whole wheat flour
2 teaspoons baking powder
1 teaspoon baking soda
1 cup chopped walnuts

Soak dried fruit bits in heated orange juice for 15 to 30 minutes, or until fruit is plumped. Beat eggs, butter, sugar and vanilla until blended. Beat in soaked fruit mixture. Combine and add the remaining 5 ingredients, and stir until dry ingredients are just moistened. Do not overmix.

Divide batter between 4 greased and lightly floured mini-loaf foil pans (6x3x2-inches), place pans on a cookie sheet, and bake in a 325° oven for 45 to 50 minutes, or until a cake tester, inserted in center, comes out clean.

Allow to cool for 15 minutes and then remove from pans and continue cooling on a rack. When cool, brush tops with Vanilla Cream Glaze. Yields 4 mini-loaves.

Vanilla Cream Glaze:
1 tablespoon cream
1/2 teaspoon vanilla
3/4 cup sifted powdered sugar

Stir together all the ingredients until blended.

Sticky Honey Gingerbread with Walnuts & Raisins

This is one of the best tasting gingerbreads, and I know you will enjoy making this often. It is especially good with hot cider or coffee with a good sprinkling of cinnamon.

- 1/2 cup butter, softened
- 1 cup brown sugar
- 2 eggs
- 1/2 cup molasses
- 1/4 cup honey
- 1/2 cup buttermilk
- 1/2 cup sour cream

- 2 3/4 cups flour
- 1 1/2 teaspoons baking soda
- 1 teaspoon baking powder
- 1 teaspoon ground ginger
- 2 teaspoons cinnamon
- 1 cup yellow raisins
- 1/2 cup chopped walnuts

- 5 tablespoons chopped walnuts

Beat together first 7 ingredients until blended. Combine and add the next 7 ingredients and stir until dry ingredients are just moistened. Do not overmix.

Divide batter between 5 greased and lightly floured mini-loaf foil pans (6x3x2-inches). Sprinkle top with additional walnuts, place pans on a cookie sheet, and bake in a 325° oven for 45 to 50 minutes or until a cake tester, inserted in center, comes out clean.

Allow to cool for 15 minutes and then remove from pans and continue cooling on a rack. When cool, brush tops with warm honey. Yields 5 mini-loaves.

Farmhouse Spiced Raisin Gingerbread

Deep, dark and delicious is this wonderful gingerbread. Old-fashioned, true, but always enjoyed.

3/4 cup molasses
3/4 cup boiling water

1/2 cup yellow raisins
1/2 cup shortening
3/4 cup brown sugar
  1 egg

  2 cups flour
  2 teaspoons baking powder
1/2 teaspoon baking soda
  1 teaspoon cinnamon
  1 teaspoon ground ginger
1/4 teaspoon ground cloves

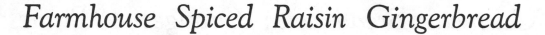

Stir together molasses and boiling water until blended. Add yellow raisins, shortening, brown sugar and egg and beat until blended. Combine and add the remaining ingredients and stir until dry ingredients are blended. Do not overmix.

Scrape batter into a greased 8-inch square pan and bake in a 350° oven for 45 minutes, or until a cake tester, inserted in center, comes out clean. Cut into squares and serve with cream cheese, sliced strawberries and chopped toasted pecans. Yields 16 2-inch squares.

Oatmeal Bread with Oranges & Prunes & Orange Honey Glaze

This is a grand loaf, very sturdy, lots of character and very delicious. It is filled with so many good things . . . that are good for you, too.

        1/2 orange, cut into 6 pieces
          1 cup yellow raisins
        3/4 cup soft pitted prunes
          1 cup pecans
        3/4 cup milk
        3/4 cup sour cream
        1/3 cup oil
          1 egg
          1 cup brown sugar

          1 cup quick-cooking oats
          2 cups flour
          2 teaspoons baking powder
          1 teaspoon baking soda

In the bowl of a food processor, place first 9 ingredients and blend for 30 seconds. Scrape down the sides and blend for another 30 seconds or until fruits are finely chopped, and not pureed.

In a large bowl, stir together oats, flour, baking powder and baking soda until nicely mixed. Add fruit and nut mixture and stir until dry ingredients are just moistened. Do not overmix.

Divide batter between 5 greased mini-loaf foil pans (6x3x2-inches), place pans on a cookie sheet, and bake in a 325° oven for 40 to 45 minutes, or until a cake tester, inserted in center, comes out clean.

Cool in pans for 15 minutes and then remove from pans and continue cooling on a rack. When cool, brush tops with warm Orange Honey Glaze. Yields 5 mini-loaves.

Orange Honey Glaze:
          5 tablespoons honey
          2 tablespoons finely grated orange peel

Heat together honey and orange peel for 1 minute. Brush glaze onto cooled loaves.

Orange Marmalade Bread

The aroma of this bread, baking in your oven, will bring friends and neighbors to your door. This is a lovely bread, very moist and deeply flavorful.

> 1 egg
> 1 cup sugar
> 1/3 cup butter, softened
> 1/3 cup milk
> 1/3 cup sour cream
> 1/3 cup orange marmalade
> 1 tablespoon grated lemon (use fruit, juice and peel)
>
> 1 1/2 cups flour
> 3/4 cup oatmeal
> 1 tablespoon baking powder
> 1/2 cup chopped walnuts

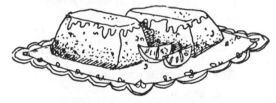

Beat together first 7 ingredients until blended. Combine and add the next 4 ingredients and stir until dry ingredients are just moistened. Do not overmix.

Divide batter between 4 greased and lightly floured mini-loaf pans (6x3x2-inches), place pans on a cookie sheet, and bake in a 325° oven for 45 to 50 minutes or until a cake tester, inserted in center, comes out clean.

Allow to cool for 15 minutes and then remove from pans and continue cooling on a rack. When cool, brush a thin layer of honey on top. Yields 4 mini-loaves.

Peanut Butter and Jam Bread with Bananas & Raisins

This wonderful little bread was created in honor of a sandwich I once ate, and which I have never forgotten. Up until that time, I must confess, peanut butter was not one of my preferred tastes. It was 2 o'clock in the afternoon, I was at the beauty shop and very, very hungry. A young lady came by selling sandwiches, but by the time she came to me, there was one, lonely sandwich left. You guessed it . . . peanut butter and jam with bananas and raisins. Well, you can imagine how dejected I was, but hunger won out and I purchased it. It was wonderful. I savored every little bite, and I look upon peanut butter now, with a newly found fondness.

    1/2 cup butter
    1/2 cup peanut butter (chunky or fine ground)
    3/4 cup apricot jam
     2 eggs
    1/2 cup sour cream
    1/2 cup sugar

     2 cups self-rising flour
     1 teaspoon baking powder
    1/2 cup yellow raisins

     2 medium ripe bananas, mashed
    1/2 cup chopped peanuts

Beat together first 6 ingredients until blended. Mix together and add the next 3 ingredients and beat until dry ingredients are just moistened. Do not overmix. Stir in the bananas and peanuts.

Divide batter between 4 greased mini-loaf foil pans (6x3x2-inches) and place pans on a cookie sheet. Bake at 325° for about 45 to 50 minutes, or until a cake tester, inserted in center, comes out clean.

Allow to cool in pans for 15 minutes and then remove from pans and continue cooling on a rack. Yields 4 mini-loaves.

Note: — *A sprinkle of sifted powdered sugar is good, to decorate. However, if you are planning this for gift giving, then brush tops with heated apricot jam and sprinkle lightly with chopped toasted peanuts.*

Danish Prune Bread with Lemon Butter Glaze

You will enjoy making this bread during the winter months when you are looking for a hardy, substantial loaf. You may use ½ cup chopped prunes for a lighter bread.

1/4 cup butter, softened
1/4 cup sour cream
2/3 cup sugar
   2 eggs
   2 tablespoons grated lemon. (Use fruit, juice and peel.
         Remove any large pieces of membrane.)

1 cup flour
2 teaspoons baking powder
1 teaspoon cinnamon
1/4 teaspoon nutmeg
1 cup chopped walnuts
1 cup chopped pitted prunes

Beat together first 5 ingredients until blended. Combine and add the next 6 ingredients and stir until dry ingredients are just moistened. Do not overmix.

Divide batter between 3 greased and lightly floured mini-loaf foil pans (6x3x2-inches), place pans on a cookie sheet, and bake in a 325° oven for 45 to 50 minutes or until a cake tester, inserted in center, comes out clean.

Allow to cool for 15 minutes and then remove from pans and continue cooling on a rack. When cool, brush tops with Lemon Butter Glaze. Yields 3 mini-loaves.

Lemon Butter Glaze:
   1 tablespoon butter, softened
   1 tablespoon lemon juice
3/4 cup sifted powdered sugar

Beat together all the ingredients until blended.

Old-Fashioned Honey Prune & Walnut Bread

This is an old-fashioned American loaf, sparkled with honey, brown sugar and prunes. Notice that it contains no butter. It is compact and dense and can be cut into the thinnest slices. No need to glaze, for this is best served with sweet, creamy butter.

      1 package (8 ounces) pitted prunes (chopped)
  1/2 cup boiling water
      1 teaspoon baking soda

      1 egg
  2/3 cup brown sugar
  1/2 cup honey
  1/2 cup buttermilk
      1 teaspoon vanilla

  2 1/2 cups flour
      1 teaspoon baking powder
      1 cup chopped walnuts

In a bowl, stir together first 3 ingredients and allow mixture to cool to lukewarm, about 20 minutes.

Beat together next 5 ingredients until blended. Beat in prune mixture. Combine and add the remaining ingredients and stir until dry ingredients are just moistened. Do not overmix.

Divide batter between 4 greased mini-loaf foil pans (6x3x2-inches) and bake at 325° for 45 to 50 minutes or until a cake tester, inserted in center, comes out clean.

Allow to cool for 15 minutes and then remove from pans and continue cooling on a rack. Yields 4 mini-loaves.

Sour Cream Walnut Tea Bread with Cinnamon-Cocoa Swirl

This lovely bread will grace a table at brunch or tea. It is especially moist and delicious and the cinnamon-cocoa filling adds just the right balance.

- 1/2 cup butter, softened
- 1 cup sugar
- 3 eggs
- 1 cup sour cream
- 1 teaspoon vanilla

- 3 cups flour
- 2 teaspoons baking powder
- 1 teaspoon baking soda
- 1 cup chopped walnuts

- 8 tablespoons chopped walnuts (for topping)

Beat together first 5 ingredients until blended. Add the next 4 ingredients, and stir until dry ingredients are just moistened. Do not overmix.

Divide half the batter between 4 greased and lightly floured mini-loaf pans (6x3x2-inches). Sprinkle 3 tablespoons Cinnamon-Cocoa Filling over each pan. Spread remaining batter evenly over the cocoa mixture. Sprinkle top with additional chopped walnuts.

Place pans on a cookie sheet and bake in a 350° oven for about 45 to 50 minutes or until a cake tester, inserted in center comes out clean. Allow to cool in pans for 15 minutes. Remove from pans and continue cooling on a rack. Yields 4 mini-loaves.

Cocoa-Cinnamon Filling:
- 1/2 cup sugar
- 1 tablespoon cocoa
- 1 teaspoon cinnamon

Stir together all the ingredients until blended. Unused mixture can be stored indefinitely for a future use.

Country Walnut & Raisin Bread with Orange Honey Butter

These few humble ingredients produce a majestic loaf. This is a rather dense bread and excellent for breakfast or brunch. Any leftover bread can be sliced and toasted in a 350° oven for about 8 to 10 minutes on each side. This will produce a dry, crisp slice, that is just wonderful for dunking.

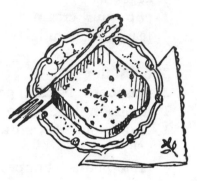

    1 egg
    3/4 cup milk
    3/4 cup sour cream
    1/4 cup melted butter
    1 cup sugar

    3 cups flour
    1 tablespoon baking powder
1 1/2 cups chopped walnuts
    1 cup yellow raisins

Beat together first 5 ingredients until blended. Combine and add the remaining ingredients and stir until dry ingredients are just moistened. Do not overmix.

Scrape mixture into a greased and lightly floured 9x5-inch loaf pan and bake in a 350° oven for about 1 hour, or until a cake tester, inserted in center, comes out clean.

Allow to cool in pan for 15 minutes and then remove from pan and continue cooling on a rack. Serve with Orange Honey Butter for special occasions. Yields 1 large loaf.

Orange Honey Butter:
    1/2 cup butter
    1/4 cup honey
    1 tablespoon frozen orange juice concentrate

Beat butter until light and fluffy. Beat in remaining ingredients until blended.

Honey Spiced Walnut Bread with Honey Butter Topping

This is a sort of sticky bread, dense, dark and delicious. The honey and spice add a lot of character.

    1/2 cup butter, softened
    3/4 cup sugar
      2 eggs
    3/4 cup honey mixed with 1 cup hot water

  2 1/4 cups flour
      1 teaspoon baking soda
      2 teaspoons baking powder
      1 teaspoon cinnamon
    1/4 teaspoon ground cloves
    3/4 cup chopped walnuts
    1/3 cup chopped yellow raisins

Beat together first 4 ingredients until blended. Combine and add the next 7 ingredients and stir until dry ingredients are just moistened. Do not overmix.

Divide batter between 4 greased and lightly floured mini-loaf foil pans (6x3x2-inches), place pans on a cookie sheet, and bake in a 325° oven for 45 to 50 minutes, or until a cake tester, inserted in center, comes out clean.

Allow to cool for 15 minutes and then remove from pans and continue cooling on a rack. When cool spoon and brush tops with Honey Butter Topping. Yields 4 mini-loaves.

Honey Butter Topping:
      2 tablespoons orange juice
    1/4 cup honey
    1/3 cup chopped walnuts

Heat together all the ingredients until butter is melted and mixture is nicely blended.

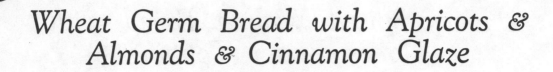

Wheat Germ Bread with Apricots & Almonds & Cinnamon Glaze

This is a dense loaf and good for breakfast. Served with some whipped butter or cream cheese and a sprinkling of chopped almonds . . . delicious.

    1 egg
1/2 cup sugar
1/2 cup brown sugar
1/2 cup butter, softened
    1 cup sour cream

1 3/4 cups flour
    2 teaspoons baking powder
1/2 teaspoon baking soda
1/2 cup wheat germ
    1 cup chopped dried apricots
1/2 cup chopped almonds
    2 teaspoons cinnamon

Beat together first 5 ingredients until blended. Combine and add the next 7 ingredients and stir until dry ingredients are blended. Do not overmix.

Spread batter evenly into a buttered 10x2-inch fluted round pan, with a removable bottom, and bake in a 350° oven for 45 minutes, or until a cake tester, inserted in center, comes out clean. Allow to cool in pan.

When cool, invert bread onto a serving platter and drizzle top with Cinnamon Glaze. Serves 8 to 10.

Cinnamon Glaze:

1/2 cup sifted powdered sugar
1/2 teaspoon cinnamon
    1 tablespoon cream

Stir together all the ingredients until blended. Add a little cream or powdered sugar to make glaze a drizzling consistency.

Bourbon Fruit and Nut Bread with Bourbon Glaze

This is a lovely bread to give as a gift from your kitchen around the holidays. Wrapped in a starburst of cellophane and pretty red ribbons it will bring best wishes the nicest way I know.

    1/2 cup butter, softened
      1 cup brown sugar
    1/2 cup sugar
      2 eggs
    1/2 cup orange juice
    1/4 cup Bourbon

      2 cups flour
      2 teaspoons baking powder
      1 teaspoon baking soda
      1 cup chopped toasted pecans
    1/2 cup chopped glaceed cherries
    1/2 cup yellow raisins

Beat together first 6 ingredients until blended. Add the next 6 ingredients and stir until dry ingredients are just moistened. Do not overmix.

Divide batter between 4 greased and lightly floured mini-loaf foil pans (6x3x2-inches) and bake in 325° oven for 45 to 50 minutes or until a cake tester, inserted in center, comes out clean.

Allow to cool for 15 minutes and then remove from pans and continue cooling on rack. When cool, brush tops with Orange Bourbon Glaze. Yields 4 mini-loaves.

Orange Bourbon Glaze:
      1 tablespoon orange juice
      1 teaspoon Bourbon
    3/4 cup sifted powdered sugar
      3 tablespoons chopped toasted pecans

Stir together all the ingredients until blended.

Spiced Raisin & Walnuts Sherry Bread with Sherry Cream Glaze

This is a fine Thanksgiving bread, not too sweet, great with pumpkin or carrot soup and frankly, just wonderful with a cup of coffee or hot spiced cider. If you are planning this for gift-giving, brush tops with glaze. As an accompaniment to soup or salad, serve unglazed.

        1/2 cup butter, softened
          1 cup brown sugar
          1 egg
        1/2 orange, grated. (About 3 tablespoons of peel,
              fruit and juice.)
        1/2 cup golden cream sherry
          2 cups flour
          2 teaspoons baking powder
        1/2 teaspoon baking soda
          2 teaspoons cinnamon
        1/4 teaspoon ground nutmeg
        1/4 teaspoon powdered cloves
          1 teaspoon vanilla
        1/2 cup, each, raisins and walnuts

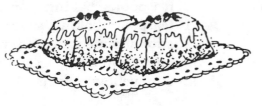

Beat together first 5 ingredients until blended. Stir together the remaining ingredients and beat these into the butter mixture until blended. Do not overmix.

Divide batter between 3 greased mini-loaf foil pans, place pans on a cookie sheet, and bake in a 325° oven for about 45 minutes, or until a cake tester, inserted in center, comes out clean. Allow to cool in pans. When cool, brush tops with Sherry Cream Glaze. Yields 3 mini-loaves.

Sherry Cream Glaze:
          1 tablespoon golden cream sherry
          1 tablespoon cream
          1 cup sifted powdered sugar

Stir together all the ingredients until blended.

Holiday Brandy Fruit & Pecan Bread with Cherry Brandy Glaze

What a nice bread to serve around the time between Thanksgiving and Christmas. And remember, this makes a lovely gift from your kitchen.

    4 ounces cream cheese, softened
    1/2 cup (1 stick) butter, softened
    1 cup sugar
    2 eggs
    1/2 orange, grated. (Use fruit, juice and peel. Remove any
           large pieces of membrane.)
    2 tablespoons Brandy
    1/2 cup sour cream

    2 cups flour
    2 teaspoons baking powder
    1 teaspoon baking soda
    1 cup chopped mixed glaceed fruit
    1/2 cup raisins
    1/2 cup currants
    1 cup chopped pecans

Beat together first 7 ingredients until blended. Combine and add the next 7 ingredients and stir until dry ingredients are just moistened. Do not overmix.

Divide batter between 4 greased and lightly floured mini-loaf pans (6x3x2-inches), place pans on a cookie sheet, and bake in a 325° oven for 45 to 50 minutes, or until a cake tester, inserted in center, comes out clean.

Allow to cool for 15 minutes and then remove from pans and continue cooling on a rack. When cool, brush tops with Cherry Brandy Glaze. Yields 4 mini-loaves.

Cherry Brandy Glaze:
    1 teaspoon Brandy
    1 tablespoon orange juice
    3/4 cup sifted powdered sugar
    2 tablespoons chopped glaceed cherries

Stir together all the ingredients until blended.

St. Patrick's Day Bread with Irish Whiskey Glaze

This is a good basic recipe for breads made with liquor. It can be varied with Bourbon, Cognac or Sherry. Currants, glaceed fruits and a variety of nuts can be substituted.

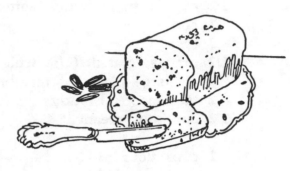

    1/2 cup butter
      1 cup sugar
      2 eggs
    1/4 cup Irish whiskey
    1/3 cup sour cream
      2 teaspoons vanilla

  1 3/4 cups flour
      2 teaspoons baking powder
      1 cup dark raisins
      1 cup chopped walnuts

Beat together first 6 ingredients until blended. Combine and add the remaining ingredients and stir until dry ingredients are moistened. Do not overmix.

Divide batter between 3 greased mini-loaf foil pans (6x3x2-inches) and bake in a 325° oven for 45 to 50 minutes, or until a cake tester, inserted in center, comes out clean. Allow to cool in pans for 15 minutes and then remove from pans and continue cooling on a rack.

When cool, drizzle tops with Irish Whiskey Glaze. Yields 3 mini-loaves.

Irish Whiskey Glaze:
      1 teaspoon Irish whiskey
      1 tablespoon cream
      1 teaspoon melted butter
    2/3 cup sifted powdered sugar

Stir together all the ingredients until blended.

Christmas Sherry Fruit & Nut Bread with Sherry Cream Glaze

The fragrance of these breads, baking in the oven, will bring the neighborhood to your door. And your home will be perfumed for hours, with the aroma of sherry and spices.

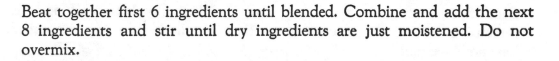

    1 egg
    1 cup sugar
  1/2 cup butter, softened
  1/2 cup golden cream sherry
  1/4 cup cream
    1 teaspoon vanilla

    2 cups flour
    1 teaspoon baking powder
    1 teaspoon baking soda
    2 teaspoons cinnamon
  1/4 teaspoon ground nutmeg
    1 cup yellow raisins
    1 cup chopped pecans
    1 cup chopped glaceed mixed fruits

Beat together first 6 ingredients until blended. Combine and add the next 8 ingredients and stir until dry ingredients are just moistened. Do not overmix.

Divide batter between 4 greased mini-loaf pans (6x3x2-inches) and bake in a 325° oven for 45 to 50 minutes, or until a cake tester, inserted in center, comes out clean.

Allow to cool for 15 minutes and then remove from pans and continue cooling on a rack. When cool brush tops with Sherry Cream Glaze and allow a little to drip down the sides. Yields 4 mini-loaves.

Sherry Cream Glaze:
    2 teaspoons sherry
    2 teaspoons cream
  2/3 cup sifted powdered sugar

Stir together all the ingredients until blended.

Health Bread with Yogurt, Oatmeal & Whole Wheat with Praline Glaze

This is a very sturdy, hardy loaf made with all manner of good things. It is dense, dark and delicious . . . and fragrant with the addition of spices.

        2 eggs
        1 cup unflavored yogurt
    1/2 cup oil
    3/4 cup brown sugar
    3/4 cup sugar

        1 cup quick-cooking oats
    3/4 cup whole wheat flour
    3/4 cup flour
        1 teaspoon baking powder
        1 teaspoon baking soda
        1 teaspoon cinnamon
    1/4 teaspoon ground nutmeg
    1/4 teaspoon ground cloves
        1 cup chopped pecans

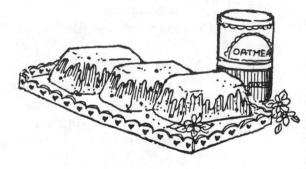

Beat together first 5 ingredients until blended. Combine and add the remaining ingredients and stir until dry ingredients are just moistened. Do not overmix.

Divide batter between 4 greased mini-loaf foil pans, (6x3x2-inches), place pans on a cookie sheet, and bake in a 325° oven for about 40 minutes, or until a cake tester, inserted in center, comes out clean.

Spread Praline Glaze evenly over the top and broil tops for about 2 or 3 minutes or until glaze is bubbling, but not browned. Allow to cool in pan for 15 minutes and then remove from pans and continue cooling on a rack. Yields 4 mini-loaves.

Praline Glaze:
        3 tablespoons butter, melted
    1/3 cup brown sugar
    1/3 cup chopped pecans

In a little saucepan, heat together all the ingredients until mixture is blended. Do not allow mixture to bubble or boil.

Whole Wheat & Buttermilk Prune Bread with Cinnamon Walnut Topping

    1/3 cup butter, softened
      1 cup sugar
      2 eggs
1 1/4 cups buttermilk

1 1/2 cups flour
      1 cup whole wheat flour
      3 teaspoons baking powder
    1/2 teaspoon baking soda
      1 teaspoon cinnamon
    3/4 cup chopped walnuts
    1/2 cup yellow raisins
    3/4 cup soft pitted prunes, chopped

Beat together first 4 ingredients until blended. Stir in the remaining ingredients until dry ingredients are just moistened. Do not overmix.

Divide batter between 4 greased and lightly floured mini-loaf pans and sprinkle Cinnamon Walnut Topping evenly over the tops. Place pans on a cookie sheet and bake in a 325° oven for 45 to 50 minutes, or until a cake tester, inserted in center, comes out clean. Allow to cool in pans for 15 minutes and then remove from pans and continue cooling on a rack. Yields 4 mini-loaves.

Cinnamon Walnut Topping:
    1/2 teaspoon cinnamon
      4 tablespoons brown sugar, sifted
    1/4 cup chopped walnuts

Stir together all the ingredients until blended. Unused topping can be stored in the refrigerator for another use.

Molasses & Buttermilk Bran Bread with Orange & Cinnamon

This recipe produces a substantial 6 loaves, and is a good choice if you are preparing for a large group. The loaves are dense and dark and simply delicious served with a little creamy butter.

```
    1 egg
  1/3 cup oil
  3/4 cup brown sugar
    2 cups buttermilk
  1/2 cup molasses
    1 orange, grated (about 6 tablespoons)

    3 cups whole wheat flour
1 1/2 cups all-bran cereal
  1/2 cup flour
    2 teaspoons baking soda
    1 teaspoon baking powder
    2 teaspoons cinnamon
1 1/2 cups yellow raisins
```

Beat together first 6 ingredients until blended. Mix together the remaining ingredients and add all at once. Beat until dry ingredients are just moistened. Do not overbeat.

Divide batter between 6 greased mini-loaf pans (6x3x2-inches), place pans on a cookie sheet, and bake in a 325° oven for 40 to 45 minutes, or until a cake tester, inserted in center, comes out clean. Allow to cool in pan for 10 minutes, and then remove from pans and continue cooling on a rack. Yields 6 mini-loaves.

Whole Wheat & Oat Bran Bread with Dates & Walnuts

This is a very dark and dense loaf, a little on the chewy side. It features oat bran which is becoming so popular these days. Whole wheat flour, buttermilk, dates and nuts all add to making it good as well as good-for-you. A fine bread to serve at breakfast.

2	eggs
1/2 cup	oil
1 cup	buttermilk
1/2 cup	brown sugar
1/2 cup	molasses

1 1/3 cups	whole wheat flour
1 cup	flour
3/4 cup	oat bran flakes
2 teaspoons	baking powder
1 teaspoon	baking soda
2 teaspoons	cinnamon
1 cup	chopped dates
1 cup	chopped walnuts

Beat together first 5 ingredients until blended. Mix together the remaining ingredients and add all at once. Beat until blended. Do not overbeat.

Divide batter between 5 greased mini-loaf foil pans (6x3x2-inches) and bake in a 350° oven for about 45 minutes, or until a cake tester, inserted in center, comes out clean. Allow to cool in pan for 10 minutes, and then remove from pans and continue cooling on a rack. Yields 5 mini-loaves.

Note: — *Oat bran can be purchased in most supermarkets or health food stores. It comes as "milled" or "stone-ground". The milled is finer in texture and the stone-ground will produce a slightly coarser crumb, which adds a little character to this country-style loaf.*

Irish Breakfast Soda Bread
with Cinnamon & Currants

What a grand bread to serve at breakfast, with a wee bit of butter and jam. This is a nice variation to the traditional soda bread.

        3 cups flour
    1/2 teaspoon salt
        1 tablespoon baking powder
        1 teaspoon baking soda
    1/2 cup cold butter, cut into 8 pieces

        1 cup sugar
    1 1/2 cups black currants

    1 3/4 cups sour milk
        2 eggs

        2 tablespoons butter, melted
        2 tablespoons cinnamon sugar

Beat together first 5 ingredients until butter is in very fine particles. Beat in the sugar and black currants. Beat in sour milk and eggs until blended. Spread batter into a greased 10-inch springform pan. Drizzle top with melted butter and sprinkle with cinnamon sugar.

Bake in a 375° oven for about 40 to 45 minutes or until a cake tester, inserted in center, comes out clean. Allow to cool in pan. Cut into wedges or slices to serve.

Bar Cakes
&
Cookies

Bar Cakes & Cookies

Rocky Road Bars 204
Rocky Road Chewies 205
Butterscotch Brownies 205
Chewy Fudgy California Brownies 206
World's Best Velvet Chocolate Brownies 207
Best Sour Cream Bittersweet Brownies 208
Chocolate Fudge Brownies 209
Chocolate Cream Cheese Bars 210
German Chocolate Bar Cookies 211
Chewy Bar Cookies 212
Goldies 213
Walnut & Butterscotch Cookie Bars 214
Friendship Caramel Pecan Bars 215
Apricot Bars with Pecan Meringue 216
Red Raspberry Butter Bars 217
Lemon Butter Bars 218
Creamy Chocolate Squares 219
Coffeecake Bars 220
Chocolate Granola Bars 221
Chocolate Chip Walnut Chewies 222
World's Best Chocolate Chip Raisin Cookies 223
Victorian Pretty Maids of Honor Bars 224
Holiday Fruit & Nut Chewies 225
Biscotti di Amaretto-Almond Biscuits 226

From my Notebook:

Bar Cakes & Cookies

Bar cakes are coffeecakes baked in a large pan, producing a low cake that is cut into bars. Bar Cookies are different, in that they can never be made into cakes. They are cookies from start to finish. But Bar Cakes and Bar Cookies are both lovely for afternoon into evening serving. Included are lots of brownies for the children when they race home from school. The ones I included show different techniques of preparation, ranging from beating the eggs until they are light and fluffy, to stirring as little as possible. Also, in this chapter, a wonderful cookie I call Goldies, which are similar to Blondies. Rocky Road Bars, Coffeecake Bars, Almond Biscuits are to be found here.

Some exquisite bar cookies for special occasions... Friendship Caramel Pecan Bars or Apricot Bars with Meringue Topping or Lemon Butter Bars... all very special.

The Victorian Pretty Maids of Honor Bars were fashioned after a marvellous little tart we enjoyed when we visited Wales. We were visiting this little coffeeshop, nestled in the countryside, and I so fondly recall the wonderful coffee and the freshly baked tarts. These are super delicious and one of my favorites in this chapter.

The World's Best Chocolate Chip Raisin Cookies is another one of my favorites. Great to include in a lunch box or picnic basket. It is very chewy with the addition of the chocolate covered raisins.

Rocky Road Bars with Sour Cream & Macaroon Crumbs

This is a wonderful bar cookie that is also easy to prepare and very tasty, indeed. Though its base is cake mix, the results are surprisingly chewy and not cakey at all.

1 package (18 1/2 ounces) yellow cake mix
    (pudding mix can be used)
1/2 cup butter, softened
1/3 cup sour cream
2 eggs
3 tablespoons brown sugar
1 cup macaroon cookie crumbs

2 cups miniature marshmallows
1 package (6 ounces) semi-sweet chocolate chips
1/2 cup chopped walnuts

In a large bowl, beat together first 6 ingredients until blended. Stir in the remaining ingredients until blended. Spread batter evenly into a greased 10x15-inch baking pan and bake in a 350° oven for about 25 minutes or until top is browned and a cake tester, inserted in center, comes out clean. Allow to cool in pan.

To serve, cut into 1 1/2-inch squares and sprinkle lightly with sifted powdered sugar. Yields 6 dozen cookies.

Rocky Road Chewies with Walnuts & Chocolate Chips

These lovely cookies are soft and chewy and totally delicious. They are incredibly simple to prepare and yield 4 dozen hefty-sized cookies. Please do not overbake or they will toughen up.

        1 can (14 ounces) sweetened condensed milk
        1 package (6 ounces) semi-sweet chocolate chips
        1 cup chopped walnuts
        2 cups vanilla wafer cookie crumbs
        1 cup miniature marshmallows

In a bowl, stir together all the ingredients until blended. Batter will be very thick. Spread batter evenly into a 9x13-inch greased pan and bake in a 350° oven for about 25 minutes or until top is lightly browned. Allow to cool in pan for 15 minutes, cut into squares, and continue cooling in pan. Serve with the faintest sprinkling of powdered sugar. Yields 4 dozen cookies.

Butterscotch Brownies with Walnuts

        3/4 cup butter (1 1/2 sticks)
    1 3/4 cups brown sugar
        3 eggs
        1 teaspoon vanilla

    1 1/2 cups flour
        1 cup chopped walnuts
        1 cup butterscotch chips

Cream butter with sugar. Beat in eggs, one at a time, until blended. Beat in vanilla and flour until blended. Stir in walnuts and butterscotch. Spread mixture evenly into a 9x13-inch pan and bake in a 350° oven for about 30 to 35 minutes or until a cake tester, inserted in center, comes out clean. Allow to cool in pan and cut into 1 1/2-inch squares. Yields 4 1/2 dozen squares.

Chewy, Fudgy California Brownies with Chocolate Buttercream

This is a dense, low, fudgy brownie, on the sticky side, that is almost like a candy. Cut into small squares, it will serve well at teatime, or as a dessert with fresh fruit. Adding the mini-morsels to the batter is truly gilding the lily. But then again, what are lilies for?

```
3/4  cup butter (1 1/2 sticks)
  1  cup sugar
  1  cup (6 ounces) semi-sweet chocolate chips
  1  tablespoon vanilla

  3  eggs, beaten
  1  cup flour
1/2  cup semi-sweet mini-morsel chocolate chips
```

In a saucepan, heat together butter and sugar until butter is melted. Add the chocolate chips and heat and stir, until chocolate is melted, about 30 seconds to 1 minute. Remove pan from heat and stir in vanilla.

Stir in beaten eggs until blended. Stir in the flour until blended. Stir in the mini-morsel chocolate chips. Do not overmix.

Spread batter into a greased 9x13-inch pan and bake in a 350° oven for about 23 minutes, or until a cake tester, inserted in center, comes out clean. Do not overbake. Remove from oven and allow to cool in pan. When cool, swirl top with a drizzle of Chocolate Buttercream, allowing some of the brownie to show. Cut into squares to serve. Yields about 4 dozen 1 1/2-inch squares.

Chocolate Buttercream:
```
1/2  cup semi-sweet chocolate chips, melted
  3  tablespoons butter, melted
```

Stir together melted chocolate and butter until blended. Drizzle while warm over the cooled brownies.

The World's Best Velvet Chocolate Brownies

This recipe first appeared in my earlier GREAT BEGINNINGS AND HAPPY ENDINGS but it is so good, I felt it worthwhile to repeat here. This is a dark, dense fudgy brownie that is my very favorite.

2/3 cup semi-sweet chocolate chips
1/3 cup melted butter

   4 eggs
   1 cup sugar

3/4 cup finely ground walnuts
1/3 cup flour
   2 tablespoons rum
   1 teaspoon vanilla

Melt the chocolate in the top of a double boiler, over hot, not boiling water. Stir in the melted butter until thoroughly blended. Set aside.

In the large bowl of an electric mixer, beat the eggs with the sugar until mixture is light and fluffy, about 5 minutes, at high speed. At lowest speed, beat in walnuts, flour, rum and vanilla until well blended. Fold in the chocolate mixture.

Pour batter into a greased 10-inch springform pan and bake in a 350° oven for about 25 minutes, or until a cake tester, inserted in center, comes out clean. Do not overbake. Allow to cool in pan. When cool, swirl Chocolate Rum Buttercream on top in a decorative fashion. A sprinkling of shaved chocolate is nice, too. Serves 10.

Chocolate Rum Buttercream:
   1/2 cup butter
   1/2 cup melted semi-sweet chocolate chips, cooled
      1 tablespoon rum
   1/2 teaspoon vanilla

Beat butter until light and creamy. Beat in the chocolate until blended. Beat in rum and vanilla.

Best Sour Cream Bittersweet Brownies with Chocolate Chips & Walnuts

What a grand cookie to have on hand for holiday giving. It is super moist, not very sweet, and delightful all around.

    3/4 cup (1 1/2 sticks) butter, at room temperature
1 1/2 cups sugar
    1 teaspoon vanilla

    2 eggs
    1 cup sour cream

1 3/4 cups flour
1/2 cup cocoa
    1 teaspoon baking powder
1/2 teaspoon baking soda

    1 cup semi-sweet chocolate chips (6 ounces)
    1 cup chopped walnuts

Beat butter with sugar and vanilla until mixture is thoroughly blended. Beat in eggs, one at a time, beating well after each addition. Beat in the sour cream.

Combine flour, cocoa, baking powder and soda and add, all at once, to butter mixture. Beat until blended. Stir in the chocolate chips and walnuts. Spread batter into a greased 9x13-inch baking pan and bake in a 350° oven for about 25 to 30 minutes, or until a cake tester, inserted in center comes out clean. (Do not overbake.) Allow to cool in pan and cut into squares to serve. Yields about 4 dozen 1 1/2-inch squares.

Note: — *These are delicious "natural." However, if it is a special celebration, you may want to decorate these with a thin coating of Chocolate Buttercream Frosting.*

Chocolate Buttercream Frosting:
    1/4 cup (1/2 stick) butter, at room temperature
    3 tablespoons sifted cocoa
    3 tablespoons cream
1/2 teaspoon vanilla
1 1/2 cups sifted powdered sugar

Stir together all the ingredients until blended. Add a little additional powdered sugar or cream to make frosting a spreading consistency.

Chocolate Fudge Brownies with Chocolate Buttercream

This is an extra-fudgy brownie that is really rich and wonderful. It is especially good for chocolate lovers. The Chocolate Buttercream is an optional, and meant for those who cannot eat brownies without frosting. The brownie is bittersweet and very moist. All ingredients should be at room temperature.

  1 cup semi-sweet chocolate chips (6 ounces)
  2 ounces unsweetened chocolate
  1/2 cup butter

  4 eggs
1 1/2 cups sugar

  1 cup flour
  1 tablespoon vanilla

  1 cup walnuts, coarsely chopped

In the top of a double boiler, over hot, not simmering water, melt together chocolate and butter until mixture is melted. Stir until thoroughly blended. Remove from heat and allow to cool.

Meanwhile, beat together eggs and sugar, until mixture is light and fluffy, about 8 minutes. Fold in the cooled chocolate mixture. Fold in the flour and vanilla, until blended. Fold in the walnuts.

Spread batter evenly into a greased 9x13-inch baking pan and bake at 350° for 25 minutes. Do not overbake, or brownies will not be moist. Allow to cool in pan. When cool, swirl top with Chocolate Buttercream. Yields 24 2-inch brownies.

Chocolate Buttercream:
    3/4 cup semi-sweet chocolate chips, melted
    1/4 cup melted butter
    1 teaspoon vanilla

Stir together all the ingredients until blended.

Chocolate Cream Cheese Bars with Chocolate Chips

This is basically a cake-type brownie (which I do not consider a brownie, at all). It is a low cake, that cuts nicely into squares and is nice for the kids after a hard day at school. The Sour Cream Chocolate Frosting is a nice optional.

    1/2 cup butter, softened
      4 ounces cream cheese, at room temperature
      1 cup sugar
      3 eggs
      2 teaspoons vanilla

      1 cup flour
      6 tablespoons cocoa
    1/2 teaspoon baking soda
      1 cup semi-sweet chocolate chips
      1 cup toasted chopped pecans

Beat together butter and cream cheese until blended. Beat in sugar, eggs and vanilla until blended. Combine and add the remaining ingredients and beat until mixture is blended.

Spread batter into a greased 9x13-inch baking pan and bake at 350° for about 25 minutes, or until a cake tester, inserted in center, comes out clean. Do not overbake. Allow to cool in pan.

When cool, spread Sour Cream Chocolate Frosting on top. Cut into squares or bars to serve. Yields about 48 (1 1/2-inch) squares.

Sour Cream Chocolate Frosting:
    1/2 cup semi-sweet chocolate chips
    1/3 cup sour cream

Melt chocolate over hot, not boiling water. Stir in the sour cream, in 3 additions, stirring well after each addition. This will produce a thin layer of frosting for a 9x13-inch cake.

German Chocolate Bar Cookies with Pecans & Coconuts

If you like the combination of chocolate, pecans and coconut, on a delicious pecan cookie crust, you will love these cookies. They are versatile, as they can be served for family dinners, afternoon coffee or tea, or with a tall glass of cold milk.

Cookie Crust:
- **1 cup flour**
- **1/2 cup sugar**
- **1/2 teaspoon baking soda**
- **1/2 cup butter (1 stick)**

- **1/2 cup chopped pecans**

Chocolate Layer:
- **2 eggs**
- **2 tablespoons flour**
- **1/4 cup sugar**
- **1 teaspoon vanilla**
- **2 cups semi-sweet chocolate chips, melted (12 ounces)**

- **1 cup chopped toasted pecans**
- **1/2 cup coconut flakes**

Beat together flour, sugar, soda and butter until mixture resembles coarse meal. Stir in the pecans. Pat mixture on the bottom of a greased 9x13-inch baking pan and bake in a 350° oven for 10 minutes.

Meanwhile, beat together eggs, flour, sugar and vanilla until blended. Beat in the melted chocolate until blended. Stir in the pecans and coconut. Pour mixture over prepared crust and spread evenly. Bake in a 350° oven for 20 to 25 minutes or until chocolate looks set. Do not overbake.

Allow to cool in pan, and then cut into squares or bars. Yields 36 (2-inch) bars or 48 (1 1/2-inch) squares.

Chewy Bar Cookies with Cherries, Dates & Walnuts

These delicious, chewy cookies can be assembled in literally minutes and are pretty and colorful around holiday time. The Creamy Glaze is the perfect accompaniment.

    1 cup flour
1 1/3 cups sugar
    1 teaspoon baking powder
1/4 teaspoon salt

    3 eggs
2/3 cup oil
    1 teaspoon vanilla

    1 cup chopped dates
1/2 cup chopped glaceed cherries
    1 cup chopped walnuts

In the large bowl of an electric mixer, place first 4 ingredients and stir to blend. Add the eggs, oil and vanilla and beat until blended. Stir in the dates, cherries and nuts.

Scrape batter into a greased 9x13-inch pan and bake in a 350° oven for 35 minutes or until a cake tester, inserted in center, comes out clean. Remove from oven and allow to cool in pan.

When cool, drizzle Creamy Glaze over the top in decorative circles, allowing some of the cookie to show. Cut into squares to serve. Yields about 4 dozen cookies.

Creamy Glaze:
1 1/2   tablespoons cream
    1 teaspoon lemon juice
    1 cup sifted powdered sugar (about)

Combine all the ingredients and stir until blended. Add a little more powdered sugar, if necessary, to make glaze a drizzling consistency.

Note: — Cookies can be frozen, properly wrapped, in double thicknesses of plastic wrap and then foil. Glaze when defrosted.

— Cookies can be stored at room temperature, securely covered with plastic wrap.

Goldies

*These are kissing-cousins of "Blondies" which are kissing-cousins of "Brownies".
They are thick chocolate chip bars that are delectable. Butterscotch chips can
be substituted and are really delicious, also. The walnuts are optional, although
I prefer adding them.*

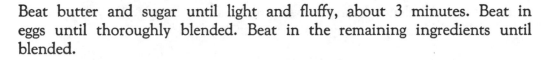

    1 cup butter, softened
    2 cups brown sugar
    2 eggs
    2 teaspoons vanilla

    2 cups flour
1/2 teaspoon baking powder
    2 cups semi-sweet chocolate chips (12 ounces)
    1 cup chopped walnuts

Beat butter and sugar until light and fluffy, about 3 minutes. Beat in
eggs until thoroughly blended. Beat in the remaining ingredients until
blended.

Spread batter evenly into a greased 9x13-inch baking pan and bake in
a 350° oven for about 30 minutes or until a cake tester, inserted in center,
comes out clean and top is golden brown. Do not overbake.

Allow to cool in pan and then cut into squares or bars to serve. A faint
sprinkling of powdered sugar is a nice optional. Yields about 48 (1 1/2-inch)
squares.

Walnut & Butterscotch Cookie Bars

This is a light, fluffy cookie bar that is surprisingly easy and very delicious. Please note there is no butter and very little flour.

    2 eggs
    2 cups brown sugar
    1 teaspoon vanilla

    1/3 cup flour
    2 teaspoons baking powder
    1/4 teaspoon salt

    2 cups chopped walnuts
    1 cup butterscotch chips

In the large bowl of an electric mixer, beat together eggs, sugar and vanilla until mixture is blended, and brown sugar is not lumpy. (If your brown sugar is not fresh, you may have to sift it.)

Stir in the flour, baking powder and salt until blended. Stir in the nuts and butterscotch. Scrape mixture into a 9x13-inch pan and bake in a 350° oven for 20 to 25 minutes, or until a cake tester, inserted in center, comes out clean. Allow to cool in pan and cut into squares to serve. Yields about 4 1/2 dozen 1 1/2-inch squares.

Friendship Caramel Pecan Bars on Butter Cookie Crust

If you love Southern Pecan Pie, you will adore these cookies. They are like miniature pecan pies, sticky and chewy and simply delicious. This recipe yields 4 dozen generous cookies, and any leftovers can be frozen.

Butter Cookie Crust:
   3/4 cup cold butter, cut into 9 pieces
1 1/2 cups flour
   1/2 cup sifted powdered sugar

   1 egg, beaten

In the large bowl of an electric mixer, beat together butter, flour and sugar until mixture resembles coarse meal. Add the egg and beat until a dough forms. Do not overbeat. Pat the dough on the bottom and 1/2-inch up the sides of a greased 9x13-inch baking pan and bake in a 350° oven for 20 minutes or until top is just beginning to take on color. Meanwhile prepare filling.

Caramel Pecan Filling:
   2 eggs
   2/3 cup sugar
   2/3 cup dark corn syrup
   1/4 cup melted butter
   1 tablespoon flour
   1 teaspoon vanilla

   2 cups chopped pecans

Beat together first 6 ingredients until blended. Sprinkle pecans over prepared crust and drizzle filling evenly over the pecans. Bake in a 350° oven for 20 to 25 mintues or until top is golden brown. Allow to cool in pan. When cool, cut into 1 1/2-inch squares and sprinkle top faintly with sifted powdered sugar. Yields 4 dozen cookies.

Apricot Bars with Pecan Meringue Topping

1 cup butter (2 sticks), softened
1 cup sugar
2 egg yolks
2 tablespoons grated lemon
2 cups flour

1 cup apricot jam

Topping:
2 egg whites
2 tablespoons sugar
3/4 cup chopped pecans

Beat together first 5 ingredients until blended. Pat dough into a lightly buttered 9x13-inch pan and spread apricot jam evenly on top. Beat whites until foamy. Gradually beat in the sugar until whites are a stiff meringue. Beat in the pecans. Spread meringue evenly over the jam. Bake in a 350° oven for 30 minutes. Allow to cool in pan and then cut into squares or bars. Sprinkle lightly with sifted powdered sugar. Yields 4 dozen cookies.

Red Raspberry Butter Bars with Coconut Meringue Topping

This is a rather glamorous cookie that serves well for brunch or tea. The base is a buttery cake layer topped with raspberry jam. A thick meringue coating covers it all and... above all, it is delicious.

Butter Cookie Crust:
2 1/4 cups flour
   3 teaspoons baking powder
1 1/4 cups sugar
  3/4 cup butter, cut into pieces
   2 tablespoons grated lemon peel
   3 egg yolks

Filling:
1 1/2 cups red raspberry jam
   1 cup chopped walnuts

Topping:
   3 egg whites
   1 cup sugar
   1 cup coconut flakes

In the large bowl of an electric mixer, beat together all the crust ingredients until mixture resembles coarse meal. Pat mixture on the bottom and 1-inch up the sides of a buttered 9x13-inch pan and bake in a 350° oven for 15 minutes. Remove from oven and allow to cool for 10 minutes.

Spoon raspberry jam on top of prepared crust and spread to even. Sprinkle nuts evenly on top of jam.

Beat egg whites until foamy. Slowly add the sugar and continue beating until meringue is thick. Beat in the coconut flakes until blended. Spread meringue evenly over all and bake in a 350° oven for about 30 minutes or until meringue is dry and lightly browned. Cover pan with foil and allow to cool.

To serve cut into 1 1/2-inch squares. Yields 4 1/2 dozen cookies.

Lemon Butter Bars with Raspberry Jam & Pecans

Flaky cookie layers filled with raspberry jam and pecans, are one of my favorites. These are a truly delicious combination of flavors and textures and I hope you enjoy them as much as I do.

1 cup butter (2 sticks), softened
1 cup sugar
1 egg
2 tablespoons grated lemon

2 cups flour

1 cup raspberry jam
1 cup chopped pecans

Cream butter and sugar until mixture is light. Beat in egg and grated lemon. Beat in flour until blended. With floured hands, pat 3/4 of the dough into a lightly buttered 9x13-inch pan. Spread raspberry jam to within 1/2-inch of the edge. Sprinkle chopped pecans evenly over the jam.

With floured hands, crumble the reserved dough on top and flatten lightly. Bake in a 350° oven for about 30 minutes or until top is golden brown. Allow to cool in pan and then cut into 1x2-inch bars. Sprinkle top lightly with sifted powdered sugar. Yields 4 dozen bars.

Creamy Chocolate Squares with Chocolate Chips & Walnuts

This is a brownie-like, very moist cookie that children will love with a tall glass of milk. They are quite chocolaty and just a little chewy. Do not overbake or cookies will not be moist.

```
1 1/4  cups  butter, softened (2 1/2 sticks)
    2  cups  sugar
    4  eggs
    1  teaspoon  vanilla

    1  cup  flour
  3/4  cup  cocoa
    1  teaspoon  instant coffee
  1/4  teaspoon  salt

1 1/2  cups  semi-sweet chocolate chips
    1  cup  chopped walnuts
```

Cream together butter and sugar. Beat in eggs, one at a time, beating well after each addition. Beat in vanilla.

Add the next 4 ingredients, all at once, and beat until blended. Stir in the chocolate chips and walnuts. Spread batter evenly in a greased 9x13-inch baking pan and bake in a 350° oven for 22 to 25 minutes, or until batter is just set. Do not overbake. (Testing is a little difficult. Cake tester should be "almost" clean.)

Allow to cool in pan and then cut into squares or bars to serve. Yields about 48 (1 1/2-inch) squares.

Coffee Cake Bars with Cinnamon, Orange & Almonds

This is a lovely cookie to serve when the neighbors drop in for coffee. It assembles easily and quickly and is quite lovely to keep on hand. The orange imparts a little "bite" and combined with the cinnamon and almonds . . . delicious.

        2 eggs
        1 cup sugar
      1/2 cup (1 stick) butter, melted
        2 teaspoons vanilla

    1 1/4 cups flour
      1/2 teaspoon baking powder

      1/2 medium orange, grated. (Use fruit, juice and peel.)
        1 cup blanched almonds, chopped and toasted

      1/4 cup chopped almonds
        2 tablespoons cinnamon sugar

In the large bowl of an electric mixer, beat together eggs, sugar, butter and vanilla until blended. (Do not overbeat.) Beat in flour and baking powder until blended. Beat in the orange and almonds until blended.

Spread mixture evenly in a buttered 9x13-inch baking pan and sprinkle top with almonds and cinnamon sugar. Bake in a 350° oven for 22 to 25 minutes or until a cake tester, inserted in center, comes out clean. Allow to cool in pan and cut into squares to serve. Yields about 4 dozen cookies.

Note: — Cookies must be wrapped securely for storing. These can be frozen. Wrap in double thicknesses of plastic wrap and then foil. Remove wrappers while defrosting.

— Almonds can be toasted in a 350° oven for 8 minutes.

Chocolate Granola Bars with Dates, Raisins & Walnuts

Now, these bars are just filled with all manner of good things. They are loaded with oats, so that the cookie is very crunchy and chewy.

    1 cup butter (2 sticks)
    1 cup sugar
    1 cup brown sugar
    1 egg
    1/2 cup sour cream
    1 teaspoon vanilla

    1 1/4 cups flour
    3 cups quick-cooking oats
    6 tablespoons cocoa
    1 teaspoon baking soda
    1/2 teaspoon baking powder
    3/4 cup chopped dates
    3/4 cup chopped raisins
    3/4 cup chopped walnuts

Beat together first 6 ingredients until blended. Combine and add the remaining ingredients and stir until nicely blended. Spread batter into a greased 9x13-inch baking pan and bake at 350° for about 35 minutes, or until a cake tester, inserted in center, comes out clean. Allow to cool in pan.

When cool, cut into squares to serve. Yields 4 dozen bars.

Chocolate Chip Walnut Chewies on Butter Cookie Base

This is a rather unusual cookie but so delicious, I know you will enjoy serving these soon. A thin cookie base topped with a chewy chocolate and nut layer, is just lovely with a glass of cold milk.

Butter Cookie Base:
- 1/2 cup butter
- 1 1/4 cups flour
- 1/2 cup sugar

- 1 egg

Topping:
- 2 eggs
- 1 can (14 ounces) condensed milk
- 1/3 cup flour
- 1 teaspoon baking powder

- 1 cup chopped walnuts
- 1 1/2 cups semi-sweet chocolate chips

Beat together butter, flour and sugar until mixture resembles coarse meal. Beat in egg until dough just holds together. Pat dough on the bottom of a buttered 9x13-inch baking pan and bake in a 350° oven for 20 minutes or until dough is set.

Beat together eggs, milk, flour and baking powder until blended. Pour over prepared crust. Sprinkle top with nuts and chocolate and press down slightly.

Continue baking in a 350° oven for 30 minutes or until topping is set and golden brown. Allow to cool in pan and then cut into 1 1/2-inch squares. A dusting of sifted powdered sugar is all it needs. Yields 4 1/2 dozen cookies.

Note: — Cookies can be frozen. Wrap securely for freezing and remove wrappers while defrosing.

World's Best Chocolate Chip Raisin Walnut Cookies

This is a variation of the world's most famous cookie. The chocolate covered raisins add a wonderful dimension that I hope you enjoy.

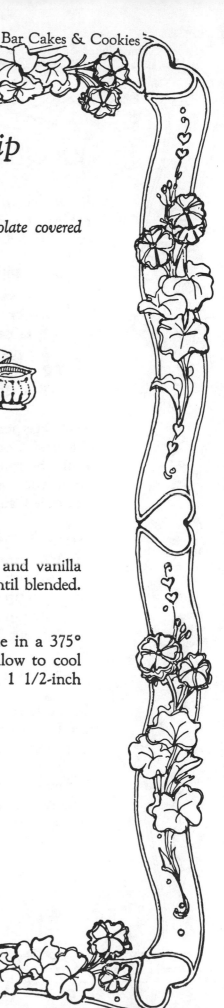

> 1 cup butter (2 sticks), softened
> 1 cup brown sugar
> 3/4 cup sugar
>
> 2 eggs
> 1 teaspoon vanilla
>
> 2 1/4 cups flour
> 1 teaspoon baking soda
> 1 teaspoon baking powder
>
> 1 package (12 ounces) semi-sweet chocolate chips
> 1 cup chocolate covered raisins
> 1 cup chopped walnuts

Beat butter and sugars until mixture is creamy. Beat in eggs and vanilla until blended. Beat in flour, baking soda, and baking powder until blended. Stir in chocolate, raisins and nuts until blended.

Spread dough evenly into a 10x15-inch jelly roll pan and bake in a 375° oven for 20 to 25 minutes or until top is lightly browned. Allow to cool in pan and cut into squares to serve. Yields about 5 dozen 1 1/2-inch squares... never to be forgotten.

Victorian Pretty Maids of Honor Bars

If you love almonds, you will love these bar cookies that are fashioned after the Maid of Honor Tarts we enjoyed when we visited Wales. The almond flavor is balanced by the tart apricot jam.

Almond Filling:
- 1 package (7 ounces) almond paste
- 1/2 cup sugar
- 1 tablespoon flour
- 2 eggs
- 2 tablespoons cream
- 1 teaspoon almond extract

Beat together all the ingredients until blended. Spread mixture evenly over Almond Cookie Crust. Bake in a 350° oven for about 25 minutes, or until the topping is set and top is browned. Allow to cool in pan. When cool, cut into 1 1/2-inch squares and sprinkle top faintly with sifted powdered sugar. Yields 4 dozen cookies.

Almond Cookie Crust:
- 1 1/2 cups flour
- 1/4 cup sugar
- 3/4 cup butter
- 1/2 cup finely chopped almonds
- 1 egg, beaten

- 3/4 cup apricot jam, sieved

In the large bowl of an electric mixer, beat together flour, sugar and butter until mixture resembles coarse meal. Beat in the almonds. Add the beaten egg and beat until a dough forms. Do not overbeat.

Pat mixture on the bottom and 1/2-inch up the sides of a greased 9x13-inch baking pan and bake in a 350° oven for 20 minutes or until top is very lightly browned. Spread apricot jam evenly over the top.

Holiday Fruit and Nut Chewies with Bourbon Glaze

This simple little "gem" will be a welcomed treat around the holidays. They are so pretty to look at with the multi-colors of emeralds and rubies . . . our Christmas colors.

      3   eggs
    3/4   cup oil
      1   teaspoon vanilla

  1 1/4   cups flour
  1 1/2   cups sugar
    3/4   teaspoon baking powder

    1/2   cup glaceed red cherries
    1/2   cup glaceed green cherries
      1   cup chopped walnuts

In the large bowl of an electric mixer, beat together eggs, oil and vanilla until blended. Beat in the flour, sugar and baking powder until blended. Beat in the remaining ingredients. (Beating time, altogether, should be about 1 minute. Do not overbeat.)

Scrape mixture into a buttered 9x13-inch pan and bake at 350° for about 28 minutes or until a cake tester, inserted in center comes out clean, and top is lightly browned.

Cut into squares while warm. When thoroughly cool, drizzle top with Bourbon Glaze and cut through again. Drizzle glaze in a decorative manner. Yields 4 dozen cookies.

Bourbon Glaze:
      2   teaspoons Bourbon
      1   teaspoon orange juice
    3/4   cup sifted powdered sugar

Stir together all the ingredients until blended, adding a little more sugar or orange juice, until glaze is a drizzling consistency.

Note: — 1 cup diced dates can be substituted for the cherries.

Biscotti di Amaretto - Almond Biscuit

This is a wonderful little cookie, so good with a hot spiced cider or even with a glass of wine. It can be cut into individual servings, but is rather dramatic when served in large sections and guests break off a piece at a time. Fillings can vary to match your dinner. Glazed fruits and nuts are especially nice around the holiday times.

      3/4 cup butter (1 1/2 sticks), softened
        1 egg yolk
      3/4 cup sugar
    1 3/4 cups flour
        1 teaspoon almond extract
        1 cup sliced walnuts
      1/4 cup finely chopped maraschino cherries
        2 tablespoons Amaretto Liqueur

        1 lightly beaten egg white
        1 tablespoon cinnamon sugar

In a large bowl, beat together first 8 ingredients until a dough forms and mixture is blended. (Do not overbeat.)

Pat dough evenly, with your fingers, in a buttered 10-inch springform pan. Brush top lightly with beaten egg white and sprinkle with cinnamon sugar.

Bake in a 350° oven for about 40 minutes, or until top is lightly browned. (Do not overbake.) Remove from the oven and cut into wedges or diamonds while still warm. Allow to cool in pan. Yields 12 servings.

Note: — *If you plan to serve this whole (like a giant cookie), then simply allow to cool in pan. Serve it on a large platter, and allow everyone to break off a piece or two. Reserve this for informal occasions.*

   — *For a more formal presentation, decorate top with whole glaceed cherries and almonds pressed into the dough before baking.*

   — *Can be frozen, securely wrapped with double thicknesses of plastic wrap and aluminum foil.*

Strudels

&

Danish

Strudels & Danish

Flaky Strudel Pastry with Apricot Jam   230
Flaky Strudel Pastry with Cinnamon Raisin   231
Flaky Strudel with Rugalach Filling   231
Flaky Strudel with Pecan Raisin Filling   231
Flaky Strudel with Chocolate Chip Filling   231
Danish Apple Strudel   232
Danish Pastry Rolls   233
Strudelettes with Walnuts & Strawberry Jam   234
Scandinavian Cinnamon Date Nut Roll   235
Danish Crescents with Strawberry Jam   236
Viennese Crescents with Cinnamon & Walnuts   237
Cinnamon Breakfast Croissants   238

Strudels & Danish

Strudels and Danish are, also, one of the most satisfying accompaniments to a cup of coffee or tea. These recipes are the stuff my memories are made of. The Flaky Pastry is one of my oldest recipes and still one of the very best. It handles easily and produces one of the finest tasting strudels. The fillings are joyous accompaniments... a superb balance of flavors.

These are included because I grew up on Strudels and Danish, and my Mom always had them ready when a neighbor dropped in for coffee. The Viennese Crescents and the Danish Crescents were always in the freezer and I must confess, many were the times when they were eaten without first defrosting... which I do not recommend... except in emergencies.

The Cinnamon Breakfast Croissant is a delightful pastry made with cottage cheese. This is another very easy dough to work with. And, of course, these strudels freeze exceedingly well, and are wonderful to have waiting for unexpected company.

Strudels and Danish do belong to the world of coffeecakes and I did want you to have them, for the ones I included are a few of the very, very best.

Flaky Strudel Pastry with Apricot Jam and Walnuts

This recipe was given to me by a dear friend, about 30 years ago. It is still one of my favorites. It is an amazingly simple dough, yet delicate and flaky. This is a wonderful dough to keep in your repertoire, for it is a good base for pies, pastries, quiches and the like. The combination of fillings is endless. Fruits, dried fruits, nuts, jams, spices, chocolate all work exceedingly well. A few are included here.

> 1 cup butter
> 2 cups flour
> 1 cup sour cream

Beat together butter and flour until mixture resembles coarse meal. Beat in sour cream until blended, about 30 seconds. Turn mixture out onto floured wax paper and sprinkle some flour over the dough, to make handling easier. Shape into a circle, wrap in the wax paper and refrigerate overnight.

Divide dough into 4 parts. Working one part at a time, roll it out on a floured pastry cloth until dough measures about 10-inches square. Spread 1/4 the filling over the dough, roll up jelly-roll fashion and end with a strudel that measures 3x10-inches and seam-side down. Repeat with remaining dough.

Place strudels in a lightly greased 12x16-inch baking pan and bake at 350° for about 30 to 35 minutes or until top is golden. Allow to cool in pan. Sprinkle generously with sifted powdered sugar and cut into slices to serve. Yields about 24 slices.

Apricot Jam & Walnut Filling:
> 1 cup apricot jam
> 1 cup chopped walnuts

Spread 1/4 cup of apricot jam over each strudel. Sprinkle with 1/4 cup of chopped walnuts. Proceed as noted above.

Flaky Strudel (continued)

Cinnamon Raisin Filling:
>   1/2 cup cinnamon sugar
>   1 cup chopped walnuts
>   1 cup yellow raisins

Sprinkle each strudel with 2 tablespoons cinnamon sugar, 1/4 cup chopped walnuts and 1/4 cup yellow raisins.

Rugalach Filling:
>   1 cup strawberry jam
>   1 cup chopped walnuts
>   1 cup yellow raisins
>   1/2 cup flaked coconut

Spread each strudel with 1/4 cup strawberry jam, 1/4 cup chopped walnuts, 1/4 cup yellow raisins and 1/8 cup flaked coconut. Proceed as noted above.

Pecan Raisin Filling:
>   1 cup chopped pecans
>   1/2 cup brown sugar mixed with
>   2 teaspoons cinnamon
>   1 cup yellow raisins

Spread each strudel with 1/4 cup chopped pecans, 2 tablespoons brown cinnamon sugar and 1/4 cup yellow raisins. Proceed as noted above.

Chocolate Chip Filling:
>   12 tablespoons Nestle's Quik chocolate powder
>   1 package (6 ounces) semi-sweet chocolate chips
>   1 cup chopped walnuts

Spread 3 tablespoons chocolate powder over each strudel. Sprinkle each with 1/4 cup chocolate chips and 1/4 cup chopped walnuts. Proceed as noted above.

Danish Apple Strudel with Cinnamon, Raisins & Walnuts

This is one of my husband's favorites. It can easily be prepared in 2 stages, making the dough early in the day (or even 1 or 2 days earlier), and rolling and baking on another day. The filling is delicious, filled with apples, raisins, walnuts, apricot jam and lemon. The pastry is flaky and tender.

        1 cup butter (2 sticks)
        2 cups flour
        1 cup sour cream

In the bowl of an electric mixer, beat together butter and flour until mixture resembles coarse meal. Beat in the sour cream until blended (about 30 seconds). Turn dough out onto heavily floured wax paper and sprinkle a little more flour over the dough. Shape it into a 7-inch circle, wrap in the wax paper and refrigerate it for several hours or overnight.

Divide dough into 4 parts. Working one part at a time, roll it out on a floured pastry cloth to measure about 10x10-inches. Spread 1/4 of the Apple Filling down the center of the dough, fold in the sides of the dough over the apples (like a letter), and place, seam-side down, on a 12x16-inch baking pan. Repeat with remaining dough.

Bake at 350° for about 30 minutes, or until top is golden brown. Allow to cool in pan. Sprinkle generously with sifted powdered sugar and cut into slices to serve. Yields 24 to 30 slices.

Tart Apple Filling:
        2 tart apples (Pippin or Granny Smith), peeled, cored
            and grated
    3/4 cup apricot jam
        1 cup chopped walnuts, toasted
        4 tablespoons cinnamon sugar
        1 cup yellow raisins
        2 tablespoons grated lemon

Stir together all the ingredients until blended. Will yield enough filling for 4 strudels.

Danish Pastry Rolls with Walnut Filling & Sour Cream Glaze

This dough is made exceedingly tender with the addition of fresh yeast. But, as the yeast does not need to rise, this can be considered a "quick" pastry. Simply beat the yeast into the dough, that is all there is to it. You cannot substitute dry yeast for this recipe.

    1 cup butter (2 sticks)
    2 cups flour
    1 package fresh yeast

    2/3 cup sour cream

In the large bowl of an electric mixer, beat together butter, flour and yeast until mixture resembles coarse meal. Beat in the sour cream until blended. Turn dough out onto lightly floured wax paper, shape into a 7-inch circle, wrap with wax paper and refrigerate for several hours or overnight.

Divide dough into 4 parts. Working one part at a time, roll it out on a floured pastry cloth until the dough measures 10x10-inches. Spread 1/4 of the Walnut Filling evenly over the dough. Roll it up, jelly-roll fashion, ending with a roll that measures 3x10-inches and seam-side down.

Place rolls on a greased 12x16-inch pan (so that you can bake the 4 rolls at one time). Bake at 350° for about 35 to 40 minutes or until tops are lightly browned. Allow to cool and drizzle tops with Sour Cream Glaze. Cut into slices to serve. Yields 36 1-inch slices.

Walnut Filling:
Beat together 1/2 cup butter, 1 cup flour, 1 cup sugar and 1 1/2 cups finely chopped walnuts, until mixture resemble fine meal. Do not overbeat or mixture will form a dough, which is OK, but a bit more difficult to work with.

Sour Cream Glaze:
Stir together 2 tablespoons sour cream, 1 teaspoon vanilla and about 1 1/2 cups sifted powdered sugar, until mixture is blended. Add a little sugar or sour cream to make glaze a drizzling consistency.

Strudelettes with Walnuts, Raisins & Strawberry Jam

This is another incredible pastry, that will grace a brunch or luncheon buffet. It can be sliced into small portions and enjoyed with a clear conscience.

      1/2 pound cream cheese
        1 cup butter (2 sticks)
        2 egg yolks
        4 tablespoons sugar
        1 teaspoon grated lemon peel

        2 cups flour

Beat together first 5 ingredients until blended. Beat in the flour until dough collects around the beaters and then a few seconds more. Turn dough out onto floured wax paper and shape into a 7-inch circle. Wrap in wax paper and refrigerate overnight.

Divide dough into 4 parts. Working one part at a time, roll it out on a floured pastry cloth until dough measures 10x10-inches. Spread 1/4 of the filling evenly over the dough. Roll, jelly-roll fashion, ending with a strudel that measures 3x10-inches and seam-side down.

Place strudel on a lightly greased 12x16-inch pan, so that the 4 strudels can be baked at the same time. Bake at 350° for about 30 to 35 minutes, or until top is lightly browned. Sprinkle with sifted powdered sugar when cool.

Walnut Raisin Filling:
        1 cup strawberry jam
        1 cup chopped walnuts
      1/2 cup yellow raisins
      1/4 cup coconut flakes
      1/2 cup marshmallow cream

Stir together all the ingredients until blended.

Scandinavian Cinnamon Date Nut Roll

Dates, walnuts, cinnamon and a hint of lemon surrounded by flaky cream cheese pastry is wonderful to serve at brunch, lunch or tea. Make this in 2 stages, for the dough must be chilled for several hours. Overnight is better.

    1/2 cup butter
      4 ounces cream cheese
      1 egg yolk
      1 cup flour
         pinch of salt

Beat butter and cream cheese until blended. Beat in the egg yolk. Beat in flour and salt until blended. Turn dough out on floured wax paper and form dough into a 7-inch circle. Wrap dough in wax paper and refrigerate for several hours or overnight.

Divide dough in half. Roll out, one part at a time, to measure a 10-inch square. Spread 1/2 of the Cinnamon Date Nut Filling over the dough. Roll it up, jelly-roll fashion, to measure a 10x3-inch roll. Repeat with remaining dough. Place in a 9x13-inch greased baking pan.

Bake at 350° for 30 minutes or until top is lightly browned. Cool in pan. Cut into slices to serve and sprinkle with sifted powdered sugar. Yields 12 slices.

Cinnamon Date Filling:
      2 cups finely chopped dates
    1/2 cup chopped walnuts
      1 tablespoon grated lemon peel
      6 tablespoons cinnamon sugar

Stir together all the ingredients until nicely mixed.

Danish Crescents with Strawberry Jam & Sour Cream Glaze

These little pastries can be stored in the freezer and are good to keep on hand in the event you are faced with unexpected company. They defrost in a matter of minutes. These are a bit more work, but very well worth the extra effort.

      2 1/2 cups flour
          1 cup butter (2 sticks), cut into 8 pieces

          2 egg yolks
      1/2 cup sour cream

Beat together flour and butter until mixture resembles fine meal. Beat together yolks and sour cream until blended and add to the flour mixture. Beat until blended and a soft dough forms, about 15 seconds. Turn dough out onto heavily floured wax paper and shape into a 7-inch circle. Wrap in the wax paper and refrigerate for several hours or overnight.

Divide dough into 6 parts. Working one part at a time, roll it out on a floured pastry cloth until dough measures a 10-inch circle. Spread with 1/6 of the filling. With a knife, cut circle into 8 triangular wedges. (Cut in half, then half again and again.) Roll up each triangle from the wide side toward the center, shape into a crescent, and place on a lightly buttered baking pan. Bake at 350° for about 25 to 30 minutes, or until tops are lightly browned.

When cool, brush tops with Sour Cream Glaze. Yields 48 crescents.

Strawberry Pecan Filling:
          2 cups finely grated pecans
      2/3 cup strawberry jam
      1/4 cup sugar
      1/4 cup finely chopped raisins
      1/3 cup finely chopped pecans

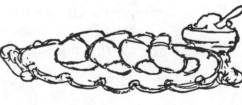

Stir together all the ingredients until blended.

Sour Cream Glaze: Stir together until blended 1 tablespoon sour cream, 1/2 teaspoon vanilla and 1/2 cup sifted powdered sugar.

Viennese Crescents with
Cinnamon & Walnuts & Vanilla Glaze

This is a divine pastry to serve with coffee. It is especially nice to serve at a ladies luncheon for the portions can be kept small and they are not sweet or cloying.

    1 cup butter (2 sticks)
    1/2 cup sugar
    2 cups flour

    3/4 cup sour cream
    1 egg yolk

Beat together butter, sugar and flour, until mixture resembles fine meal. Combine sour cream and egg yolk and beat it in until a dough forms. Do not overbeat. Turn dough out onto floured wax paper, and shape into a 7-inch circle. Wrap the dough in wax paper and refrigerate overnight.

Divide dough into 4 parts. Working one part at a time, roll it out on a floured pastry cloth until dough measures a 12-inch circle. Sprinkle 1/4 of the filling over the dough and pat it down, gently. With a knife, cut circle in half, then half again, and continue, until you have 12 triangular wedges. Roll each triangle from the wide side toward the center, shape into a crescent, and place on a lightly buttered baking pan. Bake at 350° for about 25 minutes, or until they are lightly browned.

When cool, drizzle top with Vanilla Glaze or simply with sifted powdered sugar. Yields 48 crescents.

Cinnamon Walnut Filling:
Stir together 1 teaspoon cinnamon, 1/2 cup sugar and 3/4 cup finely chopped walnuts until blended.

Vanilla Glaze:
Stir together until blended 1 tablespoon cream, 1/2 teaspoon vanilla and 1/2 cup sifted powdered sugar.

Cinnamon Breakfast Croissants with Walnuts & Raisins

These lovely, delicate croissants are assembled in minutes. They look and taste as if they were made with yeast. They freeze beautifully and are nice to have on hand. But one word of caution . . . bake these on a day when no one is around, or they will never make it to the freezer.

1 cup cottage cheese
3 ounces butter (3/4 stick)
1 cup flour

1/2 cup finely chopped walnuts
1/2 cup sugar
1/2 cup finely chopped raisins
1/2 teaspoon cinnamon (or more to taste)

cinnamon sugar

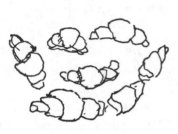

Beat together cottage cheese and butter until the mixture is blended. Beat in the flour until the mixture is smooth, about 1 to 2 minutes.

Shape dough into a ball and sprinkle with a little flour to ease handling. Divide dough into thirds.

Roll each third out on a floured pastry cloth (using a stocking on your rolling pin, too), until circle measures about 10 inches.

Combine walnuts, sugar, raisins and cinnamon and toss until blended. Sprinkle 1/3 the walnut filling evenly over the dough. Cut dough into 8 triangular wedges. Roll each triangle from the wide end toward the center and curve into a crescent. Sprinkle with cinnamon sugar and place on a lightly buttered cookie sheet. Repeat with remaining dough.

Bake in a 350° oven for about 30 to 35 minutes or until tops are golden brown. Remove from the pan and allow to cool on a brown paper bag. Yields 24 crescents.

To make Cinnamon Sugar: Stir together 1/2 cup sugar with 2 teaspoons cinnamon. Store unused Cinnamon Sugar in a jar for another use.

Savory
Dinner
Breads

Savory Dinner Breads

Easiest & Best Onion Sesame Bagels 242

Onion Kuchen with Sour Cream & Poppyseeds 243

Poppyseed Onion Rolls for Passover 244

Red Hot Pastelle with Onions & Swiss Cheese 245

Pesto Bread with Cheese & Pine Nuts 246

Pizza Bread with Tomatoes, Onions & Cheese 247

Green Onion Buttermilk Bread with Lemon & Sesame 248

Parmesan Herb & Onion Cheese Bread 249

Poppyseed Bread with Green Onions & Cheese 250

Greek Lemon Bread with Green Onions, Tomato & Feta 251

Sweet & Sour Red Cabbage Bread with Apples & Raisins 252

Sauerkraut Rye Bread with Yogurt, Onions & Bacon 253

Russian Black Bread with Sour Cream & Raisins 254

Burgundian Cheese & Chive Bread 255

Two-Minute Cheese Bread with Onions & Herbs 256

Country Kitchen Cornbread 257

Mexican-Style Cornbread with Chiles & Cheese 258

Giant Popovers with Chives & Cheese 259

Giant Popovers - Alternate Method 260

Chewy Cheese Sticks with Onions 261

Whole Wheat Raisin Soda Bread 262

Apple Cheddar Cheese Oatmeal Bread 263

Cheese & Onion Crescents 264

Cheddar Cheese Muffins 265

Bacon & Swiss Cheese Muffins 266

From my Notebook:

Savory Dinner Breads

As you probably know, not all quick breads are sweet. I was really caught up in the excitement of discovery with this chapter. My first thoughts were to include breads that would serve well with the different styles and moods of food... and once I started, I simply could not stop. I think I could write a whole book on the marvellous breads one can make with a few simple ingredients.

Many moods are reflected here... Italian, Jewish, Greek, Russian, German, French, Mexican. Onion Kuchen with Sour Cream & Poppy Seeds is a poem of flavors. The Poppyseed Rolls for Passover are a novelty and very delicious. The wonderful flatbread of Italy, Pizza Bread with Tomatoes, Onions & Cheese (Focaccio), is so exciting, it creates the biggest commotion at the table. And Pesto Bread with Cheese & Pine Nuts, fashioned after the famous sauce... incredibly delicious.

And who can resist a Greek-Style Bread with Lemon, Green Onions, Tomatoes and sparkled with Feta Cheese. Here you will find Red Cabbage Bread, Sauerkraut Bread, Cheese & Onion Breads and much, much more.

There is one recipe that I hope you will prepare soon, for it is so exciting, Easiest & Best Onion Sesame Bagels. Even though it contains yeast, it does not need to rise. It can be prepared in minutes in a mixer, thus qualifying it as a quick bread. Everybody just loves it.

The Burgundian Cheese & Chive Bread is an oldie but goodie. It is just wonderful to serve with cheese or pate and a glass of wine. And another old favorite, Popovers, sparkled with cheese and chives.

The breads in this chapter will create a good deal of excitement when you serve them. They are unusual and delicious and a lot of fun to serve. I do hope these breads bring you as much pleasure as the pleasure I feel in sharing them with you.

Easiest & Best Onion Sesame Bagels

Bagels, a quick bread??? "No way." you say. And you are probably right. But these chewy, divine "bagels" are so close to the real thing and so simple to prepare, that I had to include them. These are very chewy and can be assembled in minutes. As they do not have to rise, they qualify as a quick bread. This is truly a gem, and I hope you use it soon.

    1 package dry yeast
1/2 cup lukewarm water (110°)
    1 teaspoon sugar

    1 cup lukewarm water (110°)
    3 cups flour
    1 tablespoon sugar
    3 tablespoons dried onion flakes
3/4 teaspoon salt

    1 cup flour

    1 egg, beaten
      sesame seeds

Soften yeast in 1/2 cup water and sugar until yeast starts to foam. Place yeast mixture in the large bowl of an electric mixer. To the bowl, add the next 5 ingredients and beat, for about 3 minutes, or until dough is very smooth. (This takes the place of kneading.) Now, slowly beat in the remaining 1 cup flour until blended. Turn dough out onto a lightly floured board and knead for about 1 minute, or until dough is smooth.

Divide dough into 12 pieces. Roll each piece of dough into a 1/2-inch thick rope, pinch the ends together to form a circle and place on a lightly greased cookie sheet. Brush top with beaten egg and sprinkle with sesame seeds. Bake in a 400° oven for about 15 to 18 minutes, or until tops are golden. Makes 12 yummy bagels.

Note: — Poppy seeds may be substituted for the onions.

*   — Grated Parmesan cheese can be substituted for the sesame seeds.*

Onion Kuchen with Sour Cream & Poppy Seeds

This is a delicious adaptation of the Onion Kuchen which is basically a flat bread with a thick topping of onions. The sour cream and poppy seeds add the perfect touch. Serve this with a good, hearty beef and barley soup, or a thick, homey stew.

   1 medium onion, chopped
   1 tablespoon butter

1 1/4 cups flour
   2 teaspoons baking powder
   1 tablespoon sugar
1/4 teaspoon salt

1/4 cup cold butter (1/2 stick) cut into 4 pieces

3/4 cup milk
   1 tablespoon lemon juice

   1 egg
1/2 cup sour cream
   1 tablespoon poppy seeds

In a skillet, saute onion in butter, until onion is soft. Allow to cool. Meanwhile, beat together flour, baking powder, sugar, salt and butter until mixture resembles coarse meal. Stir together milk and lemon juice and add, all at once, to flour mixture. Stir until nicely blended, but do not overmix.

Spread batter evenly into a greased 10-inch springform pan. Spread sauteed onions on top. Beat together egg and sour cream and brush lightly over the onions. Sprinkle top with poppy seeds. Bake in a 375° oven for about 40 minutes, or until top is browned. Allow to cool in pan and cut into wedges to serve. Serves 8.

Note: — Brush egg mixture lightly and evenly over the onions. Do not let it puddle in spots or bread will get gummy.

Poppyseed Onion Rolls
for Passover Holiday

Bread for Passover? No way you say. But these are actually made with matzoh meal, instead of flour. They are leavened with eggs and delicious any time of year.

    1/2 cup margarine (1 stick), softened
      1 cup water
      2 tablespoons dried onion flakes

      2 cups matzoh meal
    1/2 teaspoon salt
      1 tablespoon sugar

      4 eggs
      1 teaspoon poppy seeds

In a saucepan, bring margarine, water and onion flakes to a boil. Stir in matzoh meal, salt and sugar until blended.

Place dough into the large bowl of an electric mixer and beat in eggs, one at a time, beating well after each addition. Beat in the poppy seeds.

With moistened hands, shape dough into 12 rolls and place on a greased cookie sheet. Cut a cross on the top of each roll. Bake in a 350° oven for about 50 minutes to 1 hour or until tops are golden brown. Yields 12 rolls.

Red Hot Pastelle with Onions & Swiss Cheese (Flatbread)

What a wonderful bread to serve with soup or salad. It is especially nice when served with Italian, French or Moroccan dishes. It is also very attractive, rustic and creates a good deal of interest. Serve it precut into wedges, or whole (for informal dinners), and allow everyone to tear off a piece or two (mostly two).

    1/2 cup butter, cut into 8 pieces
      2 cups flour
      2 teaspoons baking powder

      1 cup grated Swiss cheese
      2 tablespoons grated Parmesan cheese
    1/2 cup chopped green onions
    1/8 teaspoon cayenne pepper

      2 eggs
    1/2 cup sour cream

      2 tablespoons oil
      1 tablespoon oil
      2 tablespoons grated Parmesan cheese

In the large bowl of an electric mixer, beat together butter, flour and baking powder until butter particles are like coarse meal. Stir in the next 4 ingredients until combined. Beat eggs with sour cream and add to flour mixture, beating until a soft dough forms.

Place 2 tablespoons oil in a 12-inch round baking pan. Spread batter evenly into pan and drizzle 1 tablespoon oil on top. Sprinkle with grated cheese.

Bake in a 350° oven for 35 to 40 minutes or until top is golden brown. Allow to cool in pan. Can be served warm or at room temperature. Yields 8 servings.

Pesto Bread with Cheese & Pine Nuts

Pesto is such a favorite nowadays. Pesto with Clams, Pesto Lasagna, Pesto with Pasta, so I thought it would be nice to carry this theme into this delicious loaf. Serve this bread warm with sweet butter and it is a meal with a good peasant soup.

2 eggs
3 tablespoons sugar
1/3 cup oil
3/4 cup cream

2 cups self-rising flour
1/2 teaspoon baking powder
1 1/2 teaspoons sweet basil flakes
1/3 cup grated Parmesan cheese

1/4 cup lightly toasted pine nuts

Beat together first 4 ingredients until blended. Combine and add the next 4 ingredients and stir until dry ingredients are blended. Do not overmix. Stir in the pine nuts.

Spread batter into a greased 8x4-inch loaf pan, place pan on a cookie sheet, and bake in a 350° oven for about 45 minutes or until a cake tester, inserted in center, comes out clean.

Allow to cool in pan for 15 minutes, and then remove from pan and continue cooling on a rack. Use a serrated bread knife to cut into slices. Serve warm with sweet whipped butter. Yields 1 loaf.

Note: — If you use all-purpose flour, then increase baking powder to 3 teaspoons, and add a pinch of salt.

Pizza Bread with Tomatoes, Onions & Cheese

A wonderful blend of tomatoes, onions and cheese, this is absolutely delicious with soup or salad. This flavorful bread has all the loved qualities of pizza, yet is light and moist. I know you will love it and I do hope you have the opportunity to prepare this soon.

> 2 eggs
> 1/3 cup oil
> 2 tablespoons sugar
> 2 medium tomatoes, fresh or canned, chopped and seeded
> 1/2 cup sour cream
> 1/4 cup chopped green onions
> 3/4 cup grated Swiss cheese
> 1/4 cup grated Parmesan cheese
> 1 teaspoon Italian Herb Seasoning flakes
> 1 teaspoon sweet basil flakes
>
> 2 cups self-rising flour
> 1/2 teaspoon baking powder

In the large bowl of an electric mixer, beat together first 10 ingredients until blended, about 1 minute. Beat in the flour and baking powder and beat until nicely blended, about 1 minute.

Spread batter into an oiled 12-inch round baking pan and drizzle 1 teaspoon of oil on top. Bake in a 350° oven for about 40 minutes or until top is browned. Allow to cool in pan. Serve warm or at room temperature. No butter is necessary, just slice and enjoy. Yields 8 slices.

Note: — Bread can be prepared earlier in the day and warmed at serving time. Cover pan with plastic wrap after bread is cool.

— Pepperoni, red pepper flakes or a shake of cayenne can be added to the batter if you like the "bite."

— If you use all-purpose flour, then increase baking powder to 3 1/2 teaspoons. Self-rising flour already has the baking powder incorporated in it.

Green Onion Buttermilk Bread with Lemon & Sesame Seeds

Oh! what a nice bread to serve when the family joins for dinner. It is a great accompaniment to roast chicken or pot roast or a homey stew. The lemon imparts the gentlest flavor and the sesame seeds add just the right texture.

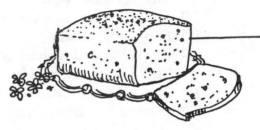

     1/4 cup oil
       1 egg
 1 1/2 cups buttermilk
     1/3 cup sugar
     1/2 cup chopped green onions
       1 tablespoon grated lemon

       3 cups flour
       4 teaspoons baking powder
         pinch of salt
       3 tablespoons sesame seeds

Beat together first 6 ingredients until blended. Mix together the remaining ingredients and add all at once. Beat until dry ingredients are blended. Do not overbeat.

Divide batter between 2 oiled 8x4-inch loaf pans, and sprinkle top with a few additional sesame seeds. Bake in a 350° oven for about 50 minutes, or until tops are golden brown and a cake tester, inserted in center, comes out clean. Allow to cool in pans for 10 minutes, and then remove from pans and continue cooling on a rack. Yields 2 loaves.

Parmesan, Herb & Onion Cheese Bread

This is a nice "conversation" bread and truly delicious. Serve it on a large platter to accompany cheese or pate. Cut it into serving pieces or let everyone tear off a piece or two. Also, this is nice served warm with soup or salad.

        3 cups flour
        4 teaspoons baking powder
        3 tablespoons grated Parmesan cheese
        2 tablespoons sugar
        1 teaspoon Italian Herb Seasoning
        2 tablespoons dried onion flakes
          pinch of salt
      3/4 cup milk
        1 cup sour cream
      1/2 cup butter, melted
      1/2 cup grated Swiss cheese

Beat together all the ingredients until blended. Do not overbeat. Spread batter evenly into an oiled 12-inch round baking pan (or a 9x13-inch rectangular pan). Brush top with a little oil and sprinkle with additional grated Parmesan cheese.

Bake in a 350° oven for about 40 to 45 minutes, or until top is golden brown. Cut into wedges (squares or diamonds) to serve. Excellent with soups or salads. Yields about 8 servings.

Poppy Seed Bread with Green Onions & Cheese

This is a great bread to serve with soups or salads. It also, serves well as a base for cheese or pate.

1 3/4 cups flour
   1 tablespoon sugar
   1 tablespoon baking powder
     pinch of salt
1/3 cup cold butter

   1 cup grated Swiss cheese
   3 tablespoons grated Parmesan cheese
1/3 cup chopped green onions
   1 tablespoon poppy seeds

   1 cup milk
   1 egg

In the large bowl of an electric mixer, beat together first 5 ingredients until butter is the size of small peas. Beat in the next 4 ingredients until blended. Beat together milk and egg and add to the bowl, stirring until dry ingredients are just moistened. Do not overbeat.

Place batter into a heavily oiled 8x4-inch foil loaf pan and bake in a 350° oven for 45 to 55 minutes, or until top is golden brown, and a cake tester, inserted in center, comes out clean. (If top is browning too quickly, then tent loosely with foil.)

Allow to cool in pan for 10 minutes, and then remove from pan and continue cooling on a rack. Yields 1 loaf.

Greek Lemon Bread with Green Onions, Tomato & Feta Cheese

This is one of the most delicious breads and perfect with a Greek salad or their famous Lemon Soup. It serves well as an accompaniment to cheese, instead of the usual cracker . . . and it generates a great deal of excitement.

3 cups self-rising flour
1 teaspoon baking powder
3 tablespoons sugar

1/2 cup chopped green onions
1 tablespoon grated lemon. Use fruit, juice and peel.
1/4 pound (4 ounces) Feta cheese, crumbled
1 tomato, peeled, seeded and chopped
1 can (12 ounces) beer

2 tablespoons oil
1 tablespoon sesame seeds

In the large bowl of an electric mixer, beat together first 3 ingredients until mixed. Add the next 5 ingredients and beat until mixture is nicely blended, about 1 minute. Do not overbeat.

Place 2 tablespoons oil in a 12-inch round baker and spread batter evenly in pan. Sprinkle top with sesame seeds. (Brush top with a little oil that collects on the sides.)

Bake in a 350° oven for 45 minutes or until top is golden brown. Allow to cool in pan. Serve warm or at room temperature. Cut into wedges or serve whole and allow friends to tear off a piece or two. Creamy whipped butter is nice with this, but not necessary. Serves 10.

Note: — *Bread can be prepared earlier in the day and heated at serving time*

— *Top can be sprinkled with additional Feta cheese, before baking, for a more intense flavor.*

— *If you are serving this as an hors d'oeuvre with a cheese or pate spread, then precut it into small squares (while in the pan) and reassemble it to look whole, on a large round platter.*

Sweet & Sour Red Cabbage Bread with Apples & Raisins

This is a most adventuresome bread and one that is just marvellous to serve with a hefty stew or soup. While it starts with a few everyday ingredients, it produces an incredible bread. The combination of apples, cinnamon and cloves is great with the red cabbage.

    2 eggs
    4 tablespoons sugar
1/3 cup oil
3/4 cup prepared sweet and sour red cabbage (usually sold
        in 1 pound jars). Drained.
1/2 cup yogurt
    1 medium apple, peeled, cored and finely chopped
1/2 cup yellow raisins

    1 cup whole wheat flour
    1 cup flour
    4 teaspoons baking powder
1/2 teaspoon cinnamon
1/4 teaspoon powdered cloves

Beat together first 7 ingredients until blended. Beat in the remaining ingredients until blended. Do not overmix.

Spread batter evenly in a heavily oiled (2 tablespoons) 12-inch round baking pan and sprinkle top with a little cinnamon sugar. Bake in a 350° oven for about 45 minutes, or until bread is nicely browned. Allow to cool in pan. When cool, remove from pan and cut into wedges to serve. Serves 8.

Sauerkraut Rye Bread with Yogurt, Onions & Bacon

Now, before you wrinkle your nose, please read this. Sounds not too great, but this is a very delicious bread, that everybody loved. The flavor of rye is strong, the flavor of sauerkraut is nil. The onions and bacon come through and this is the nicest bread to serve with a German-style dinner. Also good with hefty stews or soups.

1 cup dark rye (stone ground) flour. (Can be purchased in
    most supermarkets and all health food stores.)
1 cup flour
4 teaspoons baking powder
1 tablespoon dried onion flakes

2 eggs
2 tablespoons sugar
1/3 cup oil
3/4 cup prepared sauerkraut. Do not drain.
1/2 cup unflavored yogurt
6 strips bacon, cooked crisp, drained and crumbled

In the large bowl of an electric mixer, stir together first 4 ingredients until nicely mixed. Add the remaining ingredients and beat until mixture is blended. Do not overbeat.

Heavily oil (2 tablespoons) a 12-inch round baking pan and spread batter evenly in pan. Brush top with a little oil that collects on the sides. Bake in a 350° oven for about 45 minutes, or until top is a golden brown, and a cake tester, prodded in center, comes out clean. Allow to cool in pan.

To serve, cut into wedges. Or serve it whole (very attractive) and let everyone tear off a piece or two (mostly two). Serves 8.

Russian Black Bread with Sour Cream & Raisins

Well, of course you know where the inspiration for this bread came. This bread is dark, dense and very sturdy (perish the word "heavy"). It is a peasant bread and good with hardy soups or stews.

        4 tablespoons sugar
1 1/2 cups whole wheat flour
1 1/2 cups flour
        1 tablespoon baking powder
        1 teaspoon baking soda
1/4 teaspoon salt

        1 cup sweet and sour red beets (from a 1 pound jar),
            drained and coarsely chopped
3/4 cup sour cream
2/3 cup milk
1/2 cup oil
1/4 cup molasses
1/2 cup yellow raisins

        2 tablespoons oil

In the large bowl of an electric mixer, stir together first 6 ingredients until nicely mixed. Add the next 6 ingredients and beat until mixture is blended, about 1 minute. Do not overbeat.

Place 1 tablespoon oil in each of 2 foil loaf pans, 4x8-inches, place pans on a cookie sheet, and bake in a 350° oven for 40 to 45 minutes, or until a cake tester, prodded in center, comes out clean.

Allow to cool in pan for 15 minutes, and then remove pans and continue cooling on a rack. Cut into slices to serve and please use a sharp serrated bread knife. Yields 2 loaves.

Note: — *Bread can be prepared earlier in the day and heated at serving time. When cool, store in a plastic bag. Best served warm with sweet butter.*

Burgundian Cheese & Chive Bread
(Gougere au Fromage)

No bread book would be complete without this incredible French pastry bread. It is great to serve anytime . . . with wine, cheese, pate, soup, salads . . . the list is endless. This variation is sparkled with cheese and chives, which is not the classic bread, but pretty terrific, anyway.

1 cup milk
4 tablespoons butter (1/2 stick)

1 cup flour
3 tablespoons chopped chives
4 eggs, at room temperature

1 cup grated Swiss cheese (1/4 pound)
2 tablespoons grated Parmesan cheese

In a saucepan, heat milk and butter until mixture comes to a boil. Add the flour, all at once, and continue cooking and stirring with a wooden spoon, until the mixture forms a ball. Cook, stirring, for about 1 minute more.

Place dough in mixer bowl. Beat in chives. Add eggs, one at a time, beating very well after each addition. Beat in cheeses and beat for another minute, until dough is smooth.

Grease a 10-inch porcelain quiche baker. Spoon dough along the edge of the baker to form a 1 1/2-inch ring. Bake in a 400° oven for 15 minutes, lower heat to 350° and continue baking for about 30 minutes or until Gougere is puffed and a beautiful golden brown. Serve warm. Serves 6.

Note: — *Batter can be spooned into baker, covered with a plastic wrap, and stored in the refrigerator. Remove from refrigerator and allow to stand for 15 minutes. Then bake as noted above. Add a few minutes to baking time.*

2-Minute Cheese Bread
with Onions & Herbs

This is a variation of the popular beer bread, but highly improved with the addition of cheese and onions and herbs. Vary the herbs to match your dinner. Oregano, thyme, caraway seeds are nice variations. Excellent, served warm, with soups or salads.

- 3 cups self-rising flour
- 3 tablespoons sugar
- 1 can (12 ounces) beer, cold or at room temperature. (I have found no difference in performance using cold beer.)
- 1/4 cup minced green onions
- 1/2 cup grated Swiss cheese
- 1/4 cup grated Parmesan cheese
- 1 teaspoon sweet basil flakes

- 4 teaspoons oil

Beat together first 7 ingredients until batter is smooth and blended, about 45 seconds. Do not overbeat. Oil 2 foil pans, 4x8-inches, with 2 teaspoons oil each. Divide batter between pans and brush tops with some of the oil that collects on the sides. Place pans on a cookie sheet and bake in a 350° oven for about 45 minutes, or until tops are golden brown and a cake tester, inserted in center, comes out clean.

Cool in pans for 15 minutes, and then remove pans and continue cooling on a rack. Serve with creamy whipped butter. Yields 2 loaves.

Country Kitchen Cornbread

This is a mildly sweet, buttery cornbread . . . quite old-fashioned except for the use of sour cream. However, the sour cream imparts a moistness and delicious flavor.

- 1 cup cornmeal
- 1 cup flour
- 1/3 cup sugar
- 1 tablespoon baking powder
- 1/3 teaspoon salt

- 3/4 cup milk
- 1/2 cup sour cream
- 2 eggs
- 6 tablespoons melted butter (3/4 stick)

In a bowl, stir together first 5 ingredients until blended. In another bowl, beat together remaining ingredients until blended. Add the dry ingredients and stir until mixture is blended. Do not overmix.

Spread batter into a greased 9x9-inch pan and bake in a 350° oven for 25 to 30 minutes or until top is golden brown and a cake tester, inserted in center, comes out clean. Cut into squares and serve warm. Serves 6.

Mexican Style Cornbread with Chiles & Cheese

This is a nice bread to serve for a dinner with a Mexican theme . . . like Mexican Meatball Soup or Mexican Salad with Guacamole.

    1 cup cornmeal
    1 tablespoon baking powder
1/2 teaspoon salt

    2 eggs
1/2 cup butter, melted
3/4 cup sour cream
    1 tablespoon sugar
    1 can (4 ounces) diced green chiles
    1 cup grated Jack cheese

In a bowl, stir together first 3 ingredients until blended. In another bowl, beat together the remaining ingredients until blended. Add dry ingredients to egg mixture and stir until nicely blended, but do not overmix.

Spread batter into a greased 9x9-inch pan and bake in a 350° oven for 25 to 30 minutes or until top is golden brown and a cake tester, inserted in center, comes out clean. Cut into squares and serve warm. Serves 6.

Giant Popovers with Chives & Cheese

Did you know that the basic recipe for popovers is almost the same batter as the one for crepes, clafoutis and even Yorkshire pudding. It can be varied, slightly, thinned a little, sparkled with different herbs and cheese and is a good recipe to keep in your repertoire. If you bake these in larger custard cups, then you will have 6 to 8 popovers which should take an extra 10 minutes baking time.

Basic Recipe:
3 eggs
1 cup flour
1 cup milk
1/4 teaspoon salt

2 tablespoons chopped chives (optional)
2 tablespoons grated Parmesan cheese (optional)

Beat together first 4 ingredients until blended. Stir in chives and cheese. Divide batter between 12 heavily greased muffin cups (or custard cups) and bake in a 400° oven for about 35 to 40 minutes, or until popovers are puffed and a deep golden brown. Serve at once with sweet whipped butter. Serves 12.

Note: — *Popovers are not great reheated, so plan to serve immediately after baking. They can be held for about 5 to 10 minutes in the oven, with the heat turned off.*

— *Basic recipe can be varied with different herbs and spices.*

Giant Popovers - Alternate Method

These popovers are made by the biscuit method (cutting the butter into the flour and then adding the liquids), which, I must confess, is not orthodox. But it does produce a lovely popover, a bit more dense, but worthy of inclusion here. Serve it with creamy butter and jam for brunch.

> 1 cup flour
> 3 tablespoons cold butter, cut into 6 pieces
>
> 3 eggs
> 1 cup milk
> 1/4 teaspoon salt

Beat together flour and butter until mixture resembles fine meal. Beat together eggs, milk and salt until blended and add, all at once, to flour mixture. Beat until mixture is blended. (Butter will form the smallest particles. This is OK.)

Divide batter between 12 heavily greased muffin cups (or custard cups) and bake in a 400° oven for about 40 minutes, or until popovers are puffed and a deep golden brown. Serve at once. Yields 12 popovers.

Note: — *Place about 1 teaspoon melted butter into each muffin cup.*

— *If popovers are browning too rapidly, tent loosely with foil. Popovers should be a deep golden color.*

— *If using custard cups, popovers will be larger. This recipe will yield 6 to 8 popovers and baking time will increase by about 10 minutes.*

Chewy Cheese Sticks with Onions

*While these chewy bread sticks contain yeast, they do not need to rise
. . . thus qualifying them as a "quick bread."*

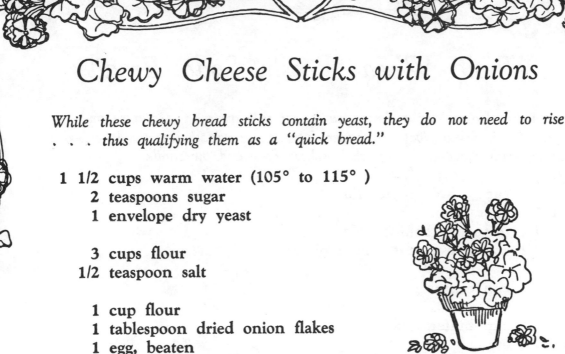

  1 1/2 cups warm water (105° to 115°)
    2 teaspoons sugar
    1 envelope dry yeast

    3 cups flour
1/2 teaspoon salt

    1 cup flour
    1 tablespoon dried onion flakes
    1 egg, beaten
      grated Parmesan cheese

In the large bowl of an electric mixer, place water, sugar and yeast and
allow mixture to rest for 5 minutes or until yeast is softened. Add 3 cups
flour and salt and beat for 5 minutes. Beat in the remaining flour and
onions, a little at a time, until a soft, smooth dough is formed.

With floured hands, divide dough into 32 balls and roll each piece into
a 1/4-inch thick rope. Place on a greased cookie sheet, brush tops with
beaten egg and sprinkle with a little grated cheese.

Bake in a 400° oven for about 15 minutes, or until bread sticks are lightly
browned. Yields 32 chewy sticks.

Whole Wheat Raisin Soda Bread

If you are looking for a dense, crusty loaf to serve with a country soup or stew, this is a good loaf to consider. It is a nice variation to the Irish Soda Bread, with the addition of whole wheat flour and buttermilk.

1 1/2 cups whole wheat flour
1 1/2 cups flour
1 1/2 teaspoons baking soda
  1/2 cup butter, cut into 8 pieces

   1 cup raisins

   1 cup buttermilk
   1 egg
   6 tablespoons sugar

Beat together first 4 ingredients until mixture resembles coarse meal. Beat in the raisins. Stir together buttermilk, egg and sugar and add all at once. Beat until batter is nicely blended, about 45 seconds. Do not overbeat.

Spread batter (batter will be thick) into a greased 8x2-inch round baking pan and with a knife, cut a cross on the top. Bake in a 375° oven for 30 minutes, reduce temperature to 350° and continue baking for about 20 minutes, or until top is a deep golden brown and a cake tester, inserted in center, comes out clean. Allow to cool in pan for 15 minutes, and then remove from pan and continue cooling on a rack. Yields 1 8-inch loaf.

Note: — *This is not an easy bread to test for doneness. Be certain to insert the cake tester in the center of the cross. When breads are very crusty, testing is a little more difficult. Rely more on color of crust. Bread should pull away slightly from the edge of the pan.*

Apple Cheddar Cheese Oatmeal Bread

Apples and cheddar cheese are a popular combination, although not one of my favorites. However, in this bread, they marry well. In fact, it is an extraordinarily delicious bread and lovely with soups or salads or omelettes. This recipe also makes a particularly fine muffin.

1/2	cup butter
1/2	cup sugar
2	eggs
2	small apples, peeled, cored and thinly sliced
1/3	cup buttermilk
1 1/2	cups flour
3/4	cup quick-cooking oats
2	teaspoons baking powder
1	teaspoon baking soda
1	cup grated cheddar cheese

Beat together first 5 ingredients until blended. Combine and add the next 5 ingredients and stir until dry ingredients are just moistened. Do not overmix.

Divide batter between 4 greased mini-loaf foil pans (6x3x2-inches) and bake in a 325° oven for 45 to 50 minutes or until a cake tester, inserted in center, comes out clean.

Allow to cool for 15 minutes and then remove from pans and continue cooling on a rack. Yields 4 mini-loaves.

Cheese & Onion Crescents
for Soups & Salads

These are marvellous little pastries, that will enhance a soup or salad course. They are truly delicious and savory.

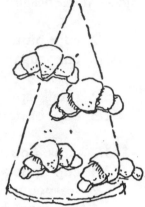

   3 ounces butter (3/4 stick)
   1 cup cottage cheese
      pinch of salt

   1 teaspoon sugar
   3 tablespoons grated Parmesan cheese
   1 tablespoon dehydrated onion flakes

   1 cup flour

In the large bowl of an electric mixer, beat together the butter, cottage cheese and salt until mixture is blended. Beat in the remaining ingredients and beat for about 2 minutes, at low speed, until mixture is smooth.

With floured hands, divide dough into thirds. Roll each third out on a floured pastry cloth (use a stocking on your rolling pin, also) until circle measures about 10 inches. Cut dough into 8 triangular wedges. Roll each triangle from the wide end, toward the center and curve into a crescent.

Place crescents on a lightly buttered cookie sheet and bake them at 350° for about 30 to 35 minutes, or until they are a deep, golden brown. Remove from pan and cool on a brown paper bag. Yields 24 crescents.

Note: — These can be frozen. Store in double plastic freezer bags and remove wrappers to defrost.

Cheddar Cheese Muffins for Soups & Salads

There are few muffins that you can make that are more delicious and tender than these. Great with soups or salads and excellent for snacking, too.

       2 eggs
       1 cup buttermilk
    1/4 cup oil
       2 tablespoons sugar

       2 cups flour
       4 teaspoons baking powder
       1 cup grated Cheddar cheese (4 ounces)
          pinch of salt

Beat together first 4 ingredients until blended. Mix together the remaining ingredients and add all at once. Beat until dry ingredients are just moistened. Do not overbeat.

Divide batter between 12 paper-lined muffin cups and bake in a 375° oven for about 25 minutes or until tops are golden brown. (These muffins are not easy to test, so make certain that the tops are a nice deep color.) Yields 12 muffins.

Bacon & Swiss Cheese Muffins

These muffins, flavored with bacon and Swiss cheese are just grand, served warm with sweet, creamy butter. They are nice with soup, salad or a hearty stew.

- 1/4 cup (1/2 stick) butter, softened
- 2 tablespoons sugar
- 1 egg
- 3/4 cup buttermilk
- 1 cup grated Swiss cheese
- 1/3 cup grated Parmesan cheese

- 1 1/2 cups flour
- 2 teaspoons baking powder
- 6 strips bacon, cooked crisp, drained and crumbled

Beat together first 6 ingredients until blended. Stir together the remaining ingredients and add all at once. Beat until dry ingredients are just moistened. Do not overbeat.

Divide batter between 12 paper-lined muffin cups and bake in a 400° oven for about 25 minutes, or until a cake tester, inserted in center, comes out clean. Serve warm with sweet whipped butter. Yields 12 muffins.

Muffins
Scones
Biscuits
Wafers

Muffins, Scones, Biscuits, Wafers

All-American Macaroon Muffins with Dates 270
Cinnamon Apple Muffins with Orange & Pecans 271
Fresh Apple & Orange Muffins 272
Buttermilk Blueberry Muffins with Pecans 273
Butterscotch Pecan Muffins 274
New Orleans Cornbread Muffins with Currants 275
Cajun Honey Bran Muffins with Raisins & Pecans 276
Cajun Jalapeno & Cheese Biscuit Muffins 277
Cajun Banana Pecan Crusty Muffins 278
Black Forest Chocolate Cherry Cupcakes 279
Sour Cream Muffins with Chocolate Chips 280
Cranberry, Orange & Apple Muffins 281
Chewy Orange Raisin Muffins 282
Best Papaya Lemon Cream Cheese Muffins 283
Currant & Oatmeal Muffins with Orange 284
Sour Cream Pumpkin Muffins with Walnuts 285
Spiced Pumpkin Muffins with Orange 286
Honey Whole Wheat & Wheat Germ Muffins 287
Maple Oat Bran Muffins with Walnuts 288
Raisin Bran Muffins with Apple & Orange 289
Honey Whole Wheat Oatmeal Muffins with Apples 290
Feather Cream Drop Biscuits 291
Chive Biscuits 291
Bacon Biscuits 291
Sesame Biscuits 291
Herb Biscuits 291
Parmesan Biscuits 291
Poppyseed Biscuits 291
Yogurt & Pecan Breakfast Wafers 292
Victorian Cream Scones with Currants 293
Whole Wheat Scones with Currants & Dates 294
Blueberry Buttermilk Scones 295
Buttery Scones with Buttermilk & Raisins 296

From my Notebook:

Muffins, Scones, Biscuits & Wafers

Muffins are quick breads baked in muffin tins. And of late, they are immensely popular. So many little shops are springing up everywhere, with ruffled, plaid curtains, selling muffins with any number of different combinations. Muffins, also, only need to be stirred (the less the better) and baked.

Now, the All-American Macaroon Muffins with Dates are an exception to the rule. While these are very untraditional, they do produce one of my very favorite muffins. These are so nice for a ladies' luncheon buffet... small and delicious and very unusual. The other muffins follow the traditional mode, but are varied with sour cream, cream cheese, yogurt.

In this chapter, you will find several muffins made with oat bran, which is becoming more and more popular lately. These are very, very good and good for you, too.

Also included are lots of muffins with fresh fruits, dried fruits, nuts and vegetables... oatmeal, bran and whole wheat.

AND, four Cajun muffins that are such a rage. While they use traditional ingredients, these muffins are baked at a much lower temperature for a longer period and they become rather crusty. My problem is which one to recommend first, since they are all so good. In any case, they are excellent served warm.

Biscuits, wafers and scones round out this chapter. Scones are also exceedingly popular these days, with so much attention being given to the Victorian Tea. The wafers are very unusual little cakes that everyone enjoyed. Quite tasty and a good choice for breakfast or mid-morning snack.

Biscuits and scones are prepared with the same technique... that of beating the flour with the butter until it resembles coarse meal. Liquids are then added, all at once, and the dough is handled minimally. As I designed all these recipes to eliminate kneading (where most catastrophes occur), you should have no trouble making light and fabulous biscuits and scones.

All-American Macaroon Muffins with Dates & Walnuts

This is a very chewy muffin, much like a macaroon and nice to serve at brunch. Let me say, at the outset, that this is a very unusual muffin and not made in the traditional manner. These are low muffins, so don't think anything went wrong.

> 3 egg whites, at room temperature
> 2/3 cup sugar
> 1 cup vanilla wafer crumbs
> 1 cup chopped walnuts
> 1 teaspoon vanilla
> 1/2 teaspoon baking powder
> 1/2 cup chopped pitted dates

Beat egg whites until foamy. Continue beating, slowly adding the sugar, until whites are stiff. Beat in the remaining ingredients until blended.

Divide mixture between 12 paper-lined muffin cups, filling each only half full. Bake in a 350° oven for 18 to 20 minutes, or until top is browned, and a cake tester, inserted in center, comes out clean.

Allow to cool in pan for 10 minutes, and then remove from pan and continue cooling on a rack. Yields 12 muffins.

Note: — These are totally delicious and everyone will be asking for the recipe.

— Can substitute chopped prunes for the dates.

— 1/4 cup yellow raisins is a nice addition.

— These are my favorite muffins to serve at brunch.

Cinnamon Apple Muffins with Orange & Pecans

These are delectable morsels to serve some Sunday night with honey-glazed chicken. They are full of flavor and need not be glazed.

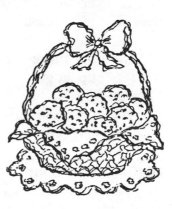

      1/3 cup butter, softened
        1 cup sugar
        2 eggs
      3/4 cup sour cream
        1 teaspoon vanilla

    1 3/4 cups flour
    2 1/2 teaspoons baking powder

        1 apple, peeled, cored and grated
      1/2 orange, grated. Use peel, fruit and juice.
      1/2 cup chopped pecans
          cinnamon sugar

Beat together first 5 ingredients until blended. Combine and add flour and baking powder and stir until dry ingredients are just moistened. Stir in apple, orange and pecans until blended.

Divide batter between 12 paper-lined muffin cups and sprinkle tops with cinnamon sugar. Bake in a 400° oven for about 25 minutes or until a cake tester, inserted in center, comes out clean. Serve with creamy butter. Yields 12 generous muffins.

Fresh Apple & Orange Muffins
with Cinnamon Topping

These delicious muffins are just grand for serving some Sunday night with Honey Glazed Chicken. Children (of all ages) love these, so it is a safe choice when there is "picky eater" around.

        1/4 cup butter, softened
        1 cup sugar
        2 eggs
        3/4 cup sour cream
        1 teaspoon vanilla

    1 3/4 cups flour
        2 teaspoons baking powder

        1 apple, peeled, cored and grated
    1/2 orange, grated. Use fruit, juice and peel. Remove any
            large pieces of membrane.
        cinnamon sugar

Beat together first 5 ingredients until blended. Stir in the flour and baking powder until blended. Do not overmix. Stir in the apple and orange until just mixed through.

Divide batter between 12 paper-lined muffin cups and sprinkle tops with 2 shakes of cinnamon sugar. Bake in a 400° oven for about 25 minutes, or until a cake tester, inserted in center, comes out clean. Yields 12 large-sized mufins.

Note: — *For smaller muffins, divide batter between 18 paper-lined muffin cups. Reduce baking time about 3 to 4 minutes. Make certain to test a little earlier.*

Buttermilk Blueberry Muffins with Pecans & Lemon Orange Glaze

This is a real fancy blueberry muffin, sparkled with pecans and the flavors of orange and lemon. A lovely muffin to serve with honey-glazed roast chicken on a Sunday night.

        1 cup buttermilk
        1 egg
    1/2 cup melted butter
    3/4 cup sugar
        3 tablespoons grated orange

    2 1/4 cups flour
        1 tablespoon baking powder

    1 1/2 cups blueberries, fresh or frozen

Beat together first 5 ingredients until blended. Beat in flour and baking powder until dry ingredients are just moistened. Do not overbeat. Stir in the blueberries.

Divide batter between 12 paper-lined muffin cups and bake in a 400° oven for 22 to 25 minutes or until muffins are lightly browned and a cake tester, inserted in center, comes out clean. Allow to cool for 10 minutes and then remove from pan and continue cooling on a rack. When cool, brush tops with Lemon Orange Glaze. Yields 12 generous muffins.

Lemon Orange Glaze:
        1 tablespoon orange juice
        1 tablespoon lemon juice
    1/2 cup sifted powdered sugar
        2 teaspoons finely grated orange peel
        1 teaspoon finely grated lemon peel

Stir together all the ingredients until blended.

Butterscotch Pecan Muffins with Sour Cream Cinnamon Glaze

These little muffins were fashioned after butterscotch brownies and children just love them.

    1/2 cup butter, softened
    1/2 cup brown sugar
    1/2 cup sugar
    1/2 cup sour cream
    1/2 cup milk
      2 eggs

  2 1/8 cups flour
      1 tablespoon baking powder
      2 teaspoons cinnamon
      1 cup chopped pecans
      1 cup (6 ounces) butterscotch chips

Beat together first 6 ingredients until blended. Stir in the remaining ingredients until dry ingredients are just moistened. Do not overmix.

Divide mixture between 18 paper-lined muffin cups and bake in a 400° oven for 20 to 22 minutes or until muffins are lightly browned and a cake tester, inserted in center, comes out clean.

Allow to cool for 10 minutes and then remove from pans and continue cooling on a rack. When cool, brush tops with Sour Cream Cinnamon Glaze. Yields 18 muffins.

Sour Cream Cinnamon Glaze:
      3 tablespoons sour cream
      1 cup sifted powdered sugar
      1 teaspoon cinnamon

Stir together all the ingredients until blended.

New Orleans Cornbread Muffins with Currants & Pecans

This is another Cajun-styled muffin that is a lovely accompaniment to a spicy soup or stew. While the ingredients are basic, the longer baking time produces a crustier muffin. These are just marvellous, served warm, with a little creamy butter.

6 tablespoons butter, melted and cooled
1 egg
2/3 cup sugar
1 cup milk
1 teaspoon vanilla

1 1/4 cups flour
1 cup yellow cornmeal
3 teaspoons baking powder
1/2 cup dried currants
1/2 cup chopped pecans

Beat together first 5 ingredients until blended. Add the remaining ingredients, all at once, and beat until blended. Do not overbeat.

Divide batter between 12 paper-lined muffin cups and bake in a 300° oven for about 45 minutes, or until tops are brown and crusty and a cake tester, inserted in center, comes out clean. Allow to cool for 10 minutes, and then remove from pan and continue cooling on a rack. Yields 12 muffins.

Cajun Honey Bran Muffins with Raisins & Pecans

These are luscious giant muffins, very spicy and flavorful. As they are baked in a low oven for a longer period of time, the tops are very crusty, but the crumb remains moist and delicious. Please note that these contain no butter.

    2 eggs
    1/2 cup sugar
    1/4 cup molasses
    1/4 cup honey
    1 cup milk
    2 teaspoons vanilla

1 1/2 cups flour
    1 cup unprocessed bran flakes
    2 teaspoons baking powder
    1 teaspoon baking soda
2 1/2 teaspoons pumpkin pie spice
    1 cup raisins
    1 cup chopped pecans

Beat together first 6 ingredients until blended. Add the remaining ingredients, all at once, and beat until blended. Do not overbeat.

Divide batter between 12 paper-lined muffin cups and bake in a 300° oven for 45 minutes or until tops are crusty and browned, and a cake tester, inserted in center, comes out clean. Allow to cool for 10 minutes, and then remove from pan and continue cooling on a rack. Yields 12 muffins.

Note: — If you do not have pumpkin pie spice, then use 2 teaspoons cinnamon and 1/4 teaspoon, each, nutmeg and ground cloves.

Cajun Jalapeno & Cheese Biscuit Muffins

Some night when you are serving a hot and spicy New Orleans Jumbalaya, you would do well to consider these divine biscuit muffins. These are moist and wonderful. Basically, it is a biscuit dough, baked in muffin tins, and a wonderful combination of cheese and peppers.

        2 1/2 cups flour
        1/4 cup sugar
          4 teaspoons baking powder
        3/4 cup butter (1 1/2 sticks), cut into 12 pieces

        2/3 cup grated Cheddar cheese
          3 tablespoons Ortega Hot Peppers (Jalapenos), seeded and
                chopped (about 1/2 of a 3.5-ounce can)
      1 1/4 cups milk

In the large bowl of an electric mixer, beat together first 4 ingredients, until mixture resembles coarse meal. Add the remaining ingredients and beat until batter is just blended. (Do this on very low speed or stir by hand.) Do not overbeat. Batter will be thick.

Divide batter between 12 paper-lined muffin cups and bake in a 350° oven for about 45 minutes or until tops are browned and crusty. (These are hard to test, so check by time and color.) Allow to cool for 10 minutes and then continue cooling on a rack. Yields 12 muffins.

Note: — *Please be careful in handling the peppers. I use a knife and fork to scrape away the seeds and to coarsely chop. You may want to use gloves and please keep your hands away from your eyes.*

— *Add more peppers if you want the extra bite.*

Cajun Banana Pecan Crusty Muffins

These New Orleans-styled muffins are pretty traditional, except for baking temperature and time. Baking these in a slow oven produces a very crusty muffin on the outside and a soft, delectable crumb on the inside. These are highly spiced and should be served warm.

    2 eggs
  1/2 cup butter (1 stick) melted and cooled
    1 cup sugar
  1/3 cup buttermilk
    2 cups flour
    2 large bananas, mashed
    2 teaspoons baking soda
    1 teaspoon cinnamon
  1/2 teaspoon nutmeg
  1/4 teaspoon ground cloves
    1 cup chopped pecans

Beat together first 4 ingredients until blended. Stir in the remaining ingredients and beat until blended. Do not overbeat. Divide batter between 12 paper-lined muffin cups and bake in a 300° oven for about 45 minutes or until tops are brown and crusty, and a cake tester, inserted in center, comes out clean. Allow to cool for 10 minutes, and then remove from pan and continue cooling on a rack. Yields 12 muffins.

Black Forest Chocolate Cherry Cupcakes with Creamy Glaze

This delicious cupcake was adapted from the Black Forest Cherry Torte which is a sophisticated combination of chocolate, cherries and creamy filling. This is a far cry from the simple little cupcakes we enjoyed when we were young.

    1 egg
    1 cup sour cream
    1/3 cup melted butter
    1 cup sugar

    2 cups flour
    1/4 cup cocoa
    1 tablespoon baking powder
    1 cup chopped walnuts

1 1/2 cups fresh or frozen pitted Bing cherries, drained

Beat together first 4 ingredients until blended. Add the flour, cocoa, baking powder and walnuts and beat until dry ingredients are just moistened. Do not overbeat. Stir in the cherries.

Divide batter between 12 paper-lined muffin cups and bake in a 400° oven for about 22 to 25 minutes, or until a cake tester, inserted in center, comes out clean. Allow to cool for 10 minutes, and then remove muffins from pan and continue cooling on a rack. Brush tops with Creamy Glaze when cool. Yields 12 cupcakes.

Creamy Glaze:
    1 tablespoon cream
    1/4 teaspoon vanilla
    1/2 cup sifted powdered sugar

Stir together all the ingredients until blended.

Sour Cream Muffins with Chocolate Chips & Pecans

These homey muffins were fashioned after the famous chocolate chip cookie and they are addicting.

- 1/2 cup butter, softened
- 1/2 cup brown sugar
- 1/2 cup sugar

- 2 eggs

- 1/2 cup sour cream
- 1/2 cup milk

- 2 1/8 cups flour
  - 1 tablespoon baking powder
  - 1 cup (6 ounces) semi-sweet chocolate chips
  - 1 cup chopped walnuts
  - 1 teaspoon vanilla

Cream together butter and sugars. Beat in eggs until blended. Beat in sour cream and milk until blended. Add remaining ingredients, all at once, and stir until dry ingredients are just moistened. Do not overmix.

Divide mixture between 18 paper-lined muffin cups and bake in a 400° oven for 20 to 22 minutes or until muffins are lightly browned and a cake tester, inserted in center, comes out clean. Allow to cool for 10 minutes and then remove from pans and continue cooling on a rack. Yields 18 muffins.

Cranberry, Orange & Apple Muffins with Orange Honey Butter

Oh, what a delicious muffin. The combination of cranberries, orange and apple all add a distinct flavor. The Orange Honey Butter is a grand accompaniment, and can be used on pancakes, waffles or a thick slice of pumpernickel raisin bread.

    1 egg
1/2 cup sour cream
1/2 cup milk
1/3 cup oil
3/4 cup sugar
    1 cup chopped walnuts
    1 apple, peeled, cored and grated
1/2 medium orange, grated
    1 cup cranberries, coarsely chopped

2 1/4 cups flour
    1 tablespoon baking powder
    1 teaspoon cinnamon

Beat together first 9 ingredients until blended. Combine and add the next 3 ingredients and stir until dry ingredients are just moistened. Do not overmix.

Divide batter between 12 paper-lined muffin cups and bake in a 400° oven for about 22 to 25 minutes or until muffins are lightly browned and a cake tester, inserted in center, comes out clean.

Allow to cool for 10 minutes, remove muffins from pan, and continue cooling on a rack. Serve warm with Orange Honey Butter. Yields 12 muffins.

Orange Honey Butter:
1/2 cup butter, softened
    2 tablespoons honey
    1 tablespoon grated orange peel

Beat butter until creamy. Beat in the remaining ingredients until blended.

Chewy Orange Raisin Muffins

These are the nicest muffins to serve for a buffet luncheon, or for afternoon tea. They are sticky and chewy (very untraditional), and faintly resembling a macaroon. Please note that they do not contain any butter or cream.

2 eggs
1 cup sugar
1 teaspoon vanilla

1/2 orange, grated (about 3 tablespoons)

1 cup flour
1 teaspoon baking powder
1 cup chopped yellow raisins

Beat together eggs, sugar and vanilla until mixture is blended, about 30 seconds. Beat in orange until blended. Mix together the remaining ingredients and add, all at once. Stir until dry ingredients are just moistened. Do not overmix.

Divide batter between 12 paper-lined muffin cups and bake in a 350° oven for about 20 to 25 minutes, or until tops are browned and a cake tester, inserted in center of muffin, comes out clean. Serve with a faint sprinkle of powdered sugar. Yields 12 muffins.

The Best Papaya Lemon Cream Cheese Muffins

These are huge cake-like muffins that are tender and delicious. Now, if you plan to serve these for a lovely Summer luncheon, I recommend that you divide the batter between 18 muffin cups, to produce a smaller muffin. Reduce the baking time by 4 to 5 minutes. (Of course, be sure to test.)

1/4 cup butter (1/2 stick)
1/4 cup cream cheese (2 ounces)
1 cup sugar
2 eggs
3/4 cup milk
2 tablespoons grated lemon
1 teaspoon vanilla

2 cups flour
2 teaspoons baking powder
1/2 teaspoon baking soda
1/2 cup chopped walnuts or yellow raisins

1 cup diced papaya

Beat together first 7 ingredients until blended. Beat in the next 4 ingredients until dry ingredients are just blended. Do not overbeat. Stir in the papaya.

Divide batter between 12 paper-lined muffin cups and bake in a 375° oven for about 25 minutes, or until tops are browned and a cake tester, inserted in center, comes out clean. Allow to cool for 10 minutes, and then remove from pan and continue cooling on a rack. Yields 12 very generous muffins.

Note: — *These are nice to bake as loaves. Divide batter into 4 mini-loaf pans and bake at 325° for about 45 minutes or until loaves test done.*

Currant & Oatmeal Muffins with Orange & Cinnamon

This is a most unusual muffin, very hardy (a nice way to say heavy) but with a good deal of character. It is full of good things, and a nice choice for breakfast.

1/2 cup butter, softened
2/3 cup sugar
  5 eggs
1/2 orange, grated (about 3 tablespoons)
  1 teaspoon vanilla

  1 cup flour
1/2 cup quick-cooking oats
  2 teaspoons baking powder
  1 teaspoon pumpkin pie spice
  1 cup dried currants
  1 cup chopped walnuts

  cinnamon sugar

Beat together first 5 ingredients until blended. Mix together the next 6 ingredients and beat in until dry ingredients are just moistened. Do not overbeat.

Divide batter between 12 paper-lined muffin cups and sprinkle tops with cinnamon sugar. Bake in a 375° oven for about 25 minutes, or until a cake tester, inserted in center, comes out clean. Cool in pan for a few minutes, and then continue cooling on a rack. Yields 12 muffins.

Sour Cream Pumpkin Muffins with Walnuts & Raisins & Orange Cinnamon Butter

These are nice to serve from Halloween through the end of the holiday season. Very moist and very tasty with the Orange Cinnamon Butter.

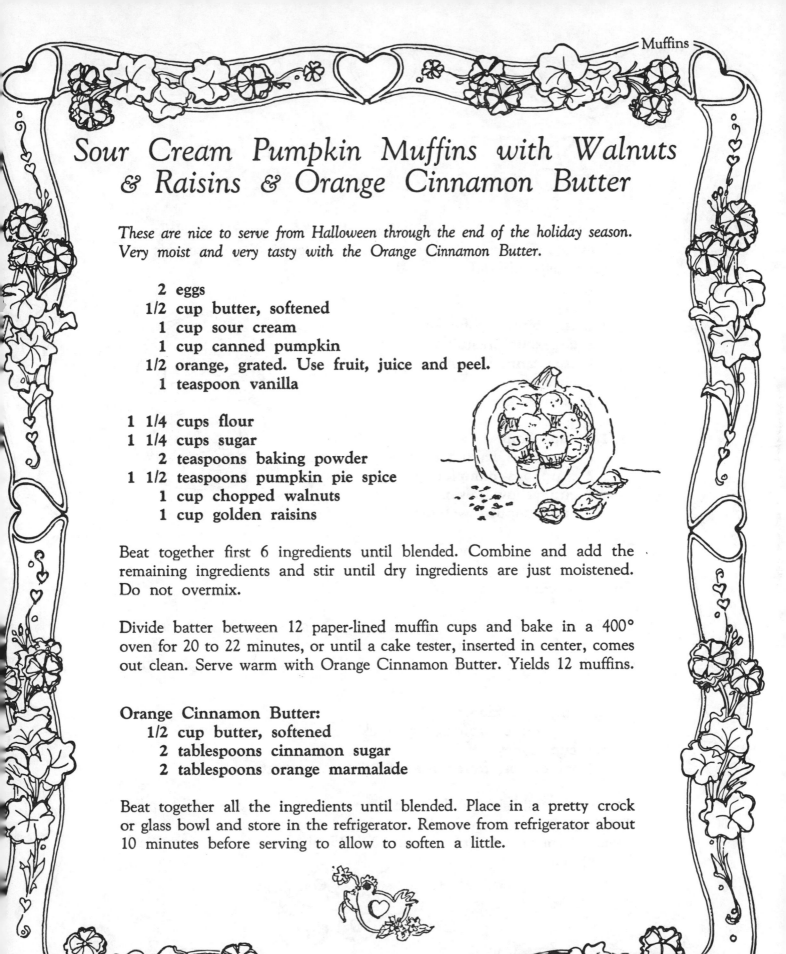

 2 eggs
1/2 cup butter, softened
 1 cup sour cream
 1 cup canned pumpkin
1/2 orange, grated. Use fruit, juice and peel.
 1 teaspoon vanilla

1 1/4 cups flour
1 1/4 cups sugar
 2 teaspoons baking powder
1 1/2 teaspoons pumpkin pie spice
 1 cup chopped walnuts
 1 cup golden raisins

Beat together first 6 ingredients until blended. Combine and add the remaining ingredients and stir until dry ingredients are just moistened. Do not overmix.

Divide batter between 12 paper-lined muffin cups and bake in a 400° oven for 20 to 22 minutes, or until a cake tester, inserted in center, comes out clean. Serve warm with Orange Cinnamon Butter. Yields 12 muffins.

Orange Cinnamon Butter:
 1/2 cup butter, softened
  2 tablespoons cinnamon sugar
  2 tablespoons orange marmalade

Beat together all the ingredients until blended. Place in a pretty crock or glass bowl and store in the refrigerator. Remove from refrigerator about 10 minutes before serving to allow to soften a little.

Spiced Pumpkin Muffins with Orange, Walnuts & Raisins

These muffins are so nice to serve during the holiday season from Halloween to Christmas. They are spicy and moist and the combination of pumpkin and orange is simply delightful.

    2 eggs
1/2 cup butter, softened
  1 cup sour cream
  1 cup canned pumpkin
1 1/4 cups sugar
1/2 orange, grated

1 1/2 cups flour
  2 teaspoons baking powder
  2 teaspoons pumpkin pie spice
  1 cup yellow raisins
  1 cup chopped walnuts

Beat together first 6 ingredients until blended. Combine and add the remaining ingredients and stir until dry ingredients are just moistened. Do not overmix.

Divide batter between 12 paper-lined muffin cups and bake in a 400° oven for 25 minutes or until a cake tester, inserted in center comes out clean. Serve warm with Sweet Butter & Honey. Yields 12 large muffins.

Sweet Butter & Honey:
    1/2 cup butter, softened (1 stick)
    1/4 cup honey
      1 tablespoon frozen orange juice concentrate

Beat butter until light and fluffy. Beat in remaining ingredients until blended. Place butter in a pretty bowl or crock and refrigerate until serving time. Remove from the refrigerator about 10 to 15 minutes before serving. Yields 3/4 cup butter.

Honey Whole Wheat & Wheat Germ Muffins with Orange & Raisins

These giant muffins are a gem to serve. They are huge and overflowing and rather attractive for breakfast or brunch. They are not too sweet, and truly delicious with the flavor of orange and raisins.

- 1/2 cup butter
- 1/2 cup honey
- 2 eggs

- 1 medium orange, grated. (Use fruit, juice and peel.)
- 1/2 cup sour cream
- 1/2 cup milk

- 2 cups whole wheat pastry flour
- 1/2 cup wheat germ (sweetened or unsweetened)
- 2 teaspoons baking powder
- 1 teaspoon baking soda
- 1 cup raisins
- 1/2 cup chopped walnuts

Beat together butter, honey and eggs until mixture is thoroughly blended. Beat in orange, sour cream and milk until blended. Mix together the remaining ingredients and add all at once, beating until dry ingredients are just moistened. Do not overbeat.

Divide batter between 12 paper-lined muffin cups and bake in a 350° oven for about 30 minutes, or until a cake tester, inserted in the center of a muffin, comes out clean. Allow to cool for 10 minutes, and then remove from pan and continue cooling on a rack. Yields 12 muffins.

Note: — These are super large with huge crowns. These can be divided into 18 muffins. Reduce baking time by 3 to 4 minutes.

Maple Oat Bran Muffins
with Raisins & Walnuts

Oat Bran, a high fiber cereal, was once only found in health food stores. But it has become increasingly popular and can now be seen in most super markets. These muffins are not traditional, but are an interesting combination of ingredients. An excellent muffin for breakfast.

      2 eggs
      1 cup sour cream
      1 cup maple syrup
      1 teaspoon pure maple extract

      1 cup whole wheat flour
      1 cup oat bran flakes
  1 1/2 teaspoons baking soda
      1 teaspoon baking powder
      1 cup raisins
    1/2 cup chopped walnuts

Beat together first 4 ingredients until blended. Mix together the remaining ingredients and add, all at once. Beat until dry ingredients are just blended. Do not overbeat.

Divide batter between 18 paper-lined muffin cups and bake in a 400° oven for about 18 to 20 minutes, or until a cake tester, inserted in center of muffin, comes out clean. Allow to cool for 10 minutes, and then remove from pan and continue cooling on a rack. Serve warm. Yields 18 muffins.

Raisin Bran Muffins with Apple & Orange

These are marvellous muffins, very moist and fruity. They are just bursting with flavor and goodness. My children love them... even though there isn't a hint of chocolate.

    1/4 cup butter (1/2 stick) softened
      1 egg
    3/4 cup milk

      1 apple, peeled, cored and grated
      1 medium orange, grated. Use juice, fruit and peel.

      1 cup flour
      2 cups Raisin Bran Cereal
      1 tablespoon baking powder
  1 1/2 teaspoons cinnamon
    1/2 cup sugar

Beat together butter, egg and milk until blended. Stir in apple and orange. Combine the remaining ingredients and add, all at once. Stir until dry ingredients are just moistened. Do not overmix.

Divide batter between 12 paper-lined muffin cups and bake in a 400° oven for 25 minutes, or until a cake tester, inserted in center of muffin, comes out clean. Allow to cool for 10 minutes, and then, remove from pan and continue cooling on a rack. When cool, drizzle top with Orange Glaze. Yields 12 muffins.

Orange Glaze:
      2 tablespoons grated orange
    3/4 cup sifted powdered sugar

Stir together orange and sugar until blended. Add a little sugar or orange juice to make glaze a drizzling consistency.

Honey Whole Wheat Oatmeal Muffins with Apples & Raisins

These are fantastic muffins that are a treat to serve. They are quite a generous size as indicated. They can be stretched to 18 muffins, but then reduce baking time by 2 or 3 minutes.

- 1/2 cup butter
- 3/4 cup honey
- 2 eggs

- 1 apple, peeled, cored and grated
- 1/2 cup milk

- 2 cups whole wheat pastry flour
- 1 cup quick-cooking oats
- 1 teaspoon baking powder
- 1 teaspoon baking soda
- 1 teaspoon cinnamon
- 1/2 teaspoon nutmeg
- 1 cup raisins
- 1/2 cup chopped walnuts

Beat together butter, honey and eggs until thoroughly blended. Beat in apples and milk until blended. Mix together the remaining ingredients and beat in until dry ingredients are just moistened. Do not overbeat.

Divide batter between 12 paper-lined muffin cups and bake in a 375° oven for about 25 minutes, or until a cake tester, inserted in center of muffin, comes out clean. Allow to cool for 10 minutes, and then remove from pan and continue cooling on a rack. Yields 12 muffins.

Note: — These can be decorated with a little sifted powdered sugar.

Feather Cream Drop Biscuits

This is my favorite biscuit, light as a feather and very easy to prepare. Biscuits are dropped from a tablespoon which eliminates kneading, rolling and cutting. Follow the directions carefully, and your biscuits will be perfect every time.

1 1/4 cups flour
1 tablespoon baking powder
1/3 teaspoon salt

1/4 cup cold butter (1/2 stick) cut into 4 pieces

1 1/8 cups cream

Place flour, baking powder and salt in large bowl of an electric mixer. Beat for a few seconds to blend. Add the butter and beat until mixture resembles coarse meal. By hand, stir in the cream until blended.

Drop batter by the heaping tablespoon onto an ungreased cookie sheet and bake in a 425° oven for 20 minutes, or until tops are golden brown. Yields 12 to 14 biscuits.

Note: — *This is the basic recipe which is great for soups and salads. But there is no end to the number of variations you can use. The following are just a few. Use an herb or seasoning to match your meal.*

Chive Biscuits: *Add to the batter 1 tablespoon chopped chives.*

Bacon Biscuits: *Add to the batter 2 tablespoons bacon, that has been cooked crisp, drained and crumbled.*

Sesame Biscuits: *Add to the batter 1 tablespoon sesame seeds.*

Herb Biscuits: *Add to the batter 1 tablespoon chopped fresh herbs or 1 teaspoon dried herb flakes (not ground herbs.)*

Parmesan Biscuits: *Sprinkle tops of biscuits with 1/2 teaspoon grated Parmesan cheese.*

Poppy Seed Biscuits: *Sprinkle tops of biscuits with 1/4 teaspoon poppy seed.*

Yogurt & Pecan Breakfast Wafers with Cinnamon Sugar

These little wafers are lovely with breakfast or brunch. Serve them warm with sweet, creamy butter and a fruity jam. Very unusual and very delicious.

```
1 1/2  cups flour
1/2  teaspoon baking soda
  2  tablespoons sugar
1/4  cup butter

1/4  cup finely chopped pecans

1/2  cup unflavored yogurt

  1  tablespoon cinnamon sugar
```

In the large bowl of an electric mixer, beat together first 4 ingredients until mixture resembles fine meal. Stir in the pecans. Beat in the yogurt until a soft dough forms.

With floured hands, divide dough into 20 balls, flatten each ball to measure 2-inches round and place them on an ungreased 12x16-inch baking pan. Sprinkle lightly with cinnamon sugar and bake in a 400° oven for about 12 to 15 minutes, or until lightly browned. Transfer wafers to a rack to cool.

Serve warm or at room temperature with butter and jam. Yields 20 wafers.

Note: — *If you would like to serve these wafers with soups or salads, omit the cinnamon sugar and sprinkle top with sesame seeds, poppy seeds or a little grated Parmesan cheese, and press it very lightly into the dough.*

Victorian Cream Scones with Currants

This very traditional scone is grand for breakfast or afternoon tea. With butter and jam, or honey butter, or fruited cream cheese . . . delicious!

- 2 cups flour
- 1 tablespoon baking powder
- 1/2 cup sugar
  pinch of salt
- 1/2 cup cold butter (1 stick) cut into 8 pieces

- 1/2 cup dried currants

- 2 eggs
- 1/3 cup cream
- 1 teaspoon vanilla

In the large bowl of an electric mixer, beat together first 5 ingredients until mixture resembles coarse meal. Stir in the currants. Beat together, eggs, cream and vanilla and add, all at once, into the flour mixture. Beat until blended and smooth, but do not overmix. (This can be stirred by hand.)

Scrape batter into a greased 10-inch springform pan and spread evenly. Sprinkle top with 2 tablespoons cinnamon sugar and pat 2 tablespoons chopped almonds (optional) on top. Bake in a 400° oven for about 20 to 25 minutes, or until top is golden brown. Allow to cool in pan and cut into wedges to serve. Yields 8 servings.

Whole Wheat Scones with Currants & Dates & Devonshire Cream

Currants and dates add character to these hardy scones made with whole wheat. These are especially good for breakfast with butter and jam. At tea time, a sweetened Devonshire-type Cream, flavored with vanilla would be just lovely.

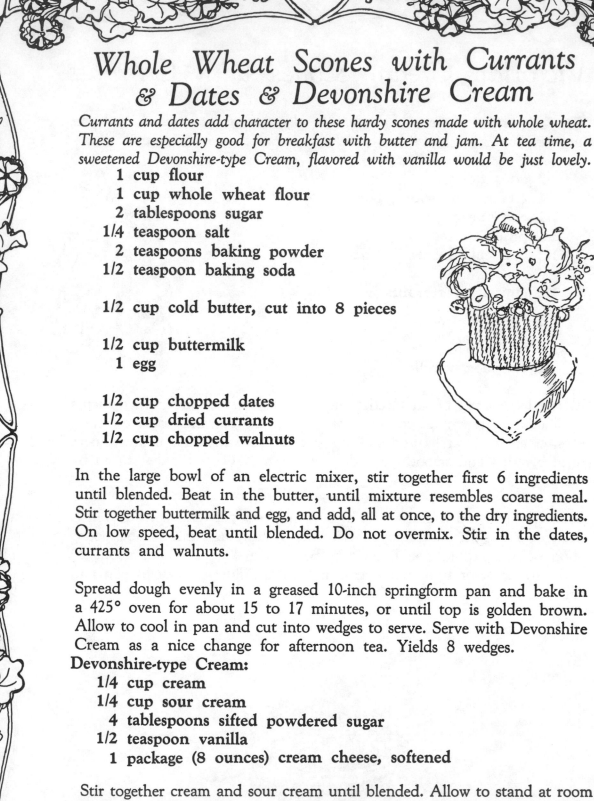

- 1 cup flour
- 1 cup whole wheat flour
- 2 tablespoons sugar
- 1/4 teaspoon salt
- 2 teaspoons baking powder
- 1/2 teaspoon baking soda

- 1/2 cup cold butter, cut into 8 pieces

- 1/2 cup buttermilk
- 1 egg

- 1/2 cup chopped dates
- 1/2 cup dried currants
- 1/2 cup chopped walnuts

In the large bowl of an electric mixer, stir together first 6 ingredients until blended. Beat in the butter, until mixture resembles coarse meal. Stir together buttermilk and egg, and add, all at once, to the dry ingredients. On low speed, beat until blended. Do not overmix. Stir in the dates, currants and walnuts.

Spread dough evenly in a greased 10-inch springform pan and bake in a 425° oven for about 15 to 17 minutes, or until top is golden brown. Allow to cool in pan and cut into wedges to serve. Serve with Devonshire Cream as a nice change for afternoon tea. Yields 8 wedges.

Devonshire-type Cream:
- 1/4 cup cream
- 1/4 cup sour cream
- 4 tablespoons sifted powdered sugar
- 1/2 teaspoon vanilla
- 1 package (8 ounces) cream cheese, softened

Stir together cream and sour cream until blended. Allow to stand at room temperature for 4 hours until thickened. Stir in the sugar and vanilla. Beat cream cheese until light and fluffy. Beat in the cream mixture until blended. Refrigerate until ready to use.

Blueberry Buttermilk Scones with Crunchy Sugar Topping

This is a great scone to serve with roast chicken, turkey or ham. It is exceedingly light, not very sweet, and a homey accompaniment to a family dinner.

3 cups flour
1/2 cup sugar
1 tablespoon baking powder
1 teaspoon baking soda
1/4 teaspoon salt

3/4 cup cold butter (1 1/2 sticks) cut into 12 pieces

1/2 cup buttermilk
1/2 cup cream

1 cup blueberries

2 tablespoons cream
2 tablespoons sugar

In the large bowl of an electric mixer, stir together first 5 ingredients until blended. Beat in the butter until mixture resembles coarse meal. Stir together buttermilk and cream and add, all at once, to the dry ingredients. On low speed, beat until blended. Do not overmix. Stir in the blueberries.

Place dough into a greased 12-inch baking pan and with floured hands, pat mixture evenly into the pan. Brush top with cream and sprinkle sugar evenly on top. Bake in a 425° oven for about 20 to 25 minutes, or until top is golden brown. Allow to cool in pan and cut into wedges to serve. Yields 12 wedges.

Note: — Testing is difficult with scones, as a cake tester does not work here. Judge by color. Top should be golden brown and edges will shrink slightly from the edge of the pan.

Buttery Scones with Buttermilk & Raisins

You will just love these light and delicious scones that have a sweet buttery flavor. These are very subtle and gentle and just lovely with honey or strawberry jam.

2 cups flour
1/2 teaspoon salt
2 teaspoons baking powder
1/2 teaspoon baking soda
4 tablespoons sugar
1/2 cup (1 stick) cold butter, cut into 8 pieces

3/4 cup buttermilk

1/2 cup yellow raisins

In the large bowl of an electric mixer, beat together first 6 ingredients until butter is the size of small peas. Beat in the buttermilk until dry ingredients are just blended. Do not overbeat. Stir in the yellow raisins.

Spread mixture evenly into a greased 10-inch springform pan. Cut through dough to form 8 wedges. Bake in a 425° oven for about 20 to 25 minutes or until top is golden brown. Serve warm with butter and honey or jam. Yields 8 wedges.

Note: — *Scones can be prepared earlier in the day and heated at serving time.*

— *If you prepare scones 1 day earlier, pan should be covered tightly with plastic wrap, and refrigerated. Heat before serving.*

— *Scones can be frozen.*

ALMOND CAKES & BREADS
—Almond Torte with Chocolate Chip Crust, 108
—Almond Torte with Glazed Strawberries, 109
—Apricot Jam and Almond Bread, 169
—Apricot & Orange Almond Bread, 168
—Black Cherry & Almond Cake, 40
—Chocolate Almond Torte, 110
—Fresh Peach & Almond Bread, 145
—Holiday Cranberry Almond Bread, 139
—Honey Almond Bread with Apricots, 166
—Red Cherry Almond Cake, 41
—Royal Raspberry & Almond Cake, 57
—Sour Cream Almond Cake, 62
—Strawberry Jam & Almond Cake, 72
—Swiss Chocolate Cake with Cherries & Almonds, 87

APPLE CAKES & BREADS
—Apple Cheddar Cheese Oatmeal Bread, 263
—Apple Orange Raisin Bread, 128
—Cinnamon Apple Cake, 30
—Easiest & Best Apple Cake, 29
—Fresh Apple Orange Pecan Torte, 111
—Fresh Apple Sour Cream Cake, 31
—Fresh Apple Spiced Cake, 28
—Fresh Apple & Walnut Honey Cake, 26
—Majestic Apple Cake with Orange, 27
—Royal Sour Cream Coffeecake with Apples, 24
—Sour Cream Apple Kuchen with Raisins, 25
—Upside Down Honey Bran Bread with Apples, 129

APPLESAUCE CAKE & BREAD
—Spiced Applesauce Bread with Currants, 130
—Spiced Applesauce Cake with Raisins, 32

APRICOT CAKES & BREADS
—Apricot Jam & Almond Bread, 169
—Apricot Jam & Macaroon Cake, 65
—Apricot & Orange Almond Bread, 168
—Apricot Pecan Yogurt Cake, 64
—Fresh Apricot & Cottage Cheese Bread, 131
—Honey Almond Bread with Apricots, 166
—Royal Apricot Cake with Raisins, 63
—Wheat Germ Bread with Apricots, 190

BAGELS
—Easiest & Best Onion Sesame Bagels, 242

BANANA CAKES & BREADS
—Banana, Orange & Raisin Bran Bread, 135
—Cajun Banana Pecan Crusty Muffins, 278
—Chocolate Banana Cake, 85
—Old-Fashioned Banana Chocolate Chip Bread, 132
—Sour Cream Banana Bread, 133
—Sour Cream & Chocolate Banana Cake, 84
—Spiced Banana Cake, 33
—Strawberry Banana Bread, 160
—Strawberry Yogurt Banana Bread, 159
—Whole Wheat Banana & Chocolate Chip Bread, 134

BAR CAKES & COOKIES
—Apricot Bars with Pecan Meringue Topping, 216
—Best Sour Cream Bittersweet Brownies, 208
—Biscotti de Amaretto-Almond Biscuits, 226
—Butterscotch Brownies with Walnuts, 205
—Chewy Bar Cookies with Cherries, Dates, 212
—Chewy Fudgy California Brownies, 206
—Chocolate Chip Walnut Chewies, 222
—Chocolate Cream Cheese Bars with Chocolate, 210
—Chocolate Fudge Brownies, 209
—Chocolate Granola Bars with Dates, Raisins, 221
—Coffee Cake Bars with Cinnamon, Orange, 220
—Creamy Chocolate Squares with Chocolate Chips, 219
—Friendship Caramel Pecan Bars, 215
—German Chocolate Bar Cookies with Pecans, 211
—Goldies, 213
—Holiday Fruit & Nut Chewies, 225
—Lemon Butter Bars with Raspberry Jam & Pecans, 218
—Red Raspberry Butter Bars with Coconut Meringue, 217
—Rocky Road Bars with Sour Cream & Macaroon, 204
—Rocky Road Chewies with Walnuts & Chocolate, 205
—Victorian Pretty Maids of Honor Bars, 224
—Walnut & Butterscotch Cookie Bars, 214
—World's Best Chocolate Chip Raisin Cookies, 223
—World's Best Velvet Chocolate Brownies, 207

BISCUITS
—Bacon Biscuits, 291
—Chive Biscuits, 291
—Feather Cream Biscuits, 291
—Herb Biscuits, 291
—Parmesan Biscuits, 291
—Poppyseed Biscuits, 291
—Sesame Seed Biscuits, 291

BLUEBERRY BREAD & MUFFINS
—Buttermilk Blueberry Muffins, 273
—Whole Wheat & Oatmeal Blueberry Bread, 136

BRAN BREADS & MUFFINS
—Banana, Orange & Raisin Bran Bread, 135

—Cajun Honey Bran Muffins, 276
—Honey Bran Bread with Peaches, 144
—Molasses & Buttermilk Bran Bread, 198
—Pineapple & Orange Bran Bread, 149
—Pineapple & Raisin Bran Bread, 150
—Upside Down Honey Bran Bread, 129

BREADS - SAVORY
—Apple Cheddar Cheese Oatmeal Bread, 263
—Bacon & Swiss Cheese Muffins, 266
—Burgundian Cheese & Chive Bread, 255
—Cheddar Cheese Muffins for Soups & Salads, 265
—Cheese & Onion Crescents for Soups & Salads, 264
—Chewy Cheese Sticks with Onions, 261
—Country Kitchen Cornbread, 257
—Easiest & Best Onion Sesame Bagels, 242
—Giant Popovers - Alternate Method, 260
—Giant Popovers with Chives & Cheese, 259
—Gougere au Fromage, 255
—Greek Lemon Bread with Green Onions, Tomato & Feta, 251
—Green Onion Buttermilk Bread with Lemon & Sesame Seeds, 248
—Mexican-Style Cornbread with Chiles & Cheese, 258
—Onion Kuchen with Sour Cream & Poppy Seeds, 243
—Parmesan, Herb & Onion Cheese Bread, 249
—Pesto Bread with Cheese & Pine Nuts, 246
—Pizza Bread with Tomatoes, Onions & Cheese, 247
—Poppyseed Bread with Green Onions & Cheese, 250
—Poppyseed Onion Rolls for Passover Holiday, 244
—Red Hot Pastelle with Onions & Swiss Cheese, 245
—Russian Black Bread with Sour Cream & Raisins, 254
—Sauerkraut Rye Bread with Yogurt, Onions & Bacon, 253
—Sweet & Sour Red Cabbage Bread with Apples & Raisins, 252
—Two-Minute Cheese Bread with Onions & Herbs, 256
—Whole Wheat Raisin Soda Bread, 262

BROWNIES
—Best Sour Cream Bittersweet Brownies, 208
—Butterscotch Brownies with Walnuts, 205
—Chewy Fudgy California Brownies, 206
—Chocolate Fudge Brownies, 209
—World's Best Velvet Chocolate Brownies, 207

BUTTERMILK BREADS & CAKE
—Buttermilk Chocolate Bread with Pecans, 171
—Chocolate Chip Buttermilk Cake, 90
—Molasses & Buttermilk Bran Bread, 198
—Whole Wheat & Buttermilk Prune Bread, 197

CARROT CAKES & BREAD
—California Carrot Cake with Pineapple & Coconut, 35
—Chocolate Carrot Cake, 86
—Cooked Carrot Spice Cake with Walnuts, 36
—Country Home Carrot & Raisin Cake, 34
—Easiest & Best Carrot Cake, 37
—Easiest & Best Carrot Torte, 112
—Farmhouse Carrot Cake with Pineapple, 38
—Spiced Carrot & Orange Bread, 137

CHEESE BREADS & MUFFINS
—Apple Cheddar Cheese Oatmeal Bread, 263
—Bacon & Swiss Cheese Muffins, 266
—Burgundian Cheese & Chive Bread, 255
—Cajun Jalapeno & Cheese Biscuit Muffins, 277
—Cheddar Cheese Muffins, 265
—Cheese & Onion Crescents, 264
—Chewy Cheese Sticks with Onions, 261
—Giant Popovers with Chives & Cheese, 259
—Greek Lemon Bread with Green Onions, Tomato & Feta, 251
—Mexican Style Cornbread with Chiles & Cheese, 258
—Parmesan, Herb & Onion Cheese Bread, 249
—Pesto Bread with Cheese & Pine Nuts, 246
—Pizza Bread with Tomato, Onions & Cheese, 247
—Poppyseed Bread with Green Onions & Cheese, 250
—Red Hot Pastelle with Onions & Swiss Cheese, 245
—Two-Minute Cheese Bread with Onions & Herbs, 256

CHERRY CAKES & BREAD
—Black Cherry & Almond Cake, 40
—Christmas Eggnog Cherry Bread, 170
—French Clafouti with Bing Cherries, 39
—Red Cherry Almond Cake, 41
—Swiss Chocolate Cake with Cherries & Almonds, 87

CINNAMON SUGAR 173,238

CHESTNUT CAKE
—Chocolate Chestnut Cake, 89

CHOCOLATE CAKES, BREADS & CUPCAKES
—Anniversary Chocolate & Raspberry Cake, 100
—Basic Chocolate Sponge Cake, 102
—Bittersweet Chocolate Fudge Cake, 95

—Buttermilk Chocolate Bread, 171
—Cafe Creme Chocolate Nut Bread, 172
—Chocolate Almond Torte, 110
—Chocolate Banana Cake with Chocolate Chips, 85
—Chocolate Carrot Almond Cake, 86
—Chocolate Chestnut Cake with Hazelnuts, 89
—Chocolate Chip Buttermilk Cake, 90
—Chocolate Chip Chocolate Cake, 92
—Chocolate Chip Graham Torte, 114
—Chocolate Pumpkin Pecan Cake, 97
—Chocolate Pumpkin Spiced Cake, 98
—Chocolate Torte with Apricot, 113
—Chocolate Velvet Cake, 103
—Chocolate Zucchini Cake with Chocolate Cream, 104
—Coffee & Chocolate Walnut Torte, 122
—Easiest & Best Torte au Chocolate, 116
—Gateau Au Chocolate with Mousse Frosting, 115
—Grand Duke's Pecan Torte with Chocolate, 117
—Hungarian Chocolate Torte with Apricot Jam, 119
—Mississippi Mud Pie Bread, 167
—Mocha Chocolate Cake, 96
—Old-Fashioned Banana Chocolate Chip Bread, 132
—Raspberry & Chocolate Chip Cake, 99
—Sour Cream & Chocolate Banana Cake, 84
—Sour Cream Chocolate Chip Chocolate Cake, 91
—Sour Cream Chocolate Fudge Cake, 93
—Sour Cream Poundcake with Chocolate Chips, 94
—Swiss Chocolate Cake with Cherries & Almonds, 87
—Vanilla Poundcake with Chocolate Chips, 101
—Whole Wheat Banana Chocolate Chip Bread, 134
—Yogurt Chocolate Fudge Torte, 123

COCONUT CAKE & BREAD
—California Carrot Cake with Pineapple & Coconut, 35
—Pineapple & Orange Coconut Bread, 151

COFFEE CAKE & BREADS
—Cafe Creme Chocolate Nut Bread, 172
—Mississippi Mud Pie Bread, 167
—Mocha Chocolate Cake, 96

CORNBREADS & MUFFINS
—Country Kitchen Cornbread, 257
—Mexican Style Cornbread with Chiles & Cheese, 258
—New Orleans Cornbread Muffins, 275

COTTAGE CHEESE BREADS
—Cinnamon Cottage Cheese

Bread with Raisins, 174
—Fresh Apricot & Cottage Cheese Bread, 131

CRANBERRY CAKES & BREADS
—Cranberry Orange & Lemon Tea Cake, 43
—Glazed Cranberry Cake with Orange & Walnuts, 42
—Holiday Cranberry Almond Bread, 139
—Pineapple Cranberry Bread with Whole Wheat & Oats, 138

DATE CAKES & BREADS
—Bara Brith - Welsh Raisin Date Nut Cake, 70
—California Date Nut Cake, 66
—Date Nut Orange Bread, 177
—Old-Fashioned Date Nut Bread, 175
—Orange Date Nut Bread, 176
—Spicy Pumpkin Bread with Dates, 155
—Whole Wheat & Oat Bran Bread with Dates, 199

EGGNOG BREAD & CAKE
—Bourbon & Eggnog Spice Cake, 74
—Christmas Eggnog Cherry Bread, 170

FIG BREAD
—Fig & Honey Pecan Bread, 178

FROSTINGS & ICINGS
—Almond Creme Fraiche, 39
—Butter Cream Cheese Frosting, 35
—Chocolate Buttercream, 85, 92, 93, 103, 108, 116, 124, 206, 209
—Chocolate Buttercream Frosting, 208
—Chocolate Cream Cheese Frosting, 86
—Chocolate Cream Frosting, 104
—Chocolate Fudge Frosting, 95
—Chocolate Mousse Frosting, 91, 115
—Chocolate Rum Buttercream, 88, 110, 207
—Chocolate Sour Cream Frosting, 90
—Chocolate Whipped Cream, 102
—Chocolate Yogurt Frosting, 123
—Cocoa Buttercream, 113
—Coffee Kahlua Cream, 75
—Cognac Cream, 55
—Cream Cheese Frosting, 36, 66
—Fluffy Vanilla Frosting, 69
—Fudge Frosting, 119
—Lemon Butter Icing, 45
—Lemon Creme Fraiche, 46
—Mocha Buttercream, 122
—Mocha Mousse Frosting, 96
—Orange Cream Cheese Frosting, 30
—Orange Pecan Frosting, 37
—Sour Cream Chocolate Frosting, 210
—Whipped Cream Chantilly, 114
—Whipped Cream Fraiche, 71
—Whipped Creme de Kahlua, 120

FRUITCAKES & BREADS
—Bourbon & Eggnog Spiced Cake, 74
—Bourbon Fruit & Nut Bread, 191

FRUITCAKES & BREADS,
Continued
—California Fruit & Nut Bread, 179
—Christmas Sherry Fruit & Nut Bread, 195
—Golden Bourbon Fruit & Nut Cake, 73
—Holiday Brandy Fruit & Pecan Bread, 193

GINGER CAKES & BREADS
—Farmhouse Spiced Raisin Gingerbread, 181
—Ginger Snap Pumpkin Cake, 55
—Spicy Nectarine Ginger Cake, 48
—Sticky Honey Gingerbread with Walnuts, 180

GLAZES
—Almond Cream Glaze, 41
—Almond Glaze, 62
—Apple Glaze, 26
—Apricot Almond Glaze, 168
—Apricot Walnut Glaze, 118
—Bourbon Glaze, 225
—Bourbon Cream Glaze, 73
—Buttermilk Glaze, 31
—Cherry Brandy Glaze, 193
—Chestnut Cream Glaze, 89
—Chocolate Coffee Glaze, 167
—Chocolate Glaze, 97, 98, 100, 133
—Cinnamon Glaze, 190
—Coffee Cream Glaze, 172
—Creamy Cherry Glaze, 171
—Creamy Glaze, 131, 134, 136, 212, 279
—Creamy Lemon Glaze, 47
—Creamy Orange Glaze, 142
—Creamy Raisin Glaze, 29
—Eggnog Glaze, 74, 170
—Honey Orange Glaze, 144
—Irish Whiskey Glaze, 194
—Lemon Butter Glaze, 185
—Lemon Buttermilk Glaze, 38
—Lemon Cream Glaze, 156
—Lemon Orange Glaze, 111, 273
—Milky Glaze, 52
—Orange Bourbon Glaze, 191
—Orange Glaze, 32, 49, 68, 139, 143, 176, 289
—Orange Honey Glaze, 178, 182
—Orange Lemon Wash, 43
—Orange Pecan Glaze, 154
—Orange Walnut Glaze, 28
—Peach Nut Glaze, 146
—Pineapple Glaze, 77, 138, 151
—Praline Glaze, 196
—Raisin Orange Glaze, 137
—Raisin Walnut Glaze, 150
—Raspberry Cream Glaze, 99
—Sherry Cream Glaze, 192, 195
—Sherry Glaze, 76
—Sour Cream Cinnamon Glaze, 274
—Sour Cream Glaze, 48, 162, 166, 233, 236
—Spicy Apple Glaze, 130
—Strawberry Glaze, 72
—Strawberry Grand Marnier Glaze, 109
—Strawberry Yogurt Glaze, 159
—Toasted Almond Glaze, 57
—Vanilla Cream Glaze, 24, 79, 179
—Vanilla Glaze, 63, 67, 101, 237
—Vanilla Yogurt Glaze, 64
—Walnut Glaze, 175

HONEY CAKES & BREADS
—Fig & Honey Pecan Bread, 178
—Fresh Apple & Walnut Honey Cake, 26
—Honey & Spice Pumpkin Cake, 56
—Honey Spiced Walnut Bread, 189
—Honey Whole Wheat Pineapple Bread, 148
—Old-Fashioned Honey Prune & Walnut Bread, 186
—Old-Fashioned Spiced Honey Cake, 78
—Sticky Honey Gingerbread with Walnuts, 180
—Two-Minute Cinnamon Swirl Bread with Honey, 173
—Upside Down Honey Bran Bread, 129

JAM & MARMALADE CAKES & BREADS
—Apricot Jam & Macaroon Cake, 65
—Orange Marmalade Bread, 183
—Peanut Butter & Jam Bread with Bananas, 184
—Strawberry Jam & Almond Cake, 72

LEMON CAKES & BREADS
—Daffodil Cake with Lemon & Pecans, 44
—Extra Tart Lemon Nut Bread, 141
—Extra Tart Springtime Lemon Cake, 45
—Lemon Cream Cheese Coffeecake, 47
—Lemon Pound Cake, 46
—Raspberry & Pecan Lemon Bread, 156
—Sour Cream Lemon Tea Bread, 140
—World's Best Orange & Lemon Spongecake, 51

MACAROON CAKES
—Apricot Jam & Macaroon Cake, 65
—Easiest & Best Macaroon Torte, 120

MOLASSES BREAD
—Molasses & Buttermilk Bran Bread, 198

MUFFINS
—All-American Macaroon Muffins with Dates & Walnuts, 270
—Best Papaya Lemon Cream Cheese Muffins, 283
—Black Forest Chocolate Cherry Cupcakes, 279
—Buttermilk Blueberry Muffins with Pecans, 273
—Butterscotch Pecan Muffins, 274
—Cajun Banana Pecan Crusty Muffins, 278
—Cajun Honey Bran Muffins, 276
—Cajun Jalapeno & Cheese Biscuit Muffins, 277
—Chewy Orange Raisin Muffins, 282
—Cinnamon Apple Muffins with Orange, 271
—Cranberry Orange & Apple Muffins, 281
—Currant & Oatmeal Muffins

with Orange, 284
—Fresh Apple & Orange Muffins, 272
—Honey Whole Wheat Oatmeal Muffins with Apples & Raisins, 290
—Honey Whole Wheat & Wheat Germ Muffins with Apples, 287
—Maple Oat Bran Muffins, 288
—New Orleans Cornbread Muffins with Currants, 275
—Raisin Bran Muffins with Apple & Orange, 289
—Sour Cream Muffins with Chocolate Chips, 280
—Sour Cream Pumpkin Muffins with Walnuts, 285
—Spiced Pumpkin Muffins with Orange & Walnuts, 286
—Yogurt & Pecan Breakfast Wafers, 292

NECTARINE CAKE
—Spicy Nectarine Ginger Cake, 48

OAT BRAN BREAD & MUFFINS
—Maple Oat Bran Muffins, 288
—Whole Wheat & Oat Bran Bread with Dates, 199

OATMEAL BREADS
—Apple Cheddar Cheese Oatmeal Bread, 263
—Health Bread with Yogurt, Oatmeal & Whole Wheat, 196
—Oatmeal Bread with Orange & Prunes, 182
—Pineapple Cranberry Bread with Whole Wheat & Oats, 138
—Rhubarb Oatmeal Bread, 157
—Whole Wheat & Oatmeal Blueberry Bread, 136

ONION BREADS
—Cheese & Onion Crescents, 264
—Chewy Cheese Sticks with Onions, 261
—Easiest & Best Onion Sesame Bagels, 242
—Green Onion & Buttermilk Bread, 248
—Onion Kuchen with Sour Cream & Poppyseeds, 243
—Parmesan, Herb & Onion Cheese Bread, 249
—Pizza Bread with Tomatoes, Onion & Cheese, 247
—Red Hot Pastelle with Onions & Swiss Cheese, 245
—Two-Minute Cheese Bread with Onions & Herbs, 256

ORANGE CAKES & BREADS
—Apple Orange Raisin Bread, 128
—Buttery Orange Walnut Coffeecake, 50
—Cranberry Orange & Lemon Tea Cake, 43
—Fantastic Spiced Orange Cake, 49
—Majestic Apple Cake with Orange, 27
—Molasses & Buttermilk Bran Bread with Orange, 198
—Orange Date Nut Bread, 176
—Orange Marmalade Bread, 183
—Orange Peach Bread, 146
—Orange Tea Bread with Walnuts & Raisins, 143
—Orange & Walnut Cake, 79

ORANGE CAKES & BREADS,
Continued
—Orange & Yogurt Cake with
Cinnamon Streusel Swirl, 80
—Peach & Orange Yogurt Bread,
147
—Poppyseed Orange Cake, 68
—Sour Cream & Orange Pecan
Bread, 142
—World's Best Orange &·Lemon
Sponge Cake, 51

PAPAYA MUFFINS
—Best Papaya Lemon Cream
Cheese Muffins, 283

PEACH CAKES & BREADS
—Fresh Peach & Almond Bread,
145
—Fresh Peach & Orange Cake,
53
—Honey Bran Bread with Peaches,
144
—Orange Peach Bread, 146
—Peach & Orange Yogurt Bread,
147
—Peach & Walnut Cinnamon
Coffeecake, 52

PEANUT BUTTER BREAD
—Peanut Butter & Jam Bread with
Bananas, 184

PEAR CAKE
—Pear Cobbler with Cinnamon &
Orange, 54

PECAN CAKES & BREADS
—Apricot Pecan Yogurt Cake, 64
—Easiest & Best Carrot Pecan
Torte, 112
—Fresh Apple, Orange & Pecan
Torte, 111
—Grand Duke's Pecan Torte with
Chocolate, 117
—Hungarian Pecan Torte with
Apricot Jam, 118
—Raspberry & Pecan Lemon
Bread, 156
—Sour Cream & Orange Pecan
Bread, 142
—Strawberry Pecan Bread, 158
—Whole Wheat Pumpkin Pecan
Bread, 154

PINEAPPLE CAKES & BREADS
—California Carrot Cake with
Pineapple, 35
—Farmhouse Carrot Cake with
Pineapple, 38
—Honey Whole Wheat Pineapple
Bread, 148
—Pineapple Cranberry Bread with
Whole Wheat & Oats, 138
—Pineapple & Orange Bran Bread,
149
—Pineapple, Orange & Coconut
Bread, 151
—Pineapple Raisin Bran Bread, 150
—Sunny California Sour Cream
Pineapple Cake, 77

POPPYSEED CAKE & BREADS
—Poppyseed Bread with Green
Onions & Cheese, 250
—Poppyseed Onion Rolls for
Passover Holiday, 244
—Poppyseed Orange Cake, 68

POUNDCAKES
—Cappuccino Poundcake, 75

—Lemon Poundcake, 46
—Old-Fashioned Marble
Poundcake, 67
—Sour Cream Poundcake, with
Chocolate Chips, 94
—Vanilla Poundcake with
Chocolate Chips, 101

PRUNE CAKES & BREADS
—Danish Prune Bread, 185
—Oatmeal Bread with Orange &
Prunes, 182
—Old-Fashioned Honey Prune
Bread, 186
—Old-Fashioned Spiced Prune
Cake, 69
—Whole Wheat & Buttermilk
Prune Bread, 197

PUMPKIN CAKES & BREADS
—Best Pumpkin Bread with Apples
& Orange, 152
—Chocolate Pumpkin Pecan Cake,
97
—Chocolate Pumpkin Spice Cake,
98
—Ginger Snap Pumpkin Cake with
Raisins, 55
—Honey & Spice Pumpkin Cake,
56
—Orange & Raisin Pumpkin
Bread, 153
—Spicy Pumpkin Bread with Dates
& Nuts, 155
—Whole Wheat Pumpkin Pecan
Bread, 154

RAISIN CAKE & BREAD
—Bara Brith-Welsh Raisin & Date
Nut Cake, 70
—Two-Minute Cinnamon Swirl
Bread with Raisins, 173

RASPBERRY CAKES & BREADS
—Raspberry & Chocolate Chip
Cake, 99
—Raspberry & Pecan Lemon
Bread, 156
—Royal Raspberry & Almond
Cake, 57

RED CABBAGE BREAD
—Sweet & Sour Red Cabbage
Bread with Apples, 252

RHUBARB BREAD
—Rhubarb Oatmeal Bread with
Ricotta & Walnuts, 157

SAUERKRAUT BREAD
—Sauerkraut Rye Bread with
Yogurt & Bacon, 253

SAVORY BREADS (See Breads
Savory)

SCONES
—Blueberry Buttermilk Scones, 295
—Buttery Scones with Raisins, 296
—Victorian Cream Scone with
Currants, 293
—Whole Wheat Scones with
Dates, 294

SHORTBREAD
—Buttery Scotch Shortbread with
Raspberries & Cream, 71

SODA BREADS
—Irish Breakfast Soda Bread with
Currants, 200
—Whole Wheat Raisin Soda
Bread, 262

SOUR CREAM CAKES &
BREADS
—Fresh Apple Sour Cream Cake,
31
—Royal Sour Cream Coffeecake
with Apples, 24
—Sour Cream Almond Cake, 62
—Sour Cream Apple Kuchen
Cake, 25
—Sour Cream Banana Bread, 133
—Sour Cream & Chocolate
Banana Cake, 84
—Sour Cream Chocolate Chip
Cake, 91
—Sour Cream Chocolate Fudge
Cake, 93
—Sour Cream Poundcake, 94
—Sour Cream & Orange Pecan
Bread, 142
—Sour Cream Walnut Tea Bread
with Cocoa Swirl, 187
—Sunny California Sour Cream
Pineapple Cake, 77

SPICED CAKES & BREADS
—Bourbon & Eggnog Spiced
Cake, 74
—Cappuccino Poundcake, 75
—Cinnamon Apple Cake, 30
—Cinnamon Cottage Cheese
Bread, 174
—Cinnamon Zucchini Bread, 161
—Cooked Carrot Spiced Cake, 36
—English Sherry Spiced Cake, 76
—Fantastic Spiced Orange Cake,
49
—Farmhouse Spiced Raisin
Gingerbread, 181
—Fresh Apple Spiced Cake, 28
—Honey & Spice Pumpkin Cake,
56
—Old-Fashioned Spiced Honey
Cake, 78
—Old-Fashioned Spiced Prune
Cake, 69
—Peach & Walnut Cinnamon
Coffeecake, 52
—Spiced Applesauce Bread with
Currants, 130
—Spiced Applesauce Cake with
Raisins, 32
—Spiced Carrot & Orange Bread,
137
—Spiced Raisin & Walnut Sherry
Bread, 192
—Spiced Zucchini Walnut Bread,
162
—Spicy Nectarine Ginger Cake, 48
—Spicy Pumpkin Bread with
Dates, 155
—Two-Minute Cinnamon Swirl
Bread with Honey, 173

SPIRITS, CAKES & BREADS
WITH
—Bourbon & Eggnog Spiced
Cake, 74
—Bourbon Fruit & Nut Bread,
191
—Cappucino Poundcake with
Coffee Kahlua, 75
—Christmas Sherry Fruit & Nut
Bread, 195
—English Sherry Spiced Cake, 76
—Golden Bourbon Fruit & Nut
Cake, 73
—Holiday Brandy Fruit & Pecan
Bread, 193

SPIRITS, CAKES & BREADS
WITH, Continued
—St. Patricks Day Bread with Irish
Whiskey, 194
—Spiced Raisin & Walnut Sherry
Bread, 192

SPONGECAKES
—Basic Chocolate Spongecake, 102
—World's Best Orange & Lemon
Spongecake, 51

SPREADS - BUTTERS
—Devonshire Cream, 294
—Honey Orange Cream Cheese,
161
—Orange Cinnamon Butter, 285
—Orange Honey Butter, 153, 188,
271
—Orange Marmalade Butter, 177
—Sweet Butter & Honey, 286

STRAWBERRY BREADS
—Strawberry Banana Bread, 160
—Strawberry Pecan Bread, 158
—Strawberry Yogurt Banana
Bread, 159

STRUDELS & DANISH
—Cinnamon Breakfast Croissants,
238
—Danish Apple Strudel, 232
—Danish Crescents with
Strawberry, Pecan, 236
—Danish Pastry Rolls with Walnut
Filling, 233
—Flaky Strudel with Apricots &
Walnuts, 230
—Flaky Strudel with Chocolate &
Chocolate Chips, 231
—Flaky Strudel with Cinnamon &
Raisins, 231
—Flaky Strudel with Pecan Raisin
Filling, 231
—Flaky Strudel with Rugalach
Filling, 231
—Scandinavian Cinnamon Date
Roll, 235
—Strudelettes with Walnuts,
Raisins & Strawberry Jam, 234
—Viennese Crescents with
Cinnamon & Walnuts, 237

SYRUP
—Orange Syrup, 112

TOPPINGS
—Almond Crumb Topping, 169
—Cinnamon Almond Topping,
145
—Cinnamon Streusel Topping, 53,
58
—Cinnamon Topping, 157
—Cinnamon Walnut Topping, 50,
197
—Honey Butter Topping, 189
—Streusel Oat Topping, 40

TORTES
—Almond Torte with Chocolate
Chip Crust, 108
—Almond Torte with Glazed
Strawberries, 109
—Chocolate Almond Torte, 110
—Chocolate Chip Graham Torte,
114
—Chocolate Torte with Apricot,
113
—Coffee & Chocolate Walnut
Torte, 122
—Easiest & Best Carrot & Pecan
Torte, 112
—Easiest & Best Macaroon Torte,
120
—Easiest & Best Torte au
Chocolate, 116
—Easiest & Best Walnut Torte
with Raspberry Jam, 121
—Fresh Apple & Orange Pecan
Torte, 111
—Gateau au Chocolate, 115
—Grand Duke's Pecan Torte with
Chocolate, 117
—Hungarian Chocolate Torte with
Apricot Jam, 119
—Hungarian Pecan Torte with
Apricot, 118
—Viennese Nut Torte, 124
—Yogurt Chocolate Fudge Torte,
123

WALNUT CAKES & BREADS
—Buttery Orange Walnut Cake, 50
—Coffee & Chocolate Walnut
Torte, 122
—Country Walnut & Raisin
Bread, 188
—Easiest & Best Walnut Torte,
121

—Honey-Spiced Walnut Bread, 189
—Orange & Walnut Cake, 79
—Sour Cream Walnut Tea Bread,
187

WHEAT GERM BREAD
—Wheat Germ Bread with
Apricots, 190

WHOLE WHEAT BREADS &
MUFFINS
—Health Bread with Yogurt,
Oatmeal, 196
—Honey Whole Wheat Muffins,
290
—Honey Whole Wheat Pineapple
Bread, 148
—Honey Whole Wheat & Wheat
Germ Muffins, 287
—Pineapple Cranberry Bread with
Oats, 138
—Whole Wheat Banana &
Chocolate Chip Bread, 134
—Whole Wheat & Buttermilk
Prune Bread, 197
—Whole Wheat & Oat Bran
Bread with Dates, 199
—Whole Wheat & Oatmeal
Blueberry Bread, 136
—Whole Wheat Pumpkin Pecan
Bread, 154
—Whole Wheat Raisin Soda
Bread, 262

YOGURT CAKES & BREADS
—Apricot Pecan Yogurt Cake, 64
—Health Bread with Yogurt,
Oatmeal, 196
—Orange & Yogurt Cake, 80
—Peach & Orange Yogurt Bread,
147
—Strawberry Yogurt Banana
Bread, 159
—Yogurt Chocolate Fudge Torte,
123

ZUCCHINI CAKES & BREADS
—Cinnamon Zucchini Bread, 161
—Chocolate Zucchini Cake, 104
—Old-Fashioned Zucchini Cake,
58
—Spiced Zucchini Walnut Bread,
162